Egyptian art

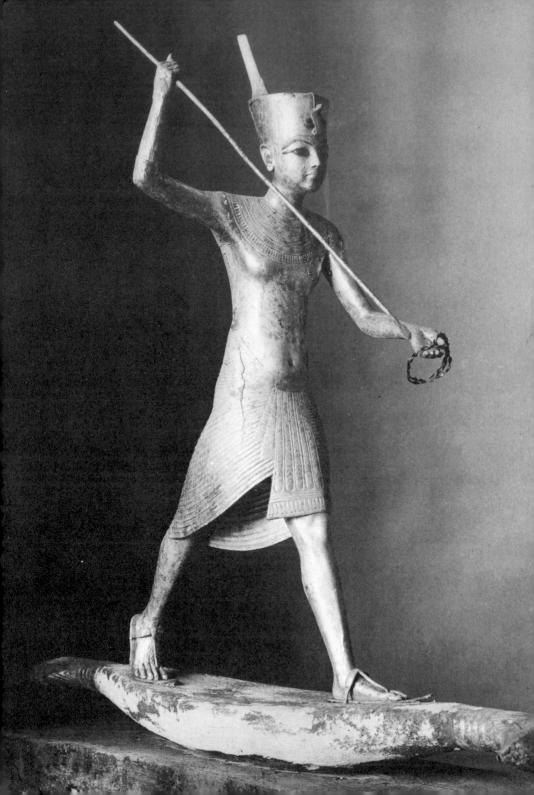

Egyptian art

in the Days of the Pharaohs
3100–320 BC

CYRIL ALDRED

NEW YORK AND TORONTO
OXFORD UNIVERSITY PRESS
1980

Frontispiece: Gilded and painted wooden statue of King Tutankhamun as the god Horus vanquishing the forces of Evil, from his
tomb in the Valley of the Kings, *c.* 1330 BC.

© 1980 Thames and Hudson Ltd, London
All Rights Reserved

Library of Congress Cataloging in Publication Data
Aldred, Cyril.
    Egyptian art.
    (World of art)
    Bibliography: p.
    Includes index.
    1. Art, Egyptian. I. Title. II. Series.
N5350.A56   709'   80–16494
ISBN 0–19–520223–6
ISBN 0–19–520224–4 (pbk.)

Printed and bound in Great Britain by
Jarrold and Sons Ltd, Norwich

Contents

Introduction
Chronology and the Dating of Egyptian Works of Art   7

1 **The Character of Egyptian Art**   11

2 **Artists, their Materials and Methods**   19

3 **The Archaic Period**   31
Dynasties I–II

4 **Imhotep and the Monuments of Djoser**   45
Dynasty III

5 **The Pyramid Age**   59
Dynasty IV

6 **The Pyramid Age**   78
Dynasties V–VI *Relief Sculpture*

7 **The Pyramid Age**   91
Dynasties V–VI *Statuary*

8 **The First Intermediate Period**   106
Dynasties VII–X

9 **The Middle Kingdom**   113
Dynasties XI–XIII

10 **The Second Intermediate Period; the Character of the New Kingdom**   139
Dynasties XIV–XX

11 **The Early New Kingdom**   147
Dynasty XVIII

12 The New Kingdom: Ramesside Period 187
Dynasties XIX–XX

**13 The Character of Late Egyptian Art and
the Tanite Period** 203
Dynasty XXI

14 The Libyan Period 206
Dynasties XXII–XXIV

15 The Kushite Period 215
Dynasty XXV

16 The Saite Period 225
Dynasty XXVI

17 The Late Period 233
Dynasties XXVII–XXX

Epilogue 240

Select Bibliography 241

List of Illustrations 242

Index and Glossary 248

Chronology and the Dating of Egyptian Works of Art

Manetho, the learned High Priest in Heliopolis who was commissioned by Ptolemy I in the third century BC to write a history of Egypt, divided into thirty-one dynasties the entire chronicle of events, from the unification of Upper and Lower Egypt under Menes, the first pharaoh, to the conquest of Alexander the Great in 332 BC. Although Manetho's work has not survived, his list of kings and their years of rule have been extensively preserved in the writings of early Christian chronographers. Modern historians still make selective use of these, and accept the numbering of Manetho's dynasties, which seems to follow very ancient practice. They also often render the names of the pharaohs in his Greek versions, where they exist, a system which is followed in this book.

Surviving records, in which the ancient Egyptians noted certain celestial phenomena as occurring on specific days in their calendars, have enabled correspondences to be made with the modern calendar; but even so, the chronology of ancient Egypt before the first millennium BC is still not settled, particularly for the remoter and more troubled periods. The system adopted in this book follows that proposed by the Oriental Institute of the University of Chicago, with some modifications in the dating of the Eighteenth Dynasty.

The thirty-one dynasties of Manetho have been further grouped by modern historians into larger time-spans, coinciding with periods when a distinct cultural pattern prevailed, separated by obscure interludes of political upheaval. In the following pages they are defined as follows:

Dynasty	Period	Approximate Date BC
I–II	Archaic	3168–2705
III–VI	Old Kingdom	2705–2250
VII–X	First Intermediate	2250–2035
XI–XIII	Middle Kingdom	2035–1668
XIV–XVIII	Second Intermediate	1720–1550
XVIII–XX	New Kingdom	1552–1070
XXI	Tanite	1070–946
XXII–XXIV	Libyan	946–712

Dynasty	Period	Approximate Date BC
XXV	Kushite	712–664
XXVI	Saite	664–525
XXVII–XXXI	Late	525–332
Greek	Ptolemaic	332–30

Sometimes these periods are further sub-divided. Thus in the New Kingdom, Dynasties Nineteen and Twenty are frequently referred to as *Ramesside*, after the predominant name of their kings; and the reign of Akhenaten (*c.* 1356–1339) is often designated the *Amarna* Period, after the name of his own residence-city at modern Tell el-Amarna. The Twenty-first Dynasty is occasionally called *Tanite* from Tanis, the chief residence-city of its rulers. Similarly, the epithet *Bubastite* is applied to the Twenty-second Dynasty, as *Saite* is to the Twenty-sixth, from the Delta towns of Bubastis and Sais, the seats of their power. In the Late Period, Dynasties Twenty-seven and Thirty-one are also known as *Persian*, from the nationality of their kings who twice made Egypt part of their empire.

When precise dating is not required, as is often the case in this work on Egyptian art, reference is usually made to the period or dynasty in question, or more specifically to the king in whose reign the object was made. Dates for the dynasties are given below, those before the Twenty-sixth Dynasty being approximations. The dates of individual kings, queens and private persons mentioned in the text will be found against their entries in the index.

Dynasty	Dates BC	Dynasty	Dates BC
I	3168–2857	XX	1185–1070
II	2857–2705	XXI	1070–946
III	2705–2630	XXII	946–712
IV	2630–2524	★XXIII	828–712
V	2524–2400	★XXIV	740–712
VI	2400–2250	XXV	712–664
VII–X	2250–2035	XXVI	664–525
XI	2035–1991	XXVII (Persian)	525–404
XII	1991–1784	XXVIII	404–399
XIII	1784–1668	XXIX	381–343
★XIV–XVII	1720–1552	XXX	381–343
XVIII	1552–1296	XXXI (Persian)	343–332
XIX	1297–1185		

★ *These dynasties were partly contemporaneous with others, different kings ruling in different places in Egypt at the same time.*

The order of kings has survived from Manetho and from such fragmentary documents as the Turin Canon, the Palermo Stone and the selective lists in the temples at Karnak and Abydos, and in the tomb of an architect Tjenry at Saqqara. But such records are often incomplete or tendentious and the correct order is dubious in one or two places.

Fortunately, most works of art from ancient Egypt can be ascribed to the reign of a particular king, since it was for royalty that the most enduring and splendid monuments were made. It is also often possible to attribute objects to a specific reign from the archaeological context in which they were found, although this is sometimes subject to error owing to an incomplete excavation record, or a misinterpretation of *cf. 37, 101* the evidence. Inscriptions may also mislead, having been added later to an earlier work left unfinished or uninscribed.

Lastly, Egyptian works of art may be dated on stylistic grounds. This system, which is commonplace with art historians, is regarded by many Egyptologists as too subjective to be trustworthy, but in the case of uninscribed fragments, found out of their proper context, there is no alternative method that can be employed. *cf. 90*

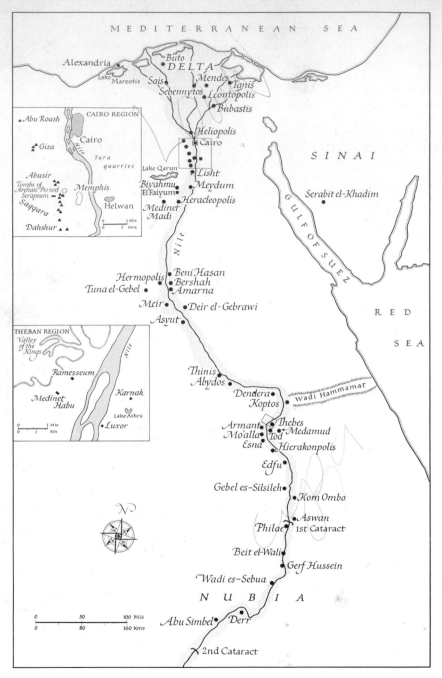

1 Ancient Egypt and the principal sites mentioned in the text.

CHAPTER ONE

The Character of Egyptian Art

Art, in the sense in which that word is generally employed today, did not exist in ancient Egypt, though artists certainly flourished and played a vital role in inventing and developing the forms of its material culture. If the ancient Egyptian was aware of 'art', it could not have been above the consciousness of his religious experience, and that indeed was wide enough to encompass almost every human activity. Egypt, like all the other nations of antiquity, was profoundly influenced by magic, by a belief in the existence of all-pervading, invisible and superhuman forces that had to be propitiated if their aid was to be secured, or neutralized if their enmity was to be avoided. Only continuous worship of these mysterious powers could keep the universe in an equilibrium favourable to the survival of man and his institutions. It was the constant affirmation of the pharaoh, the divine king who presided over the destiny of Egypt and its people, that he had restored the harmony (*maet*) of an ideal world as it had been established at the First Time, but which could easily be jangled out of tune by human neglect or wrongdoing.

Art for the ancient Egyptian rather had that secondary meaning, which still exists in English, of 'skill in execution', in particular a superior ability to fashion material things with tools. In this context, Egyptian art is of a high order. The mastery which the artist displays over a variety of intractable materials has rarely been equalled by other peoples of the ancient world, and is hardly surpassed elsewhere.

This creativeness was not divorced from the creative process by which the Egyptian universe had come into being and was daily maintained. In historic times the great productive power was the god Ptah of Memphis, the 'Creator' who in his more active and seminal *81* form was depicted as a ram-headed craftsman, fashioning mankind upon his potter's wheel. In a song current in the New Kingdom, he is described as 'making this with his two hands as balm to his heart'. *141* According to the peculiar belief of the ancient Egyptian, Ptah was also the primordial mound of earth that arose from the waters of elemental Chaos and on which all life began, just as after the annual inundation of the Nile, a narrow spit of land first emerged from the flood, soon to be covered with vegetation and busy with animal life. Besides the flora and fauna of nature, Ptah, the New Risen Earth,

II

North — Lower Egypt
South — Upper Egypt (more unified)

contained within himself all the products from which man under his inspiration could also create things: clay, stone, metals and minerals. It is not surprising, therefore, that the High Priest of Ptah should bear the title of Greatest of Craftsmen, and was originally responsible for the design and execution of all Egyptian works of art. Even in later times, when other gods shared the creative power of the demiurge, craftsmen in far-off Thebes, the city of Amun, the god of light and air, still worshipped Ptah in their local shrine and acted as his priests in their leisure hours.

56, 57

Of the Egyptian artist it might be claimed, with as much truth as Johnson's epitaph on Goldsmith, that nothing that he touched he did not adorn. The wealth of art objects that has survived by chance from the three millennia of ancient Egyptian civilization is so bewildering in its volume and diversity that in these limited pages we shall have to confine our study to the fine arts of painting and sculpture, with a brief side-glance at architecture. It is in this context that our references to 'art' should be understood. But it should also be stressed that the so-called 'minor', or applied arts are hardly less important, since all art in Egypt served a practical purpose; and in essentials a wall painting and a libation vessel are informed with the same creative intention, in as much as they are both meant to perform practical though different functions, and might very well have been designed by the same artist.

In examining any large collection of ancient Egyptian art, the spectator cannot but be conscious of its unique quality which is usually instantly recognizable, apart from the exotic charm of its ethnic features and fashions. The dominant impression is of its humanity. The main subject of this art is man and his many activities in an Egyptian milieu. Colossal figures may exist (though they are rarer than is commonly supposed and most Egyptian statues, even of

Frontispiece, 19

gods, are of less than life-size), but they magnify only the heroic and beneficent qualities of divinities and kings, and not the horrific power of tyrants or demons. Sinister and hostile forces are tamed into intellectualized concepts and often reduced to a contemptible size, with little power to impress by their intrinsic appearance, but able to terrify only by what they symbolize. With few exceptions Egyptian art mirrors an ideal aspect of the natural world in which calm,

35, 69, 129, 134, 195

successful men and women are shown acting in a rational manner. The scenes that are depicted express for the most part piety, family affection and social harmony amid a sympathetic nature. Scenes of violence and disorder are confined to the butchery of the sacrificial

37, 53, 79, 140, 156, 186

ox, the gala fights of the clownish boatmen or the overthrow of the forces of evil, whether in the form of the animals of the wild or the human marauders of the Nile Valley. Egyptian art at its best reflects the restraint and sense of proportion of a sophisticated society that in its formative period was counselled by its philosophers to follow moderation in all things, to beware of the passionate or sensual man, and to cultivate 'silence' or the qualities of temperance, patience and benevolence.

In his rational and disciplined approach to life and art, the ancient Egyptian was repeating the rule that had been imposed by the Creator upon Chaos at his epiphany. This orderly system was re-established on the land and its inhabitants during every reign by the god incarnate in the pharaoh. Every year Egypt was remade in the old mould after the subsidence of the inundation had left the fields with fresh deposits of fertile silt ready to sprout into new life. These cultivable tracts, on which old landmarks had often been obliterated by the flood, formed a vast *tabula rasa* that had to be demarcated anew to re-establish the limits of fields and estates. If the Egyptian, even from earliest times, could impress a system of mensuration upon his environment and reduce it to a rational and finite pattern, it is no wonder that he also devised a canon of proportion to which his works of art should *2* conform. Thus in ground-plan and elevation his buildings reveal a mathematical order based upon the use of such geometrical figures as the 'sacred' right-angled triangle, with sides of three, four and five units.

This mathematical framework that underlies the structure of his artworks is but one aspect of the Egyptian concept of space. The Egyptian was highly conscious of the box-like structure of his world, traversed by two co-ordinates at right angles: the generally south–north flow of the Nile, and the east–west passage of the sun across the ceiling of the heavens, which was supported by a third axis. The contiguous planes of this environment are carefully defined as separate entities and are to be found in the fully developed Egyptian temple, which is strictly cubic and is a model of the universe at its creation. Every temple relief is framed by a geometrical figure, the baseline being the earth-glyph (⊏⊐) and the ceiling line the sky-sign (⊂⊃) which is sometimes supported by *was*-sceptres (⌡⌡) at the ends, standing for the poles that keep the heavens aloft at its four corners. Such an orthogonal feeling for space is seen even in *122* such decorative features as the block-pattern border which often frames compositions, or the rectangular word-groups of hierog- *108, 124* lyphic inscriptions, or the units that comprise scenes in reliefs and paintings or even the disposal of elements within a circular area. *9*

The careful definition of the separate planes of this cubic universe is revealed in an art which is essentially two dimensional. The basis of Egyptian art lies in its drawing which, while it has barely survived as

13

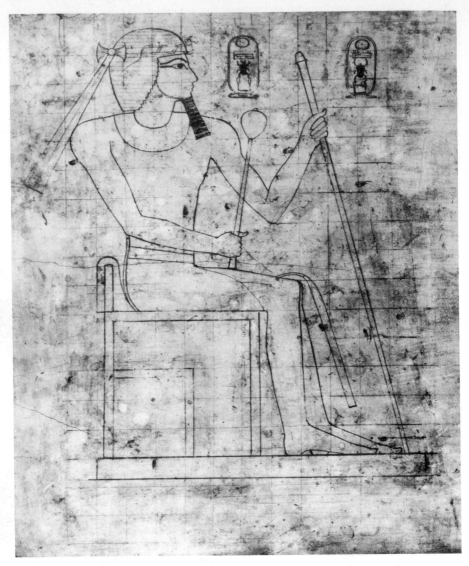

2   Gesso-coated wooden board with line drawing of King Tuthmosis III seated on a throne, overlaid with a grid for transfer to a larger scale, *c.* 1460 B C.

an independent genre, is explicit in reliefs and statuary. In seeking to represent three-dimensional objects on a plane surface, whether a drawing board or an area of wall, the Egyptian avoided the perspectival solution of the problem which alone of the nations of antiquity, the Greeks ultimately reached by the fifth century BC. Their vision of the natural world, seen from a certain standpoint at a certain moment of time, would have seemed to the ancient Egyptian as presumptuous, and concerned only with illusion, a mere distortion of reality. The Egyptian was concerned not with presenting an evanescent personal impression, caught in an instant, but with what he regarded as eternal verities. He represented not what could be seen transiently, but what he expected to exist for perpetuity. This vision was not peculiar to an individual artist, but was part of that immutable order of things that had been established as an institution of the Egyptian state at the First Time. What was important was not the expression of an individual view of reality, but the conforming to a sanctified creative mode; and Egyptian art was adjudged good when this had been achieved by the highest technical skill at the artist's command.

His non-perspectival vision placed the Egyptian artist in harmony with a world that he knew to exist. His perception of the forms of nature was derived from a fusion of several aspects recollected in the tranquillity of his mind and not captured as an instant revelation to the seeing eye. Thus the Egyptian represented the palace of King Serpent (Djet) as the rectangular ground-plan of the entire residence with its façade rising along the baseline. These are the coordinates of his perception. The serpent within the enclosure identifies the owner and so distinguishes the palace from those of other kings. Similarly, the figure of a man might be represented by the integration of the front and side views. Such figures become symbols rather than images, standing for 'palace' and 'man' respectively; but it should be noted that each element in the representation is orthographically rendered without distortion, and in the case of the human figure the various parts have a natural proportion to each other. The success of the artist rests in the skill he has shown in depicting naturalistic details, such as the collar-bones and the muscles of the limbs of the man, and the architectural features of the elaborate façade of the palace.

The use of symbolic forms in Egyptian art is intimately associated with a characteristic of Egyptian culture, the employment of hieroglyphs in a system of writing which has no exact counterpart in other civilizations. Egyptian hieroglyphs are the most attractive forms of writing ever devised, and it may be that their aesthetic appeal as well as their religious sanction contributed to their retention,

2, 25

11

3

especially for monumental inscriptions, throughout the course of pharaonic history. Each great cultural period produced its special attempt to maintain a pure style in the grouping, drawing and carving of the signs, and no renaissance of art in Egypt took place without a parallel revival in the style of hieroglyphic writing.

Since such writing consisted of an assemblage of concrete images, some phonetic in character, and others ideographic, a number of standard signs had to be designed which were instantly recognizable and differentiated, the one from the other, even in schematic form. Such glyphs were invented at an early stage of Egyptian artistic development and their origins are lost to us. It may be that the final forms surviving at the dawn of historic times had evolved by natural selection, displacing any signs that made a lesser impact or produced ambiguities. Certain it is that in design, hieroglyphs are unsurpassed for the information they convey, giving an immediately recognizable aspect, usually in profile, of the thing represented, and thus the sound or meaning that the writer intended to convey. Designers of logos for modern industry have been unable to produce any symbols having greater significance, elegance and clarity. Egyptian hieroglyphs must have been first developed by drawing them on papyrus or pottery with a pen or brush. Later they were incised on ivory or wood and carved in relief or intaglio.

8
3, 27, 69

The form of a hieroglyph, with its attendant meaning, could influence the design of objects of art, so that, for instance, a libation vessel could be ingeniously made in the shape of the *ankh* ('life') sign, symbolizing that the liquid poured from the container was imbued with life-giving virtues. But a closer association between Egyptian art and hieroglyphic writing ('the god's words') was the divine potency of both, since pictures and signs could be animated by magic. For a period at least, the Egyptians believed that hieroglyphs of men and animals, carved in proximity to the burial place, could come alive and work the dead a mischief. They were, therefore, mutilated or incompletely drawn to render them harmless. Similarly, some of the later Theban tombs bear witness to spiteful damage inflicted upon the image of the deceased by someone who owed him a grudge.

124

Yet there is a still more intimate connection between hieroglyphs and the drawing on which Egyptian art is based: the ideograms of hieroglyphic writing, signs expressing ideas rather than sounds, were but the models for Egyptian drawings on a larger scale with more detail and enrichment. The repertoire of signs, once established, was little altered through the centuries, just as modern alphabets differ only marginally from their archetypes. Because they, too, had to be read like the signs of an inscription, the elaborate ideograms that form the elements of Egyptian iconography also remained unchanged in form over the centuries, though they do show modifications in style and proportions. The success of the Egyptians in devising a corpus of signs that showed human or animal figures at rest or in action in a variety of postures that were clear and immediately recognizable, inhibited any desire for experimentation by succeeding generations of artists. Children, for instance, are represented unsentimentally as adults in miniature, their immaturity symbolized by their absence of clothes, or by the long lock of hair worn before puberty on the right side of the head or by their having their forefinger held to their mouths, and these conventions ruled throughout Egyptian antiquity except during the atypical Amarna interlude.

37, 63

140

An old man is represented with a slight forward stoop as he leans upon a staff. Mature and successful men are shown in all the pride of physical well-being, or in the corpulence of good living. The comely wife is represented as slight in stature and elegant in her finery. The peasant or other menials may appear with a little more realism as unkempt and deformed by toil or disease; and the foreigner is usually depicted in an undignified or servile posture, his ethnic features slightly exaggerated for the sake of immediate recognition. All in fact are types of humanity, determined by the minuscule form of hieroglyphs; only in the details possible in a large-scale drawing is some attempt made at individual portraiture or the depiction of peculiarities. But grotesque representations of the human species are extremely rare, and largely confined to ephemeral scurrilities sketched on flakes of limestone or pottery to while away an idle hour. There are also bizarre phallic figures which were evidently popular as *ex votos*, especially in the Ptolemaic and Roman Periods.

3

14, 25, 30

44

164

3, 108, 139, 185

When once a scribe had learnt to draw the full range of ideographic signs with requisite skill he had become *ipso facto* an artist, since the composition of his pictures is the assemblage of a number of ideographs with some interaction between them, often expressed in strong rhythmic patterns. This relationship has been fully discussed recently by Dr Henry G. Fischer of the Metropolitan Museum of Art, New York, who has pointed out that the dominant rightward orientation of Egyptian writing has influenced the scenes depicted on the earliest monuments, and this remains true for as long as the ancient culture persisted.

25, 45, 46, 69

112, 133, 141

The rightward direction of the signs of most hieroglyphic inscriptions may not appear to have had much effect upon the composition of paintings and reliefs where an orientation can be reversed at will to indicate confronted figures or scenes, but it has certainly had its effect upon statuary. At first sight such sculpture

Terms   hieroglyphs

Papyrus   the gods' words

might be thought to be little affected by the conceptual character of Egyptian drawing, and instead of a synthesis of front and side elevations, there is a separation of a left and a right profile drawn on opposite sides of a block of stone or wood and worked into the front elevation drawn on the front surface. Further examination will show, however, that the features of Egyptian drawing on a flat area are just as dominant in the carving of figures in three dimensions. As Dr Fischer remarks, Egyptian statues normally put the left foot or arm forward when a limb has to be advanced. 'They nurse or hold children with the left arm, or carry burdens on the left side. Similarly lions and sphinxes normally show the tail on the right side, corresponding to the rightward orientation of the hieroglyphic image of a lion.' Of course there are exceptions to this rule, such as statues worked as pairs in some balanced arrangement; but the influence of drawing in two dimensions may be seen on the left side of most standing statues of men where the advanced leg is the only one to be represented, whereas on the right side both legs are shown, corresponding to the rightward orientation of such figures in relief or in painting. Such a convention is closely associated with the idea of 'negative space', about which more will be said later. The spectator must imagine that the stone fillings of the statue are transparent and he can see through them.

cf. 118, 184

If Egyptian works of art, therefore, represent ideograms writ large – the idea of objects rather than their exact realization in a spatial context – that is because, like the 'god's words', or the writing that conditioned them, both are concerned with the practical functions of making a statement, as Ptah fashioned the world by making a creative utterance. It is exceptional for a work of art in ancient Egypt not to be accompanied by an inscription that sets the scene, or describes the action or defines its purpose and names the actors. Even a statue which might be thought to exist independently in its own right, is not complete, and represents nobody without its inscription. Sometimes the statue may act as the determinative hieroglyph in three dimensions of that inscription.

The purpose of such statements is to cast a spell, to impose a favourable order upon the universe under the inspiration of the Creator who first brought it into being out of Chaos. The position of such a work of art in the world of Creation is seen in the magic ritual, the Opening of the Mouth, that each statue, painting, relief or building had to undergo on its completion to ensure that it was transformed from an inanimate product of man's hands into a vibrant part of the divine order charged with numinous power.

CHAPTER TWO

Artists, their Materials and Methods

While to our modern understanding Egyptian art may be an elusive manifestation, the recognition of the Egyptian artist is a simpler matter since the names of some of them have survived. We even have a few signed pieces. The ruins of artists' studios have been excavated, and there are reliefs and paintings of artists at work.

47
102, 170
146–8

In the workshops pictured in the Old Kingdom reliefs, or the New Kingdom wall paintings, craftsmen of different trades, from sculptors and metalsmiths to joiners and jewellers, are shown working side by side. It is clear that they are under the direction of an educated supervisor, familiar with the techniques of several crafts, able to recognize an inferior standard of work and to correct errors. He is, in short, what would be called today a designer, concerned with planning the main design and the details for the specialist craftsman to execute under his guidance. Most of the commissions would follow a traditional pattern long hallowed by use and religious sanction; but occasionally a fresh design would be demanded, as on the advent of a new king, and especially during the New Kingdom when a taste for exotic novelties arose among the patrons.

As mentioned above, such chief designers in earlier times were the High Priests of Ptah of Memphis, and their responsibility for designing works of art is explicit in the directions given to them by Mykerinus and Sahurē when these kings had tomb furnishings made for favourite courtiers. In the case of the latter pharaoh, the High Priest was commissioned to make a double portal of Tura limestone for the tomb of the King's chief physician. A room of the palace was utilized as a studio so that Sahurē could inspect the daily progress of the work and give instructions about its colouring. The portal has happily survived and is now in the Cairo Museum. It is obviously made of fine materials by superior craftsmen.

The first recorded High Priest of Ptah was the son-in-law of Shepseskaf, the last king of the Fourth Dynasty, but it is highly probable that the office had been held by near relations of the pharaoh from earliest times. The tradition was observed sporadically in later ages, sons of both Amenophis III and Ramesses II holding the appointment. But the Egyptian ideal of advancing the son to the place of his father encouraged a tendency for such offices to become hereditary, like that of the craftsmen whom they directed. In the Third Dynasty, the Greatest of Seers, or the High Priest of the influential sun-god, Rē of Heliopolis, some twenty-five miles north of Memphis, undertook the office of Master of the King's Works. The most celebrated of these priests was Imhotep, the Chancellor of King Djoser, who not only designed the Step Pyramid at Saqqara, the first stone building worthy of the name, but also as Chief of Sculptors produced some of the sculpture with which it was furnished.

The sun cult of Heliopolis was greatly concerned with star watching and the movement of heavenly bodies. Its priesthood became adept at astronomy, time measurement and the associated mathematics, and was well fitted to supervise the layout and orientation of buildings, and to make the calculations needed for estimating the amount of materials and the size of the labour force required for their construction. By the early Fourth Dynasty such important offices were also held by sons of the king, such as Rēhotep and Hemon.

In the New Kingdom it was usually the Overseers of All the Works of the King who were responsible for directing craftsmen on the royal building projects; but other institutions, such as the Great Temple of Amun at Thebes, which had risen to great wealth and influence, also had its Master of Works, usually the Second Prophet. Under Ramesses II, it was the First Prophet, Bekenkhons, who was responsible for some of the extensive building schemes of his king, including the great court, with its pylons and obelisks, that was added to the temple of Amenophis III at Luxor. A century or so later, another First Prophet, Ramesses-nakht, also acted as the King's Master of Works and was in charge of a considerable force of workmen and a pioneer corps cutting and hauling greywacke in the Wadi Hammamat for the monuments of Ramesses IV.

The king's stewards, such as Senenmut and Kenamun, also directed bodies of labourers and craftsmen. Indeed, the former has been accredited with the design as well as the construction of the mortuary temple of Queen Hatshepsut at Deir el-Bahri. Following after him was a King's Scribe, Minmose, who had acted as a military secretary to Tuthmosis III during his campaigns in Asia. He raised temples for his king in various parts of the country, particularly in Lower Egypt, and even in distant Byblos in the Lebanon. The high official largely responsible for the enormous constructions of Amenophis III was another expert in military logistics, the Scribe of the Recruits, Amenhotep-son-of-Hapu.

The special ability of all these architects and Masters of Works, like that of the canal diggers of the earliest dynasties, was their experience in handling large bodies of men and supplies. Great engineering works in Egypt depended for their successful completion on the most effective use of materials and the labouring force to handle them. Only in Imhotep do we find a functionary equally proficient in the design and execution of a great monument. Thus although it was Amenhotep-son-of-Hapu who was responsible for the tremendous feat of transporting the monolithic colossi of Amenophis III upstream from the quarries near Heliopolis and erecting them on the west bank at Thebes, it was the King's Chief Sculptor, Men, who was doubtless responsible for fashioning them, as well as other mighty monuments in the granite of Aswan.

The evidence for the position and importance of Chief Sculptors is stronger in the New Kingdom. Bak, the Chief Sculptor of Akhenaten, was a royal favourite, as was his successor, Tuthmose. Yuti, the Sculptor of Queen Tiye, had his studio within the precincts of the royal palace. At the same period wealthy patrons of art, apart from the court, existed in the great temples where workshops were established for the production of statuary and artworks of all kinds needed for sacerdotal use. The close connection between the priest and the artist, which is evident in the Old Kingdom with the office of chief craftsman held by the High Priest of Ptah, continued throughout Egyptian history. In the Middle Kingdom the sculptor Iritisen, who has left us in his tomb stela an obscure account of his knowledge of traditional processes, boasts also of his knowledge of liturgical matters. The architect Minmose was appointed to lucrative priesthoods in several of the temples that he erected, though it may well be that these rewards were bestowed upon him after his retirement from the active list. Many of the craftsmen employed on the construction of the royal tombs at Thebes also held priesthoods in the local cults. The two sculptors who made the statue of Sennufer 102 bear the titles of ordinary priests as well as designers in the House of Gold (workshops) of the temple of Amun. The sculptor who cast the bronze statue of Karomama was a priest of Amun as well as an official 170 of the God's Wife of Amun, a lady of great eminence in Thebes during his time.

Such religious duties were not in conflict with a secular calling since all such activities were inspired by the gods and discharged in their service. As we have seen, on completion, all works of art, such as statues and reliefs with their accompanying inscriptions, had to undergo a religious rite, the Opening of the Mouth, in order to animate them, and this ceremony was repeated periodically.

The workmen who were directed by these architects, chief sculptors and master craftsmen were for the most part modest artisans, working in studios attached to palaces or temples, or, in the feudal period, to the residences of local magnates. It is doubtful if they had the same wide understanding of the principles of Egyptian art as their supervisors; they probably followed rule-of-thumb formulae that they had learnt from their fathers and would pass on to their sons. Egyptian art reflects the conservatism of hereditary crafts in many of its technical features. Processes were continued with little change over the centuries, apart from the substitution of bronze for copper tools in the New Kingdom, and the introduction, possibly in Saite times, of iron, which may account for the fine cutting of inscriptions in hard stones during this period.

Moreover, the intense specialization of Egyptian crafts, in which a workman perfected his skill in a limited field of endeavour, tended to inhibit any rapid change in style, though it did not entirely eliminate originality, as is seen in the free modelling of plaster while wet, which the sculptors introduced into the tomb reliefs at Amarna where the rock was too poor to allow fine detail to be carved with the chisel. An Egyptian work of art is often the result of a collaboration between several different specialists. Draughtsmen, stonemasons, sculptors, painters, goldsmiths and lapidaries may all play their part in the production. It is evident that in such circumstances any changes in iconography and style could only have been effected by the master craftsman who designed the work and superintended its execution.

27, 59, 112, 146, 168

The geological resources of Egypt, with its wealth of different rocks, from soft sedimentary limestones and sandstones near the waterway of the Nile, to hard igneous and metamorphic rocks in the deserts and cataracts, very early encouraged the Egyptian to exploit stone as a prime material for his crafts. The process began in the prehistoric age when boulders selected for their intrinsic beauty were fashioned into stone vessels by means of a special tool, the 'wobbly drill', a cranked device with weights acting as a flywheel and actuating flint borers that ground out the interiors. So characteristic of stone-working was this drill that in the form of a hieroglyph it became the ideogram for any craftsman, craft or ingenious device. Expertise in the working of stone with stone tools was handed down as a traditional skill and was never superseded by the introduction of metal tools at the dawn of history.

The material *par excellence* in the Old Kingdom, which never lost its popularity throughout Egyptian history, was the limestone of the Memphis region, particularly the fine-grained stone from the quarries of Tura. This material could be easily cut and split from its bed in almost naturally occurring blocks. Limestone, sandstone, gypsum, steatite, serpentine and similar soft stones could be shaped with the same tools as those employed by woodworkers. These consisted of copper (later bronze) chisels of various weights and sizes, bow-drills, saws and adzes, the blades and points of which were hardened by cold hammering. Such implements were soon blunted and made brittle by use, and had to be frequently sharpened and reworked by specialist coppersmiths attached to the gangs of workmen. Hard stones such as granite, basalt, diorite, quartzite, greywacke, alabaster and indurated limestone had to be worked by different methods, principally by lighting fires contained within mud-brick walls on the larger areas, quenching the heated stone with water and pounding away the shattered surfaces with naturally occurring dolerite balls, flint mauls held in a withy, or hard pebbles. Modern experiments have demonstrated that it is possible to carve a granite head in a comparatively short time using flint tools.

The tools in the hands of craftsmen shown carving hard stone monuments in the tomb of Rekhmirē appear to be of flint or stone *126* and are used without hammers. By striking the hard stones in a certain way with even harder stone tools, unwanted pieces were jarred off by vibration. In his *Reminiscences* the Rev. Archibald Sayce has described how his boatmen, finding their way impeded by a granite outcrop during one of their porterages through the First Cataract, searched around until they had found pieces of a certain stone, which unfortunately he does not identify, and using these as hammers soon reduced the obstacle to a heap of small chips. He realized that they were using an ancestral technique of stoneworking.

In the late periods, iron punches appear to have been used for stunning the surface of hard stones, particularly for the extremely crisp cutting of the inscriptions. In all these methods, employing *190-2* pounders of stone or metal, the aim was to pulverize the stone and to remove the powdered surface with scrapers of flint or bronze. Work in both hard and soft stones was finished by smoothing and polishing with rubbers made from quartzite, or similar hard granular stones, using finely sifted quartz sand as an abrasive. Quartz sand, in fact, was an important adjunct to many tools in ancient Egypt, and was used with copper drills and saws. Particles of quartz were driven by the rotating or reciprocating motion of the tools into the soft metal, giving them cutting edges similar to those of modern gem-set tools. Sir Flinders Petrie found marks on the granite sarcophagus of King Kheops which led him to postulate that it must have been cut with copper saws over two metres long.

The heavy pounding that hard-stone statues sustained during the course of manufacture occasionally caused damage and fracture at a late stage of production. Rather than troubling to discard the work

and begin again, the sculptors refitted broken pieces with dowels of
wood or metal. They were also expert in cutting out blemishes or
damaged areas and inserting close-fitting insets before continuing the
carving. Two statues of Amenophis III which reveal these techniques
quite clearly are in the Metropolitan Museum of Art, New York,
where there is also a statue of Sesostris I which shows that the missing
head was broken off and reattached with a dowel in antiquity.

Wood was employed extensively for statuary, and not in-
frequently for reliefs decorating panels, doors and the sides of shrines.
It was worked chiefly by the adze and chisel. The saw and axe were
used for lopping, splitting and rough shaping; but the main work was
done with the adze, which, as the boat builders of Micronesia have
demonstrated with stone examples in modern times, is a versatile
instrument in the hands of skilled craftsmen. An adze in black bronze
inlaid with gold, found in the tomb of Tutankhamun, has suffered
the theft of its blade of gold or silver, and although a presentation
piece not intended for practical use, is admirably designed to fit the
hand. With such a tool it was possible to cut and shape wood and to
plane it smooth. Detail was added with a chisel, and a finish imparted
with an abrasive, where the natural surface was to be left exposed.

The native timbers of Egypt, chiefly the acacia and sycamore-fig,
were too fibrous, knotty and contorted to permit fine joinery, and the
highest standards of execution are found in objects made from
imported timbers, such as the coniferous woods of the Lebanon and
the ebony of tropical Africa.

Most sculpture in wood and soft stone was made to be covered
with a thin layer of gesso, a mixture of glue and whiting capable of
taking a very smooth finish like a polish. Afterwards, the surface was
painted in dense colours from a limited palette or covered with gold
leaf. Statues in such fine woods as ebony and boxwood were usually
left in the raw state. Objects in hard stones such as granites, basalt and
quartzite were occasionally coloured or gilded, but usually only in
certain parts such as lips and eyes, and details of dress such as jewels,
belts and headgear.

References to statues made of copper are found in the records as
early as the Second Dynasty, and probably apply to figures of gods
and kings made by hammering copper plates over a wooden core.
Only two examples of this technique have been found and they are
greatly corroded. One shows King Phiops I larger than life-size, the
other, on a much smaller scale, probably represents the same king
supporting his Horus name, now missing. A few statuettes in solid
copper have survived from the Old Kingdom, but they are invariably
crude owing to the technical difficulty of casting in this metal; and it

145

3

59, 68, 146
Frontispiece

144

52

was not until the introduction of bronze in the Middle Kingdom that metal statues are found that have been cast with a fair degree of skill, using the *cire perdue* method. In this process, the object was modelled in beeswax, fitted with sprues and invested with a very fine clay in a semi-liquid form. When this coating had dried hard, it was carefully heated in a brazier, the wax burning away to leave a hollow impression in the clay which had been fired to the condition of terracotta. Molten metal was poured from a crucible down the tubes left by the volatilized wax sprues to produce a cast of the original model. Finally the mould was broken away, the surplus metal removed and the cast polished. By such means figurines in gold, silver and bronze were cast solid.

During the New Kingdom, if not earlier, larger statues were cast in bronze round a clay core retained within, supported on chaplets of copper. An example showing this technique is the kneeling statue of Tuthmosis IV in the British Museum, which is lighter in weight, of 131 course, than a solid example, less bronze (an expensive metal in antiquity) having been used in its manufacture. To judge by the fragment of a statue of Ramesses V in the Fitzwilliam Museum, Cambridge (no. E.213.1954) such casts were substantially thick at this period; but by Libyan times, greater skill and longer experience had succeeded in achieving casts of much thinner metal. In the Late 169, 170 Period, votive statuettes, using heavily leaded bronze with a low melting-point, were mass produced, the best of them being worked with great competence. Although most of those surviving are covered with a green patina where they have not been cleaned in modern times, there is little doubt that in their pristine state they were burnished to resemble gold. Some of them in fact were covered with a thin skin of gilded gesso.

The design of metal sculpture owes nothing to the practice of modelling the archetype rather than carving it. Similarly, wood and ivory sculpture is uninfluenced by the cylindrical shape of the log or tusk from which it is carved. In the wooden statues of women the head, body and legs, but not the forepart of the feet, were carved in one piece, and the same process was generally employed for statues of men. In the unique statue of King Hor advantage has been taken of a 100 divergent limb from the trunk of the tree to form the right leg as an extension of the torso, the advanced left leg being attached separately. This technique may have been employed more frequently than has been noted, any joins being hidden in most examples under clothing applied in gesso. Arms were usually made separately and tenoned into 100, 101 the body at the shoulders, though if both arms were held straight to the sides they were carved *en masse* with the body. 59, 60

Figures in wood, ivory and metal differ from contemporary stone statues in that the more tractable nature of the media enabled the sculptor to release limbs from fillings, to bend arms at the elbows and to drill the clenched hands so as to hold staves and sceptres. In this way statues could assume the postures of figures represented in two dimensions in painting and relief. For the rest, the Egyptian concept of form is imposed on the medium – wood, ivory, metal or stone – with little regard to its inherent qualities.

Sculptors also carved in relief, usually in soft limestone during the Old and Middle Kingdoms, but more often in sandstone during the New Kingdom and Late Period. In addition alabaster, granite, quartzite and other hard stones were worked in relief, particularly for shrines and sarcophagi. Walls were lined with fine limestone or sandstone blocks, and dressed *in situ* to a uniform flatness, usually by means of adzes and pounders, using for the purpose of achieving a plane surface boning-rods, i.e. a set of three rods of equal length, the two outer joined by a string at their upper ends, the third free to move along the line of the string to indicate high spots. Blemishes and joints were filled with plaster and tinted to match where necessary; the whole was finally rubbed down to a smooth finish.

On this prepared surface, a grid was laid out by snapping a string dipped in paint and stretched at vertical and horizontal intervals. Figures and objects were drawn on this grid by the outline draughtsman, scaling up the work from designs in pattern books of which no traces have survived, though there are vague references to them in the inventories of temple libraries in the Ptolemaic Period. A drawing board in the British Museum, dating to the reign of Tuthmosis III, gives an idea of their appearance.

A similar grid was applied to each face of the block of stone from which a statue was to be carved, so as to receive a left and right profile, a front and rear view, and a top view which were worked into each other by the stonemason, more detail being added by the master draughtsman as the work progressed. The same system was doubtless used on an enormous scale for hewing colossi, such as the statues of Memnon at Thebes, or those of Ramesses II at Abu Simbel. No account was taken of foreshortening from the standpoint of the spectator, since in conformity with the Egyptian ideal, the optical impression of the near observer was subservient to the need to carve a statue which was perfect in itself.

In both relief and statuary, the initial outlines were subjected to a scrutiny by the master sculptor who corrected where necessary in ink of a different colour. Such modifications reveal that the final appearance of a composition was not a mechanical result, but was

26

dependent on the personal judgment of the master artist as to the proportion of the figures and their position in relation to each other. Here his sensibility and experience had full scope. Similarly, in the production of a statue, the half-finished works found in the studios at Amarna show that control was exercised by the master throughout the carving process, areas to be removed being indicated by bold shading in black or red ink, and lines of reference being constantly redrawn.

148

In relief, after the outline drawing had been completed and approved, it was the turn of the specialist stone cutters to take over with their chisels and rubbers. This stage appears to have been often a somewhat mechanical process, for examples of relief exist showing that the sculptor has misinterpreted the lines drawn by the draughtsman and mistakes have had to be rectified in plaster.

Relief was of two kinds: raised relief (*bas-relief*), in which the entire background was lowered, leaving the figures and inscriptions raised from the field, and sunk relief (*relief en creux*) in which the outlines are deeply incised into the background and the subject modelled within these contours, inscriptions also being incised. In general, raised relief is used in work of high quality, and is particularly in evidence upon interior walls where the lighting is diffused. Sunk relief is usually reserved for exterior walls in strong sunlight; but it also appears commonly on monuments in granite, alabaster, quartzite and other hard stones in which the entire sinking of the background would prove a long and laborious process. Nevertheless, examples of raised relief in hard stones do exist, particularly in the royal stelae of the Archaic Period. Sunk relief was extensively used by Akhenaten at Karnak and Amarna, as this allowed his sculptors to decorate his large monuments in a relatively short time. A development of sunk relief is the sinking of the background for a distance round the contours of subjects, and the tapering of it gradually to the surface of the stone producing a kind of bastard raised relief in which less stone is removed from the field.

43, 75, 133
194
69, 122, 140,
166

cf. 4, 7

138, 139, 142

In addition to carvings in relief, a third type of linear representation is sometimes encountered, particularly in the earlier periods, when virtual engravings in stone, wood and ivory are found. In large-scale monuments such examples are usually incised upon hard stones, like granite or alabaster, but on rare occasions soft limestone may be used. Thus the elegant outlines of the scenes of King Mentuhotep II before the gods, from his dismantled temple at Tod, are cut in the limestone blocks with only a minimum of subtle enhancement given to the interior contours. This closely approaches engraving, though technically the process is a sort of very shallow sunk relief.

8

72, cf. 105

27, 45 Like statuary, the soft-stone reliefs were brilliantly painted. In the case of sandstone, such pigments were applied to a thin coat of gesso so that in their original condition the grey-buff sandstone monuments of the later periods would have differed little in surface appearance from their white limestone prototypes. Today, this painted skin of thick whitewash has disappeared except in some interior chambers that have escaped weathering, or in the sandstone blocks of the temples of Akhenaten at Karnak which were dismantled before their painted surfaces could be denuded.

Where painted relief could not be used, as, for instance, in the walls of tomb-chapels hewn in areas of poor rock, the subjects were 79, 80 represented in paintings on plastered surfaces. In the hills of the Theban necropolis during the New Kingdom strata of good rock were found only exceptionally, and it is in such areas that sculpture is 133–4 used for decorating the walls of tomb chapels. Elsewhere, and in the more modest tombs on this site, a thick coating of straw and mud was applied to the rough-hewn walls and covered with an outer skin of plaster. On surfaces so prepared, and squared with a grid, the outline draughtsmen drew their scenes and decorations, to be followed by the painters who applied colour in broad masses. Finally, the draughtsmen restored the outlines, usually in a dark red-brown, but 124, 125, 129 sometimes in a dense black, especially during the Ramesside Period. In this way detail was added and the contours sharpened. A scribal draughtsman drew the inscriptions, which in the best examples are 141 painted in an elegant blue-grey silhouette or in polychrome detail. The resilient straw-and-mud support of these pictures has preserved them from bad shrinkages and earth tremors, so that many of them have survived in an astonishingly fresh condition, though frequently 124 damaged by the hand of man.

Early in the Eighteenth Dynasty the background was usually painted a French grey colour, but exceptionally it was yellow, as in the tomb of Kenamun. Later a white ground was preferred, but in Ramesside tombs yellow is often found. The colours came from a limited palette. Yellow, red and brown ochres are earth pigments which have altered little over the years. A lime white played very much the same role as Chinese white in modern gouache painting, being used alone and mixed with other colours to lighten their tones and make them more opaque. Green was obtained by mixing blue with yellow ochre or orpiment. It was also made from copper salts, usually carbonates, but this pigment has not always lasted well and has sometimes changed to a rusty hue. Blue was a difficult colour to manufacture, most of it being obtained from a copper-based frit which was ground to a fine powder and which often tends to green. A

28

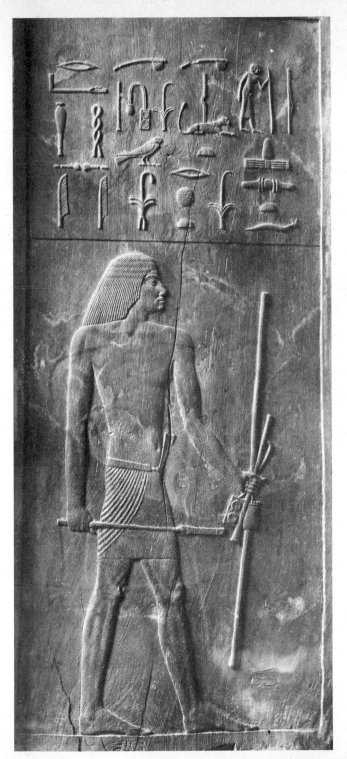

3　Wooden stela of Hesy,
from Saqqara, *c.* 2670 B C.

more successful result was achieved by grinding to powder another artificial substance, 'Egyptian Blue', or copper-calcium-tetrasilicate, which produces an ultramarine shade of blue. The vehicle in all cases was a water-soluble gum and Egyptian painting is, therefore, a form of glue tempera. Black pigment was usually made from soot, and sometimes from plumbago which has not always combined with the vehicle, but has fallen away from the wall, leaving only a faint stain behind. Its loss is particularly evident in paintings of wigs and hair, which occasionally are a pale straw colour rather than a dense black.

Paint was applied to walls in flat tones, though a textural effect is frequently achieved by chance circumstances, such as blemishes and roughness in the plaster surface, impurities in the pigments and scrubbing by a brush not always fully charged with colour. Shading is very rarely indicated, but does exist in some early Ramesside pictures. In general, the chosen pigments imitate the natural colour of the object represented. Thus herbage was painted green, mud black, water blue, linen garments white, gold yellow and silver white. Flesh tones were determined more by convention, the skin of Egyptian men being painted red-brown and that of their womenfolk pale ochre. Nubians and Negroes were usually represented as black. Asiatics have light yellow skins, yet Aegeans are as red-brown as the Egyptians. Nevertheless there are some departures from these norms, some women being depicted with yellow-brown skins, and some Asiatics appearing with the red-brown colouring of the Aegeans. In a group of men drawn with overlapping contours, alternate forms may be coloured in light and dark tones to distinguish them.

The only near-illusionist colouring in which the Egyptian painter indulged was in his representation of the fur of animals, the plumage of birds and the scales of fish. He could also, in depicting architectural features, imitate quite skilfully the graining of knotty wood, or the speckle of red granite. He could illustrate, too, the veining and pebbly surface of vessels made of breccia or porphyry, and the wavy banding of his polychrome glass flasks. In the tomb of Ti at Saqqara he has tried to indicate the legs of cattle and herdsmen beneath the waters of a ford.

All these efforts to represent vividly in paint the appearance of things, are not, however, aberrations from his essentially non-perspectival view of reality. They are more the exuberance of an artist exulting in his ability to depict detail, just as the sculptor of the panels of Hesy has lovingly carved the musculature of the torso and limbs, the appearance of the collar-bones and the waves of the hair. The essential drawing remains intact, representing the subject as it was known to exist in the mind's eye.

CHAPTER THREE

The Archaic Period
Dynasties I–II

There is a clear gap between the prehistoric periods in ancient Egypt and the culture of the dynastic age that succeeded them. There is even a suggestion of a racial difference in the predominance of a broad-headed ruling caste with a more massive physique in pharaonic times than that of the slighter, long-headed people whose skeletons are found in the Upper Egyptian prehistoric cemeteries.

Tradition affirmed that near the end of the fourth millennium BC Egypt was divided into two independent kingdoms. The North, or Lower Egypt, comprised all the Nile Delta and part of the Valley a little to the south of Dahshur. From there the South, or Upper Egypt, extended to Gebel es-Silsileh, some forty miles north of the First Cataract. It is possible that while Upper Egypt was united under the rule of a paramount chief or king, Lower Egypt consisted of a loose federation of Delta city states under the leadership of an overlord. The union of these 'Two Lands' for the first time was probably effected very much in the same manner as subsequent reunions in the twentieth, sixteenth and eighth centuries BC – an aggressive king from the harsher and more unified South defeated the local rulers of the North, and made himself master of the entire country.

The success of the political settlement that was made by the first ruler to assume the crowns of Upper and Lower Egypt, the legendary Menes, ensured that reunification after periods of anarchy would repeat the same pattern. Menes is reputed to have founded his new capital, White Walls (later called Memphis), on land reclaimed by diverting the Nile flood near the junction of the two kingdoms, thus recognizing the most important responsibilities of the unitary state under its sole ruler, the control of the entire Nile flood and the extension of the cultivable land by drainage schemes and hydraulic works. Lower and Upper Egypt remained thereafter separate entities but united in the person of the divine king.

Lower Egypt was virtually the Delta region, with its stretches of pastures separated by thickets of rushes and reeds from the marshes around the pools and branches of the Nile, a land eminently suitable for the raising and herding of cattle, sheep, goats and pigs. Its flowery meadows produced honey as well as milk, and its creeks abounded in fish and pond fowl. It was along the banks of the western branch of the Nile that the choicest vineyards were situated. Its population, too, was constantly reinforced by a drift of Libyan peoples on its western borders and infiltrations of Asiatics on the east. Its seaports traded with the Aegean and Levantine worlds, importing ideas as well as products.

By contrast Upper Egypt was more homogeneous, its population less diversified and more united by the easily navigable main stream. It was a region devoted to the raising of crops, such as grain and flax, to the hunting of the animals of the river margins, and to the exploitation of the deserts, particularly their minerals and gold deposits. It also controlled the oases in the Western Desert and the products imported from tropical Africa such as ebony, ivory, exotic pelts and feathers. Both regions shared a common language, though it was proverbial that the largely Nubian population on the southern frontier would be unable to understand a man from the Delta. Above all, they enjoyed the same material culture and believed in the same fundamental religious ideas. The underlying sympathy in the thought and purpose of the peoples of both lands is evident in the vigour with which Egyptian civilization flourished during periods of reunion after interludes of schism. The prime factor in the absence of discord was the rule of a sole divine king, the incarnation of the Creator who had fashioned the Egyptian universe in the 'First Time', and whose advent reaffirmed *maet*.

Evidence for the political activity that brought about a unified pharaonic Egypt comes from the few works of art that have survived from the remote First Dynasty. The furnishings that have been recovered from the rifled royal tombs and cenotaphs of this period are mostly fragmentary but they give tantalizing glimpses of highly accomplished work in wood and ivory, rock-crystal and other hard stones, flint, gold, and copper. In this they show the persistence of traditions dating from prehistoric times. The novel creations of the time are the series of shield-shaped slate palettes, and the large, votive, pear-shaped mace-heads, unfortunately mostly fragmentary, that commemorate successes on the field of battle. They, too, are developments of designs that appear in the immediate predynastic period.

One such fragment is the 'Battlefield Palette' from Abydos, now divided between museums in London, Lucerne and Oxford, which commemorates the defeat of a Libyan people in the eastern Delta. A fragment of another palette, in Cairo (no. C. 14238), probably dates to the reign of Scorpion, perhaps the immediate predecessor of Menes, and records the conquest of fortified settlements also on the Libyan borders of the Delta with a rich booty of animals and plants.

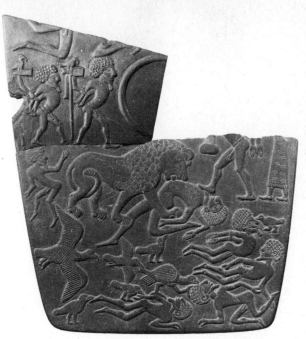

4 The 'Battlefield Palette', a fragment of slate carved with figures of a ravening lion among the corpses strewn on a battlefield, and personified districts led captive, from Abydos, *c.* 3170 BC.

These memorials of the king's victories are distinguished by the clarity of their designs.

Other, earlier palettes, of the predynastic period, were probably used in a magic ceremony to ensure success in the hunt. They show animals of the wild, the predators of the domesticated cattle and cultivated crops, and regarded by the Valley dwellers as tangible manifestations of evil, like the marauding bedouin. The most complete example comes from Hierakonpolis, the ancient capital of Upper Egypt, and is expertly carved in relief with a rout of animals, 5 leopard, lion, gazelle, giraffe, ibex, oryx and bull, as well as the mythical serpopard, gryphon, and an animal-headed flautist. The field is enclosed by a coursing wild dog on each side. Among these beasts all is disorder and violent action.

By contrast, the palette of King Narmer, also from Hierakonpolis, 6, 7 which commemorates a victory over human foes is calm, logical in its arrangement, and restrained in the actions depicted. This, the most important of these early monuments, even at the dawn of history, exhibits the essential characteristics of pharaonic art. The shield-shaped field is divided into registers, a means of organizing the picture space according to an intellectual concept. The reverse shows 6

33

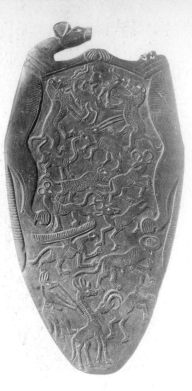

5 Reverse of the Oxford slate palette, showing creatures of the wild, from Hierakonpolis, *c.* 3200 BC.

6 Reverse of the slate palette of King Narmer, from Hierakonpolis, *c.* 3168 BC.

7 Obverse of the slate palette of King Narmer, from Hierakonpolis, *c.* 3168 BC.

Narmer, probably the legendary Menes, wearing the White Crown of Aphroditopolis, which was soon to become the emblematic headgear of the pharaoh as King of Upper Egypt, Narmer is clubbing a foeman who sinks helpless before his divine might. He is followed by his foot-washer, shown on a smaller scale and standing on a separate register line, as befits his relative unimportance. The sacrifice is performed before the supreme sky-god Horus, of whom Narmer is also an incarnation, represented as a falcon with a human arm holding captive a personified papyrus thicket, probably symbolizing the inhabitants of the Delta. Below, in contrast to this orderly scene, is a contorted design representing two fallen Asiatics in death-throes.

7   On the obverse of this palette, Narmer wears the Red Crown of the Delta city states, Sais and Buto, in his capacity of King of Lower Egypt, and he inspects a battlefield near Buto, the northern capital, with the decapitated bodies of pinioned foemen. He is preceded by his four standard-bearers and his priest, and followed by his foot-washer. The middle register of this highly organized design shows a circular depression round which are disposed two long-necked lionesses and

34

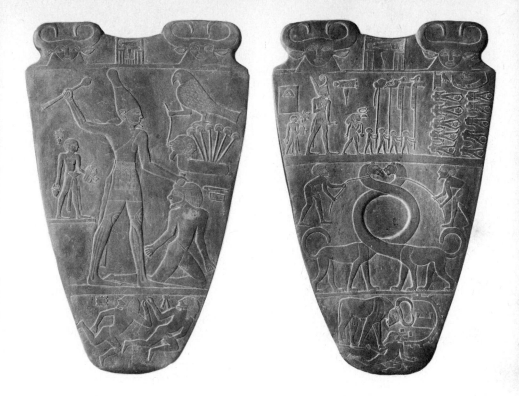

their attendants, perhaps symbolizing the idea of union. In the lower register Narmer, in the guise of a bull, breaks down a fortified place and tramples upon its fallen chief, probably a Libyan.

This palette may represent, as many have claimed, the conquest of all Egypt by Narmer and its unification under his rule; but it also illustrates what was to be the dominant theme of much pharaonic iconography, the victory of the god incarnate over the forces of evil and disorder. Here, as man, falcon and bull, he subdues rebellious subjects as well as Asiatic and Libyan neighbours of Egypt. The skilful carving of the piece, with its mastery of design and precise delineation of minor details, entitles us to regard it as the work of a supreme craftsman, probably also the sculptor of the 'Bull Palette' in the Louvre (no. E. 11255), specially commissioned to produce a work which would worthily commemorate the king's triumph. It was doubtless dedicated at the shrine of the sky and mother goddess whose woman's face emerges from the cow heads at the top of the palette, flanking the name of Narmer written within the palace-glyph. cf. 11

The palette, however, shows other features which are significant.

The eyes are carved in relief and not hollowed out as blind depressions, a characteristic of the earlier predynastic palettes. But perhaps the most striking novelty is the appearance of hieroglyphic labels attached to the actors in the drama depicted. The figures of the king, his foot-washer and priest, as well as his foemen, are accompanied by signs which may spell out their various names. The rebus formed by the falcon surmounting the personified thicket on the reverse and having the meaning, 'Horus leads captive the Delta', has often been remarked as a notable step in the development of hieroglyphic writing.

The production of a repertory of such glyphs evolved in step with the iconography of the new pharaonic art. The rapid development of both can be seen in the ivory label of King Den, the fifth king of the First Dynasty, in which the design of the conquering king, smiting the enemy of the Egyptian state, has reached its classic pose, while the accompanying caption, 'first time of smiting the East', is unambiguous, unlike the pictographs on similar labels of earlier kings. In the reign of Den, whose appearance marks a distinct advance in the evolution of Egyptian culture, the figure of the hound biting its quarry emerges for the first time in Egyptian iconography. In earlier hunting scenes, as on the slate palettes, the predatory animal merely nuzzles or licks its victim; here the association of two figures, hitherto separately conceived, is complete. The disposition of the animals within the picture area is an early example of the Egyptian predilection for squaring the circle and thus giving expression to the essential Egyptian feeling for space as rectilinear.

Apart from such votive pieces as the slate palette of Narmer, some statues and carved ceremonial mace-heads which have been

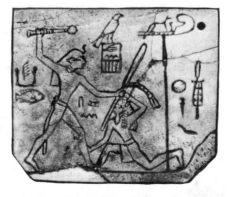

8   Ivory label of King Den smiting an Asiatic foe, from Abydos, *c.* 2950 BC.

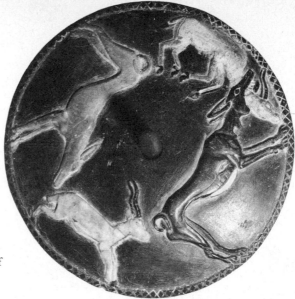

9 Steatite and alabaster disc of
King Den, showing dogs
hunting gazelle, from Saqqara,
c. 2950 BC.

excavated from temple precincts, the monuments of the Archaic
Period have nearly all come from funerary contexts.

The constructions of the prehistoric period, whether the shrines of
gods or the dwellings of man, were built of flimsy and perishable
materials, and are better examined in the more permanent versions of
the Third Dynasty (see below). The chief features of the mortuary
architecture of the First Dynasty as it has been preserved in the royal
tombs at Saqqara and the cenotaphs at Abydos, the birthplace of the
ancestors of the early pharaohs, is the *mastaba*, the rectangular, bench-
like superstructure, with its long axis running north and south, built
over a complex of burial and storage chambers below ground. The
walls of these superstructures have a slight slope, or 'batter', a
reminder of an earlier mode of construction, when woven reed
hurdles, forming the sides of buildings, were daubed with mud which
had a tendency to flow downwards forming a thicker coating at the
base of the wall. This batter is a feature of all external walls of
Egyptian dynastic buildings, even those made of stone, though the
interior space is strictly orthogonal, and the angle of the external
inclination may vary.

The external decoration of these superstructures is based upon the
so-called 'palace façade' decoration – the design of the ceremonial
entrance to the king's palace, which was a doorway, flanked by cf.10
towers or bastions. The exterior walls of the mastaba were interrupted

by a series of such dummy entrances, perhaps corresponding to the storage chambers within the mass of the superstructure, but reduced in width and increased in number so as to form alternating recesses and projections. The design was admirably adapted to construction in sun-dried rectangular bricks.

A similar form of building is found in the slightly earlier temples at Uruk in Mesopotamia; and this has encouraged the view that it was from this source that brick construction was introduced into Egypt. There were indeed trade contacts between the two river valleys in predynastic times. The lapis lazuli of which a number of early artefacts are made must have been imported from Afghanistan, the nearest source, by middlemen, since it is doubtful whether the deposit in the Dakhla oasis was worked in remote antiquity. Four cylinder seals of Jemdet-Nasr type have also been found on Egyptian sites. Cylinder seals, common in the early dynastic period in Egypt, together with pictographic writing and such decorative motifs as the hero seizing two lions and the opposed animals with long necks intertwined, have been accredited to a Mesopotamian source. Egypt, even at this remote period, was not isolated. Imported pottery, recovered on early dynastic sites, shows that there was trade with both Palestine and Syria, but influences from abroad were probably more in the realm of ideas and techniques introduced by a drift of broad-headed peoples from Asia into Egypt. These immigrants brought with them new skills and knowledge, as was the case in later historic times. Once such ideas as picture-writing and rectangular mud-brick construction reached Egypt, they developed rapidly on native lines.

The mud-brick walls of the royal mastabas rose to an average height of over 20 feet (6 metres) and were coated with a thick lime-wash painted in imitation of woven hangings. From this it has been inferred that such constructions are renderings into mud brick of tent-like archetypes built of wood and polychrome coverings of matting or textile. Such tomb superstructures may have imitated the homes of nomadic ancestors, and must have presented a colourful and even gay appearance in marked contrast to their mortuary purpose.

With the interior arrangements of such tombs and their development, which have little architectural significance, we are not concerned. It is apparent that the thick exterior walls enclosed other structures such as a rectangular mound, sometimes stepped, of brick filled with rubble over the burial chamber. Additional storage chambers above ground level were also incorporated into the superstructure. A sand-and-rubble filling covered all, and was doubtless capped by a cambered brick roof below a parapet. The finished effect resembled a contemporary palace, a 'house of eternity'

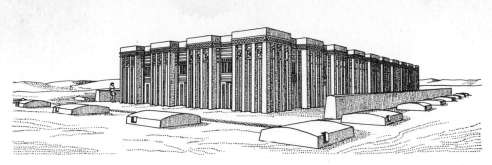

10   Reconstruction of the mastaba tomb of Queen Merneith at Saqqara, *c*. 3000 BC.

for the dead king and his retainers, a concept that appears to be of Lower Egyptian origin. But such a palace also contained within its mass the mound above the grave-pit, an Upper Egyptian feature, representing the primeval mound that arose at the First Time above the waters of elemental Chaos and from which Creation began, and in which re-creation or resurrection was therefore possible.

Subsequent development during the Archaic Period reveals an enlargement and elaboration of the substructures into long galleries with many chambers. The treatment of the exterior of the mastaba as the façade of a palace was abandoned in favour of a plain surface. The royal examples have a design of panels separated by pilasters, with a niche or dummy entrance at each end of the east face, the larger at the southern extremity being the place where offerings were presented. With the relegation of all magazines to the subterranean regions, the need of a sand-and-rubble filling to the superstructure disappeared and the palace façade decoration was transferred to the outer faces of the boundary walls of the tomb, as at the so-called 'forts' of the last two kings of the Second Dynasty at Abydos.

The mastaba tombs, both the great edifices of the kings and some of their queens, and the more modest structures of their high officials and retainers, are in too ruinous a condition to give much idea of their architectural appearance except in reconstructions. The contents of *10* their burial chambers and magazines, apart from the hard stone vessels, are also generally in too fragmentary a state to give more than an impression of an opulent yet restrained taste for articles of luxury. *9* The decoration of such tombs was limited to painted mat patterns in black, red, yellow, blue and green on a white ground, but except for the fragment of a limestone lintel with a frieze of recumbent lions from the burial chamber of Djer at Saqqara, little stone-work carved in relief has been recovered. The most notable sculptural adjunct of

39

these tombs are the round-topped stelae that were erected in pairs, probably on the east side of the building. The earlier examples are in limestone, and the finest in the series is the stela of Djet, the fourth king of the First Dynasty now in the Louvre. The excellent condition of this monument reveals crisply carved details. The masterly drawing of the falcon, poised as though for flight, is yet in conformity with the sculptor's conceptual vision: the tail is shown in a rear elevation on a profile view of the head and body. From the reign of the next king, Den, the fashion is introduced of carving such stelae in a hard stone. All the examples so far recovered come from Abydos, with the exception of the red granite stela of Rēneb of the Second Dynasty, now in New York, which doubtless originally came from the king's unlocated tomb at Saqqara.

In the reign of Qa'a, the last king of the First Dynasty, the tombs of his officials, Merka at Saqqara and Sabef at Abydos, were each marked by a stela on which the figure of the deceased, seated upon a stool, appears in raised relief, together with a fully developed hieroglyphic inscription giving his name and titles. Such stelae are indeed little better than a slight elaboration of the rudimentary grave-stones carved with silhouettes and names of retainers buried in the subsidiary tombs around the cenotaphs of their kings at Abydos.

The rapid development of relief carving, however, is evident in the slab stela, the Northern version of the round-topped stelae of Abydos, that appears during the Second Dynasty, set in the exterior niche of private mastaba tombs at Saqqara, or in the roof of the burial chamber at Helwan. In both, the owner is represented seated upon a chair before a funerary meal of bread and beer, the staples of the Egyptian diet, supplemented with cuts of meat and poultry and jars of wine. By the Fourth Dynasty such slab stelae had reached their full development, with the more disciplined arrangement of the signs, the elegant drawing and accomplished cutting of the relief, which in the best examples retains its colour. But the central feature is still the deceased seated before a table or altar on which are shown the ceremonial slices of bread, and below which usually stand jars of beer. This essential icon persists thereafter through centuries of funerary art in Egypt, changing only in style and elaboration over the unfolding years.

Such representations, of course, reveal the increasing influence of the written word, and the power of magic, since images of offerings, after the consecration rites had been performed upon them, were considered as effective as the actual food and drink entombed with the deceased, or as viable substitutes for them. Already as early as the late Archaic Period a tabulated list appears, enumerating the kinds and

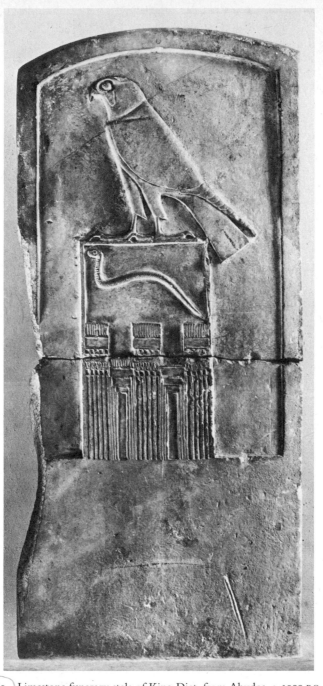

11   Limestone funerary stela of King Djet, from Abydos, *c.* 3000 B.C.

quantities of bread, cakes, beer, wine, incense and oils required by the deceased for a full life in the hereafter. A similar list is an essential part

27 of the Fourth Dynasty slab stelae from Giza.

Another need, for which magic particularly operated, was fulfilled by the provision of a statue of the deceased. There is little doubt that the Egyptians, like many peoples both ancient and modern, believed that the statue of a person or animal could in certain conditions become animated, if not dynamically alive. Statues of important and

137 influential men, such as Amenhotep-son-of-Hapu have been found with parts worn smooth by the hands of petitioners importuning them for favours as though they were living beings. A statue could also receive food offerings, like the spirit of the deceased person or living god whom it represented. With the exception of the sun-god during the Amarna Period (see below), all the gods of Egypt were

Frontispiece animate in graven images which were treated as living notables, being attended by special servants (priests), awakened, washed, censed, clothed, fed and put to rest daily. On holy days they were carried around their domains on litters, or they visited other gods in their temples elsewhere, and could give oracular answers to petitioners during such perambulations. Colossal statues of some kings such as Amenophis III and Ramesses II were worshipped as gods and had their own attendant clergy. On occasion, statues could act as substi-

cf. 166 tutes for the kings at ceremonies which they could not attend in person.

The idea of the correspondence of a statue to the person or thing it represents is not confined to the ancient Egyptians. Even a sophisticated modern audience can suspend disbelief when the statue of the Commendatore drags Don Giovanni off to Hell. But the ancient Egyptians were alone in emphasizing the identity of the subject and its image by the magic ritual of the Opening of the Mouth, whereby the statue was thought to be imbued with the five senses. That identity, moreover, was not complete until the name of its owner had been inscribed upon the statue, even though the piece had originally been made for another person and bore little if any resemblance to its usurper.

The animation of such sculpture was of a passive kind, the statue or relief became a repository of numinous power, though certain specialized statues, such as the servant figures which were designed to

66, 76 work for their owners in the Otherworld, could be shown in vigorous action. But the concept of the statue as a substitute for the living person necessarily imposed upon the ancient sculptor the ideal of creating an object which conformed to the proportions and appearance of nature. Thus the statue may be painted in quasi-

59, 21, 65 naturalistic colours and provided with realistic artificial eyes.

A tradition of sculpture in wood and ivory existed from prehistoric times and persisted throughout the dynastic period, though carvings in such organic materials have been highly susceptible to the ravages of man and nature. A damaged statuette from Abydos in the British Museum (no. 37996) shows an early king in his jubilee robe. Some fragments of statues in wood now in Boston and Oxford come from the cenotaphs at Abydos, but perhaps the most remarkable of such vestiges are the bases of two wooden statues from the mortuary temple attached to the tomb of King Qa'a at Saqqara. These remains show that already by the end of the First Dynasty, wooden statues were being produced with the left foot advanced in the conceptual tradition of most subsequent male statuary. Indeed the disjointed annals of the earliest kings, as partly preserved in the Palermo Stone and similar fragments, record as remarkable events 'the birth' of various gods, by which we may understand that the definitive forms given to images of Egyptian gods in their particular shrines were already being established, like their hieroglyphic determinatives. It was to such archetypes that later designers had recourse, such as those of Neferhotep I (c. 1750 BC), who searched ancient records in Heliopolis so that a statue of Osiris could be made in its true and pristine form.

12   Schist statue of King Khasekhem, from
Hierakonpolis, c. 2710 BC.

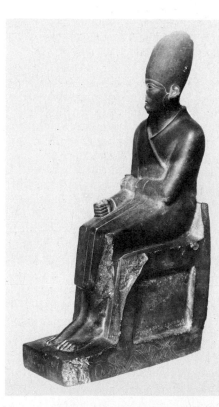

The bases of the statues of Qa'a and fragments of ebony furniture found in the tombs of the First Dynasty reveal that a high degree of skill had been reached by the Egyptian wood-carver. But the deliberate setting fire to the tombs of this dynasty, both at Abydos and Saqqara, must have exposed the vulnerability of monuments made of wood and ivory, and encouraged the sculptor to turn his attention increasingly to the carving of statues in stone.

Very little sculpture has survived that can with certainty be dated to the first two dynasties, and statues have mostly been attributed to this period by the crudity of their workmanship (which is no sure criterion of date) and the archaic kind of stool with bent wood

cf. 20

reinforcements on which the owner is usually seated. Of these the most complete, and probably the earliest in date, is the limestone statue in Berlin (no. 21839) of a man seated with his right hand on his knee and his left clenched on his chest. He wears a cloak with a diagonal fold that exposes the right shoulder. There is little doubt that inspiration for such a piece was derived from a royal prototype and

12

we do not have to look far for examples in the statues of Khasekhem from Hierakonpolis. The schist specimen in Cairo, like its restored limestone specimen in the Ashmolean Museum, Oxford (no. E. 517), represents the work of a master sculptor of the reign and is already moving away from the style of wooden figures to develop the distinctive character of monolithic statuary. The throne has become massive and rectilinear, the hands are clenched as though to hold the sceptres that would have been provided as separate adjuncts on a wooden version, and the head is thrust forward to balance the mass of the White Crown. The details of the features, particularly the eyes and the muscles at the corners of the lips, which have been plastically rendered, and the modelling of the mass of the body beneath its long jubilee robe, show that a tradition of working stone was steadily being established among the hereditary craftsmen who were employed in the royal ateliers.

The statues of Khasekhem were found in the ruins of an early temple, and the bases of the statues of Qa'a were also excavated in a temple, though it was a modest brick-built structure attached to his tomb. The complete examples of contemporary private statues have not been recovered as a result of careful excavation and the details of their finding have not been disclosed. Some apparently came from the site of the temple of Ptah at Memphis and are *ex votos*. If any came from tombs, the circumstances in which they were housed, whether in the chapel or in a special sealed statue chamber, the *serdab* (Arabic for 'cellar'), or whether with the coffin in the burial chamber, are entirely unknown.

CHAPTER FOUR

Imhotep and the Monuments of Djoser
Dynasty III

The achievement of the first two dynasties of kings in Egypt was immense. Under the guidance of a god incarnate, a centralized government organized the Two Lands into a rich agricultural state, independent of the caprice of the local weather for its prosperity. The annual Nile flood was utilized, though it could not be completely controlled, by massive hydraulic works undertaken by armies of conscribed peasants made idle by the inundation of their fields. Every year the extent of the cultivable land was increased by draining the marshy verges and irrigating the desert margins. Censuses of men and domestic animals were made. Writing was developed as a means of recording data and transmitting information and commands afar. Learning and speculative thought were pursued in the large religious centres, as at Memphis and Heliopolis, where theologians attempted a syncretism of ancient beliefs to match the unification of political forces. By the end of the Archaic Period religious differences had been reconciled and the political direction of the economy established on firm grounds.

Increasing prosperity and confidence is reflected in the technical progress of the arts. The cenotaph of King Den at Abydos had been floored with granite brought from Aswan on the far southern frontier. The burial chamber of King Khasekhemwy was built of limestone blocks rather than mud brick. Even private tombs at Helwan and Saqqara used cut limestone in their construction. During the Second Dynasty, the Palermo Stone records that a royal statue was made of copper and a temple was built entirely of stone. All this achievement was accomplished by an élite of technocrats, men of learning and skill who controlled a docile workforce capable of great discipline.

cf. 52

One of the earliest of such administrators whose name has survived is also the greatest, a genius that the Egyptians recognized during his own lifetime and throughout their history as the heroic initiator of their culture, eventually deifying him as a god of wisdom, astronomy, architecture and, above all, medicine. This was Imhotep, the Chancellor of King Neterikhet (Djoser), the first great ruler of the Third Dynasty. As High Priest of the sun-god, Rē of Heliopolis, Imhotep was versed in the learning and beliefs of that religion, and it is from the time of his advent that sun-worship assumes a dominant position in the Egyptian state, being closely associated with the kingship. During his reign, Djoser was worshipped as the sun-god incarnate. (Later in the Old Kingdom the idea prevailed that the pharaoh was begotten on the chief queen by the sun-god and ruled as his son, his soul flying at death as a falcon to the horizon, where he was assimilated to his begetter.)

In the twenty-seventh century BC Imhotep created for Djoser at Saqqara, the necropolis of the capital Memphis, a funerary monument that served as the wonder of its age and an inspiration to Egyptian architects at later periods. Even today, in all its ruin, it still dominates the Saqqara skyline. The mass of the monument was built of local limestone, the facing being the fine limestone quarried in the hills at Tura on the opposite bank of the Nile. The site of the monument was on an escarpment on the desert verges west of Memphis. Although the basic plan was a development of the layout of the tombs of the last kings of the preceding dynasty, there are several innovations, apart from its all-stone construction, that make it a work of great originality. In the changes which its design underwent during its building, and in the progressive improvement in the quality of the masonry, it is evident that both architect and craftsmen were feeling their way towards an ultimate realization, and gaining confidence and mastery in the process.

The rectangular area enclosed by the girdle wall was over sixty times the extent of the largest of the Second Dynasty cenotaphs at Abydos, the perimeter being more than a mile long. The outer face of this wall was in the familiar palace-façade pattern, and rose to a height of some 33 feet (10 metres). Of the fourteen great gateways that interrupted the rhythm of the bastioned wall, only one is a true entrance, the rest are dummies.

Within this vast temenos, Imhotep erected a number of buildings, some of which, as far as we can judge, were new in purpose in a funerary monument, while others followed tradition. Of the latter, the mound over the subterranean burial chambers of the King and members of his family, was planned as the usual mastaba, although it was built of stone on a novel square ground-plan. It rose to a height of 26 feet (7·9 metres), and thus lay concealed behind the enclosure walls. This nucleus, however, underwent six changes of plan, and eventually there appeared on the Saqqara horizon, above the line of the long white girdle wall, a white stone pyramid rising in six unequal steps, on a base 411 × 358 feet (125 × 109 metres), to a height of 204 feet (62·3 metres). Although a stepped brick structure had been erected above the burial shaft of the tomb of King Andjib in the First Dynasty, it was

46

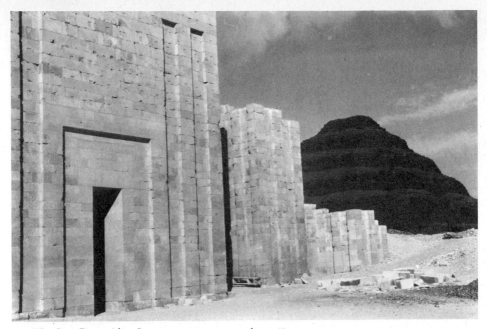

13   The Step Pyramid at Saqqara, entrance portal, *c.* 2680 BC.

enclosed in the mass of the mastaba. The Step Pyramid of Djoser, an independent feature, was on a much greater scale, each face orientated to a cardinal point, and dominating its environs. The casing blocks of the individual steps were set on their beds inclined towards the interior, producing a structure of great stability. It was by means of this giant staircase that the spirit of the dead king would mount up to the sky-realm to join the crew of the solar barque in its path across the heavens, and to become one of the circumpolar stars.

Another traditional feature of the Djoser monument is the store of provisions and furnishings that was concealed in chambers below the pyramid and in magazines above ground on the west side. But these supplies were on a very lavish scale, and included about 40,000 costly stone vessels, a number of them made in the reigns of preceding kings, and inscribed with their names.

A startling innovation was the transfer of the cenotaph, hitherto located at Abydos, to the southern extremity of the complex, thus incorporating the tomb of Djoser as King of Upper Egypt with his Lower Egyptian tomb in the same precincts. The south tomb, however, was not surmounted by a stepped edifice but by a simple

47

mastaba, largely built into the mass of the southern enclosure wall with its long axis running from west to east. Associated with this tomb was a chapel with panelled exterior walls crowned by a frieze of cobras, the first appearance of this royal decorative and protective element in Egyptian architecture.

The entrance-port lay open, the leaves of its great stone doors carved as though folded back against the walls of the corridor, and led into a colonnade with forty fasciculated columns engaged into the walls so as to form recesses, some perhaps housing statues of the king. It was in this area that the base of a statue was found showing the king's feet treading upon nine bows, symbols of the contiguous nations, while before them crouched figures of adoring *rekhyt*-plovers representing the populace of Egypt, all peoples alike subject to the divine might of the pharaoh. The remarkable feature of this fragment, which is now in the Cairo Museum (no. J.49889), is that the name and titles of Imhotep by a unique honour accompany those of Djoser on the front of the pedestal, thus confirming the late tradition that associated him with the king in the building of this pyramid complex.

The entrance colonnade led by a door, carved as though half-open, into a vast court, lying between the south tomb and the pyramid and containing two B-shaped erections near each end, evidently the

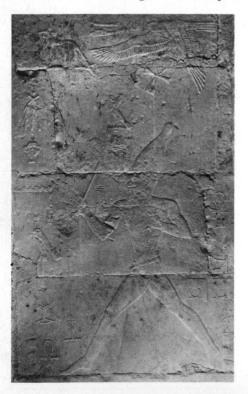

14   The Step Pyramid at Saqqara, relief panel of King Djoser in the south tomb, *c.* 2680 BC.

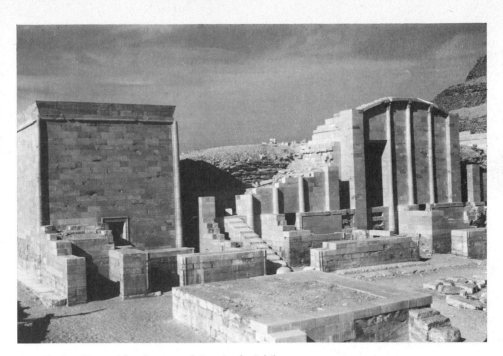

15   The Step Pyramid at Saqqara, shrines in the jubilee court, c. 2680 BC.

markers for a course that the king paced out when he took possession cf. 14
of his kingdom at his coronation, and repeated at his jubilee. The
decoration of the early royal monuments of Egypt is much concerned
with the rite of the Sed festival, or jubilee, which was a ceremony
designed to rejuvenate the powers of the king after a reign of thirty
years. Few pharaohs ruled for so long a span, but many of them are
represented as celebrating the Sed as much in some eternal heyday as
in actuality. Djoser, in fact, is so pictured in delicate low relief on
panels framed by doorways in chambers beneath both the pyramid 14
and the south tomb, though he ruled for a mere nineteen years.

The chief indication of the importance of this festival in the idea of
kingship in Egypt, however, is to be found in the adjacent jubilee
court, where the ceremony of the coronation could be re-enacted
during the jubilee rites. This court is furnished with the great stepped
podium on which the thrones of the pharaoh, as King of Upper Egypt
and again as King of Lower Egypt, were placed under canopies.
Adjoining it are the remains of a columned structure which was

49

probably the temple used as a robing room for these rites. But the dominant features of this court are the two rows of shrines flanking the podium on the western and eastern sides, some of which have been rebuilt in recent years under the brilliant direction of the French archaeologist, J.-P. Lauer. These shrines are of three kinds: those with a flat roof surmounted by a primitive form of the cavetto cornice, so characteristic of later Egyptian architecture; others of similar designs but with a cambered roof crowned by a fan-shaped cornice; and the remainder, also with an arched roof supported on a curved architrave upheld by a pilaster at each end and three thin fluted columns, with capitals having the form of leaf-like pendants. These buildings represent the national shrines of Upper and Lower Egypt, and in actuality would have contained images of the gods of the various *nomes*, or districts, brought to attend the coronation of the King and give him their acclaim. Each shrine had a small cubicle for housing the statue approached by a narrow passage skirting a baffle wall which obscured the sacred image from profane view.

Two other buildings, known today as the House of the North and the House of the South, stand in adjacent courts and are of a similar design to the shrines with the arched roofs, but on a larger scale. Presumably they imitated the palaces of Djoser as King of the North and the South. Their inner niches also can be approached only obliquely, and probably housed small statues of the king. Other structures include a mortuary temple of labyrinthine plan on the north side of the pyramid, similar to the temple that was found in the same position at the brick mastaba of Qa'a (see above), and a large altar, also in the same area.

It is apparent that in his design of the Step Pyramid complex, Imhotep had two major aims in view. The first was to incorporate in one huge enclosure the southern or Abydene cenotaph of the king, and his northern or Memphite tomb, and to include in it such traditional features as subsidiary tombs for members of the royal family, two mortuary temples and magazines for food and funerary stores, both below and above ground. His most striking innovation in the mortuary concept was to transform the mound over the burial shaft into a great stepped pyramid rising above the summit of the boundary walls.

The second aim that Imhotep cherished was the creation for Djoser of a vast city of the dead, a kind of funerary replica of White Walls, the capital founded by Menes four centuries earlier. Within the white limestone enclosure walls was built the royal compound, containing palaces, national shrines and jubilee courts, most of them in two distinct versions for a pharaoh who wore a different costume when he

50

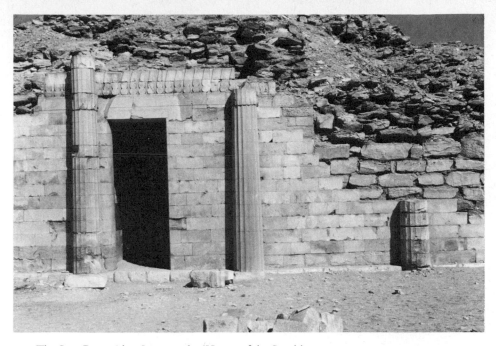

16   The Step Pyramid at Saqqara, the 'House of the South', *c.* 2680 BC.

officiated as King of Upper Egypt from that which he assumed as King of Lower Egypt. But these mortuary buildings served their purposes by magic only, and were mere dummies, façades behind which lay solid rubble cores. Stone imitations of wooden doors, with their cross-battens, hinges and bolts, stand open where approach is permitted. Elsewhere access is barred by imitation stake fences carved in high relief on blocking walls.

But the great revolutionary feature of this complex, marking a turning-point in the history of architecture, was that it was built entirely of quarried stone, the first large building in the world to be so raised. It was, however, a structure of a special kind, petrification of a system of building that belongs entirely to construction in wood and vegetable products coated with argillaccous mud, such as bundles of reeds, stalks of papyrus rushes and palm fronds stripped of all but their uppermost leaves. Some of the stone-work is massive, as in the burial chambers of the pyramid and south tomb, built entirely of Aswan granite, but the fine masonry of the outer facings is in small limestone blocks no bigger than their mud-brick counterparts. A curved wall appears, an element proper only to wattle-and-daub construction. In

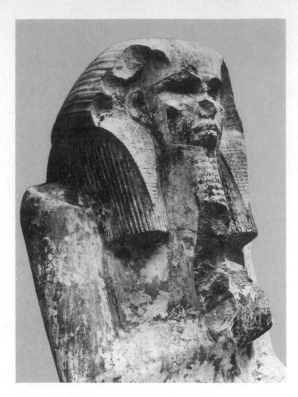

i° Statue

17 Statue of King Djoser, from
the mortuary temple to the Step
Pyramid at Saqqara, *c.* 2680 BC.

wide façades, doorways are placed off-centre for extra stability, one
16   jamb being adjacent to a reinforcing pillar. Engaged columns copy
15   faceted, tapering tree-trunks, or tied bundles of palm ribs with their
leaves folded over the top. Ceilings are channelled on the underside to
represent a roofing of palm logs. Ornamental panels copying original
mat hangings are made of blue faience tiles of rectangular plano-
convex shape, cemented into cells cut into interior limestone walls.
The cambered roofs of the shrines on the west side of the jubilee court
are crowned with an arched cornice imitating the feathery tops of
reed archetypes. As a decorative element, the *kheker* finials now make
their appearance, and form a characteristic Egyptian frieze, derived
from an alternative method of treating the feathery tops of reed
16   palisades by tying them into bundles at regular intervals.

    The domestic architecture which Imhotep immortalized in stone
belonged to a style of building never again seen in Egypt. It is
doubtful whether it was even contemporary, but seems to belong to
a remote past, perhaps deliberately recalling the prehistoric occasion
of the First Time, when Creation began and to which Djoser returned

52

on death. The later temples preserved only in their adyta the form of the primeval shrine in which the Creator had first manifested Himself, and this was also a stone imitation of the prehistoric wattle-and-daub hut with its cavetto cornice.

The buildings in the courts of the Step Pyramid, with their elegant proportions and their details based upon plant forms, have an appearance of naturalism and vitality which is in contrast to their mortuary purposes. For all their original features, in that respect they represent an end rather than a beginning. Imhotep's greatest contribution to architecture was the establishing of a tradition and technique of building in stone which inspired subsequent generations of visitors, Egyptians and foreigners alike. The great reservoir of economic activity, architectural practice and artistic skill, created by building the Step Pyramid during the nineteen years of Djoser's reign, was available to his successors, and step pyramids were built by the other kings of the dynasty, though only that of Huni(?) at Meydum ever reached near-completion. Sekhemkhet, the successor of Djoser, planned a higher pyramid, rising in seven stages within an enclosure two-thirds the size of his predecessor's in the same area of Saqqara, but it was never finished. The rapid progress in the craft of the mason, however, is seen in the greater height of the courses of its stone-work, which are twice the size of those in the earlier monument.

Of the sculpture that was once housed in the pyramid complex of Djoser, little has survived, but what remains is significant. Life-sized statues, found lying in the jubilee court, are only roughly blocked out, but would evidently have represented the king wearing the short jubilee cloak. One statue-base showing the pharaoh supreme over mankind has already been mentioned. Another, still in place, shows only the feet of four persons ranged in echelon, suggesting the presence of Djoser standing beside deities, or more likely members of his family, the first example of a group statue in Egypt.

The most famous piece of sculpture from the site, however, is the life-sized seated statue found enclosed in the serdab, a stone chamber 17 adjacent to the mortuary temple with two holes cut in its front wall, through which the statue could look on the offerings or sniff the incense burnt before it. Egyptian statuary was originally designed to reside within such a shrine, either separate from or integral with the temple or tomb in which it functioned. The volumetric nature of cf. 100 Egyptian statuary is cubic, deriving not only from the Egyptian concept of the universe, but also from the nature of the space that actually enclosed it. While the idea of the statue may derive from a conceptual view of reality, the architectural frame ensures that it is the

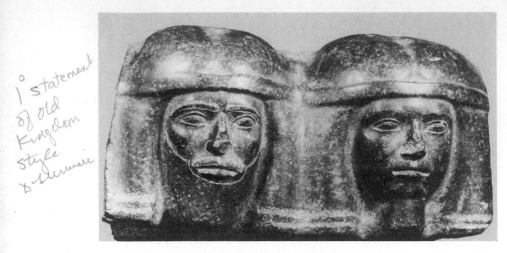

18 Granite corbel with heads of northern foes, from the Step Pyramid at Saqqara, *c.* 2680 BC.

front view which makes the essential, and often the only impact, in contrast to the profile views preferred in two-dimensional representation. In most examples, the side and front views of Egyptian statues remain distinct: it is only the head, in which the exigences of portraiture (see below) demand a specific identity rather than a symbolization, that the working of the profiles into the front view of the head achieves an integration.

17   The great statue of Djoser is carved with considerable skill to achieve a monumental effect, with the body enveloped in the jubilee cloak, the right hand clenched beneath the chest, and the left flat on the thigh. Nevertheless, like the style of the architecture, this statue looks back to its Archaic antecedents with its enclosed form and massive, brooding head, given even greater weight by the heavy wig and beard. Only the distinctive portrait is new, with the pronounced cheek-bones and down-turned mouth, setting the fashion for *3* contemporary portraits such as that of the official, Hesy, for example. The loss of the inlaid eyes, which would have given the statue an alert animation, cannot entirely detract from the formidable air of a reserved and powerful majesty.

All such sculptures are in limestone designed to be painted; but it is remarkable that the best work in ancient Egypt is often found in the hard stones, carved only with difficulty. Three such artefacts from the site (now in the Cairo Museum) are two alabaster embalming tables

54

(nos. C. 1321–2) with sides in the form of lions (the first appearance of a ritual object which was to preserve its essential design for centuries), and a black granite corbel with the heads of foreigners (no. J. 49613). *18* This latter piece gives so developed an aspect of an architectural feature, which is better known from later, similar pieces, that it has generally been dated to a later period, though the type of the foreign prisoner, filling an abject caryatid role, exists from the time of Khasekhem, when a stone door socket carved as the head of a Nubian is known.

The sophistication and the style of the Djoser corbel allow us to attribute the statuette of a god in the Brooklyn Museum to this same *19* period. This specimen and a companion fragment in Brussels are fashioned from an extremely dense diorite (*anorthositic gneiss*), probably brought from quarries deep in the Nubian desert. They are of a size to have occupied a similar niche to those found in the chapels of the jubilee court. Unlike the life-sized statue of Djoser, the Brooklyn statuette does not look back to the Archaic Period, but is

19   Diorite statue of a god holding a knife, *c.* 2680 BC.

20   Granite statue of the shipwright Bedjmes, *c.* 2700 BC.

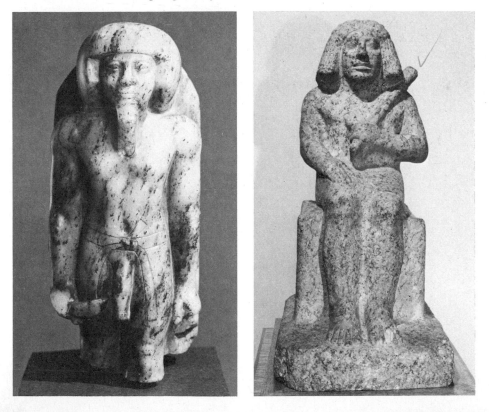

the first complete statement of the Old Kingdom style in stone sculpture to have survived.

Most standing statues in ancient Egypt were conceived of, originally, in the same way as relief representations of men and women. Usually the men stand with the left foot advanced, the women with both feet together. In statues of stone, as distinct from wooden statues, the idea of 'negative space' operates, except in some rare examples on a small scale. By 'negative space' is meant the separation of the various volumes within which the limbs of the body exist, the form being incompletely released from the matrix, or remaining invisible within it. This is particularly evident in the statues of men, where on the left-hand side only the advanced leg is shown, and the remainder of the space is occupied by the stone filling of that leg. We have already traced this feature from the two-dimensional concept of the figure existing essentially in a side-view facing right. Moreover, while the front view of a human figure may appear occasionally in ancient Egyptian drawing, only one example of a rear drawing is known at a much later date and it is significant that a tendency to hide the back is found in stone statuary. It is usually placed against a slab, or high-backed throne, and ultimately against a pillar.

These features are already present in the Brooklyn statuette. The left profile shows the advanced leg only. The back slab takes the form of a round-topped stela, probably representing a shrine with an arched roof. The back slab or pillar, in fact, stresses the architectural setting of the statue which is essential to its use. Only the knife, held obliquely in the right hand of the god, seems to defy the separation of the planes of the limbs and body; but this is a compromise dictated by the technical difficulty of carving a knife held forward in the hand and released entirely from the very hard matrix. Later solutions to the problem were to be reached by excluding all objects grasped in the hand apart from a rolled-up cloth, or handkerchief. When, however, the arm was folded across the body, support was provided for a sceptre or weapon carved in high relief, and advantage has been taken of the special design of a triad in Boston, to introduce a mace into the king's right hand, resting on the seat of the throne.

The private statuary of the late Second and early Third Dynasties, with the exception of a kneeling figure of a funerary priest in Cairo (no. C. 1), follows the pattern of Khasekhem and Djoser in showing the owner seated upon a stool, one arm held across the torso and the other upon the thigh. Only the pose of the hands may vary in being either open or closed. All are characterized by the carving of the back to reveal an unrestricted view of dress or musculature, and a

21   Painted limestone statues of Rehotep and his
wife Nofret, from Meydum, *c.* 2630 BC.

Found in a mastaba tomb near
pyramid accredited to Snofera 4ᵗʰ Dyn.

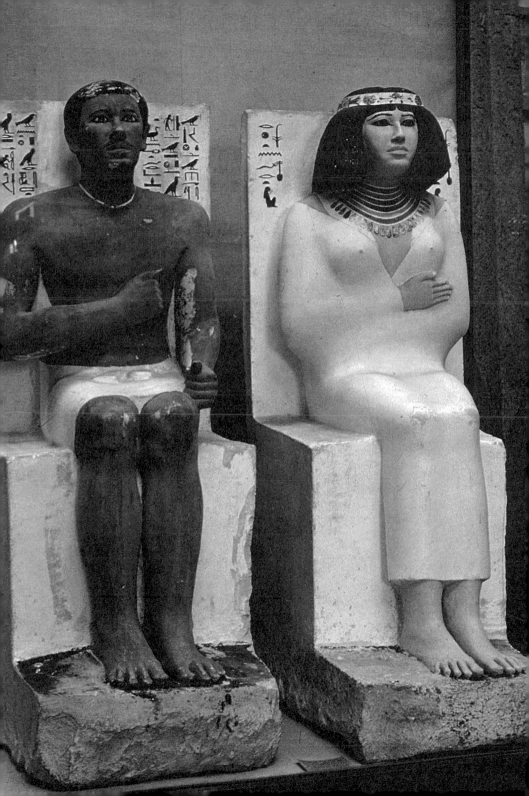

disproportionately massive head, with a well-defined coiffure, set upon a short neck. With the exception of the Berlin example in limestone, all are in hard stone (which may have been largely responsible for their survival). Perhaps the most accomplished example in this group is the red granite statue in the British Museum of the shipwright Bedjmes, where the left hand holds the adze of his trade over his shoulder like a royal sceptre.

The apogee of this early style, however, is found in the life-sized statues of Rēhotep and Nofret, carved in limestone and painted in the conventional colouring for the flesh tones and dress. The eyes, with their rock-crystal pupils, are inlaid within metal frames, a tradition that begins with Djoser and persists in the case of statues in wood and soft stones well into the Fifth Dynasty; and it is frequently revived thereafter, being also used occasionally for hard-stone sculpture. This gives such a vivid appearance of life to the face that in many cases robbers have prised them from their sockets before daring to begin their depredations.

Since the statues of Rēhotep and Nofret were found in a mastaba tomb at Meydum, near the pyramid formerly accredited entirely to Snoferu of the Fourth Dynasty, they have generally been dated to the years of that reign; but the possibility remains that they belonged to the family of Huni, the last king of the Third Dynasty, and the putative builder of the step pyramid at Meydum. Their portraits reveal the family face of the ruling class whose authority directed the prosperity of this age of the great pyramid builders. Nofret, with her heavy wig and enveloping cloak, wears the dress popular in the Archaic Period, but the details such as the diadem and collar relieve the massiveness of her form, seen particularly in the thick ankles so characteristic of the statues of women during the earlier Old Kingdom. Rēhotep has his right hand clenched below his left breast and his left hand closed on his thigh. Nofret has her hands folded across her torso, both poses developments of the Archaic style. The inlaid hieroglyphic titles and names of the owners, however, display a developed orthography, and their elegant form and layout set the standard for similar inscriptions in later reigns.

CHAPTER FIVE

The Pyramid Age

Dynasty IV

King Snoferu

With the Fourth Dynasty comes the first coherent statement of the mortuary style in Egyptian architecture. The later step pyramids of the Third Dynasty are now too ruined to show whether their enclosures contained buildings similar to those that Imhotep constructed for Djoser, but the presumption is that other designs were being evolved. During the reign of Snoferu, the first king of the Fourth Dynasty, the funerary monument of the dead king reaches its complete realization. The mound above the burial chambers develops from the step pyramid, a staircase to the sky, into the familiar pyramid on a square base, a large-scale model of the *ben-ben* stone of Heliopolis, a pyramidal or conical object, probably of meteoric origin, revered in that city as the High Sand on which Atum, the demiurge of the sun-cult, appeared above the waters of Chaos at the Creation of the World. An intermediate form is found in the Bent (or Rhomboidal) Pyramid which Snoferu built at Dahshur. Later in his reign, the first true pyramid was erected a mile to the north at the same site, and reached a height of 325 feet (99 metres) on a base 709 feet (216 metres) square. Snoferu also added a casing to the step pyramid of his predecessor at Meydum, so converting it to a true pyramid, but this mantle has collapsed and now lies as mounds of rubble at the base of the monument.

mastaba
v
step
v
Bent
v
Pyramid

With the pyramids of Snoferu also appear the adjuncts that are features of similar complexes throughout the Pyramid Age. The four-sided geometrical mass of the primeval mound, each face orientated to a cardinal point, rises above the tomb chambers. The entrance to the burial vault is usually on the north side, facing the polar stars. On the east side is the mortuary temple, leading by means of a causeway beyond the enclosure wall to a valley temple at the edge of the cultivation. On the south side is a subsidiary pyramid, probably representing the Abydene south tomb. In the vicinity are two or more boat-pits for the installation of barques, either imitations of the solar ships in which the king sailed over the waters of heaven in the train of the sun-god, or the actual state barges used by the king during his lifetime. Within the precincts of the pyramid rose the smaller pyramids of his chief queens and the mastaba tombs of members of his family, or his favoured officials.

No monument of the Old Kingdom preserves all these features in a sound condition. Only at the Bent Pyramid is the original casing substantially intact and the subsidiary pyramid not grossly dilapidated. The valley temple of Khephren is the most complete of all such surviving structures. The mortuary temple of Sahurē, though sadly ruined, has yielded valuable data which have enabled other pyramid temples to be restored, on paper at least. The causeway of Unas is the best preserved, enough of its roof with an open continuous lighting slot having survived to allow the rebuilding of a short stretch. A few blocks carved in raised relief that once decorated the walls have also been replaced. The burial chamber of the pyramid of this same king is in the best condition and largely intact. In its original state it must have been very handsome, its white limestone walls carved with elegant blue-filled glyphs in silhouette, giving the earliest version of the Pyramid Texts that assured the apotheosis of the king and his assimilation to the demiurge. The black basalt sarcophagus lay within an alabaster niche at the western end of the chamber, carved and painted with designs to represent the mat-hung walls and panels of a house interior. The inclined, massive, limestone slabs that formed the pitch roof of the chamber were carved with five-pointed yellow stars in raised relief on the blue ground of the night sky. While the pyramid represented the primeval mound, the sarcophagus in its decoration imitated the 'house of eternity' of the king, thus combining the two ideas of the mortuary destiny, the corpse below in the eternal habitation on earth, the soul aloft in the sky as a star or in the following of the sun-god. Since the sarcophagus of Unas was a plain, undecorated stone box, the tectonic features of his palace were transferred to the alabaster walls that surrounded it on three sides.

The architecture of the Fourth Dynasty pyramid complexes at Dahshur and Giza, with the geometric shapes of royal pyramids and private truncated pyramids (mastabas) predominating, shows a mastery over the management of large simple masses. Throughout the first four reigns of the dynasty there is a progressive increase in the size of the blocks of limestone and granite used in their construction. It has been calculated that some of the core blocks of the Khephren valley temple weigh nearly 135 tons, while some of the granite ashlars that clad it weigh 40 tons or more. The use of such materials on so huge a scale seems determined by the need for creating a monument to last for ever.

The mortuary temples of the Meydum and Dahshur pyramids are very modest structures, scarcely more than small stone chapels giving oblique access to a courtyard containing an altar and two tall round-topped limestone stelae with the names and figures of the king. They

24

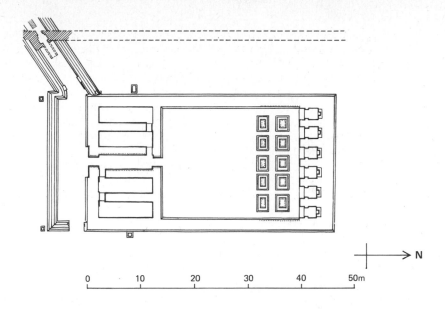

0   10   20   30   40   50m

22   Plan of the Valley Temple of the Bent Pyramid of King Snoferu at
Dahshur, *c.* 2610 BC.

may, however, have been supplemented by larger structures built in
the vicinity. Such a building, which has been identified, perhaps
wrongly, as the valley temple of the Bent Pyramid, has been
excavated at Dahshur, and proves to be quite different in design from
any of the dummy buildings of the Djoser complex. Its ground-plan   *22*
is strictly rectangular and comprises an entrance hall on the south,
flanked by two rooms on each side, probably store-rooms, leading to
an open court closed at the northern end by a double colonnade of
five square pillars in front of six shrines, which evidently housed
statues of the king, not free-standing, but carved three-quarters in the
round, *en masse* with the rear walls of the shrines. This is the nucleus of
the design of all subsequent mortuary temples of the Old Kingdom.
   The most austere and monumental of these Fourth Dynasty
temples, however, is the valley temple of Khephren, the builder of the
second pyramid at Giza. The massive limestone core-blocks were clad   *23*
inside and out with granite blocks, their faces dressed into outer and
inner walls, with twin entrances on the eastern façade. The building
had the slight batter of mud-brick archetypes, but the plain exterior
walls were unrelieved by any panelling. The severity of the roof-line,
however, was mitigated by an early version of the Egyptian cavetto

61

cornice, having the torus moulding at its lower extremity, but lacking the upper string-course to soften the sharp top edge. Around each entrance doorway was carved a band of bold glyphs giving the name and titles of the king and describing him as beloved of two aspects of the universal mother and sky-goddess.

The architectural impact of this austere building, essentially a rectangular mass of stone with a slight batter, was achieved by the elegance of its proportions and the richness of its materials. The two entrances, each flanked by a pair of recumbent sphinxes or guardian lions, gave access to each end of a transverse vestibule leading to a T-shaped hall with the ceiling upheld by rows of square monolithic granite pillars supporting massive architraves. Light was admitted to the interior obliquely, through louvres cut at the tops of the walls at the line of the ceiling, and fell in shafts upon the alabaster pavement below. This diffused light played upon twenty-three seated statues of Khephren in green diorite, alabaster and schist, but of these, only one is substantially intact.

The uncompromising spirit that raised the pyramids at Dahshur and Giza in all their geometrical perfection and majesty, did not hesitate to use the hardest of stones in their construction; polished basalt, granites, quartzites and diorites, as well as alabaster and the fine

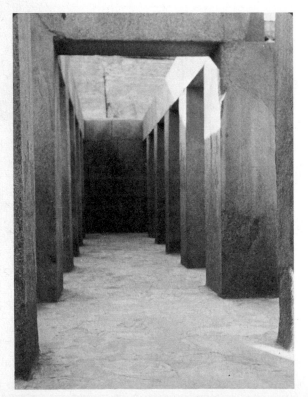

23 Hall with red granite piers and architraves in the Valley Temple of King Khephren at Giza, *c.* 2565 BC.

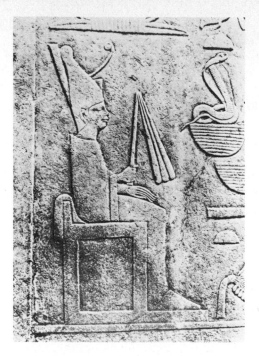

24   Limestone funerary stela of King Snoferu, from Dahshur, *c.* 2605 BC, detail: the king enthroned.

limestone of Tura. Today in their ruin, they hardly present a true picture of their pristine appearance, since much of their severity of form would have been softened by decorative details, by the statuary and delicate reliefs for which they were once the setting. Of the reliefs, only a few fragments have survived, notably in the valley temple of the Bent Pyramid, where the faces of the square pillars were decorated with figures of Snoferu before various gods, and where the walls of the entrance corridor were lined with personifications of his estates in the form of elegant women bringing trays of bread and water as offerings to his tomb. This is the first known version of a theme which is common in the later royal and private tombs of the Old Kingdom.

cf. 43

The almost total loss of the reliefs in the royal tombs of the Fourth Dynasty is particularly grievous, since without them we are unable to trace the development of iconography during the period. In contrast to this silence, the scanty remains in the pyramid complexes of the next dynasty are eloquent and may give a false impression of their originality. The decoration of the contemporary private mastaba tombs at Giza is of little assistance, since it is sparse and confined almost entirely to the restricted offering niche.

The stela which had been the only example of relief carving in the private tombs of the Archaic Period, is repositioned in the Third

63

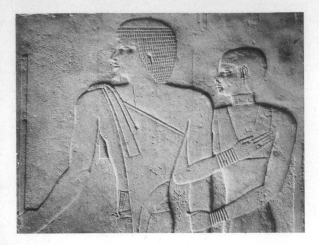

25 Limestone relief of Prince Khufukaf and his wife at Giza, *c.* 2560 BC.

26 Frieze of geese painted on plaster, from the mastaba of Itet at Meydum, *c.* 2630 BC.

Dynasty to the east side of the mastaba, and incorporated in the southernmost of two false doors. This blind doorway was now considered as the main 'entrance' to the tomb, and before it were laid the funerary offerings. By the end of the dynasty, this portico had developed into a stone-lined cruciform chamber, the false door occupying a niche in the rear wall, the essential relief of the owner seated at a table of offerings being carved on the tympanum above the lintel of the door. The subsequent development of tomb decoration during the Old Kingdom is an elaboration of these two features. The small cruciform chapel was expanded in size and complexity until it occupied almost the whole of the superstructure with suites of stone-built rooms not only for the owner but sometimes for his wife or son as well. The walls of such chambers offered ample scope for decoration with painted relief, or, where that was not possible, with paintings.

The false door remained the focal point of the chapel but underwent two artistic developments. The first is the increased elaboration of inscriptions to give the titles, names and affiliations of the owner and his wife. Such texts became too long for the limited space of the jambs and lintel of the door and were continued or repeated on the square pillars and architraves of the main chamber. But the importance of such texts, in presenting the dignity and power of the owner to his posterity, is seen in the care with which they have been laid out and drawn, and the precision of their carving.

The second stylistic development that the false door underwent was an elaboration of the panel scene of the deceased seated before a table of offerings. Quite early in its history it is accompanied by a tabulated list of offerings which are extended in range from the staple

49

27

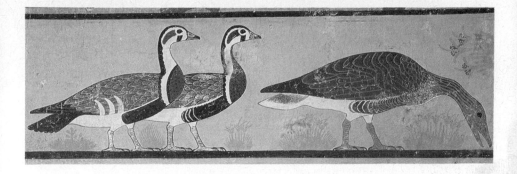

bread and beer to include beef and fowl, vegetables, clothing and sacramental oils. The wife or mother of the deceased may also be included in the scene as a counterpoise to the figure of the man, and the altar with its slices of bread may be supplemented by other tables containing offerings or libation vessels.

In the Third and Fourth Dynasties, the side walls of the cruciform chapels were carved with figures of the owner and his wife, and perhaps one or more of their children receiving the offerings brought by relatives or servants. This simple theme undergoes a considerable expansion during the Fifth and Sixth Dynasties, eventually filling the walls of a complex of rooms with coloured reliefs, or with painted versions of the same subjects. Such scenes illustrate an everyday life such as the deceased had passed on earth and which he expected to repeat for ever in the Hereafter. They are also concerned with the cult of the dead, the proper observance of which would ensure such a blissful eternity. For the magic inherent in these reliefs and their inscriptions would secure the welfare of the dead, even though the offerings should fail through the lapse of their endowments or the extinction of their posterity. 25

The early elaboration of the subject of the panel scene in the tympanum of the false door is seen in the eleven wooden stelae which were incorporated into niches along the mud-brick wall of a corridor in the great mastaba of Hesy, an official of King Djoser at Saqqara. Most of these panels have suffered damage and decay and have lost their painted gesso coatings. They show the owner in standing or seated poses before a table of offerings. The relief is shallow and the modelling is subtle, recalling the work of Djoser in the Step Pyramid. But later in the dynasty a deeper, bolder relief also appears and is still present in the figures carved on the faces of the pillars in the valley temple of the Bent Pyramid, early in the next dynasty. Thereafter a deeper relief appears sporadically, especially in such elements as pillars, the reveals of doorways and the sides of thrones. 3

cf. 14

65

The reliefs of the deceased in a standing pose and wearing different fashions of dress, such as one finds in the panels of Hesy, also appear soon afterwards on the jambs of the false door, thus representing the owner coming forth to receive the funerary offerings. The most developed realization of this idea is seen in the Sixth Dynasty chapels of Mereruka and Iteti where the figure of the owner is carved almost in the round, in a frontal aspect stepping out over the threshold of the door.

49

The stela within the false door, which was the focal point of the tomb chapel, where offerings were brought by the deceased's relatives or funerary priests, was supplemented in the great tomb of Hesy by paintings on the plastered mud-brick walls of adjacent corridors. The detailed pictures of furniture, games, tools, weights, measures, looms and toilet objects, give not only an inventory of the household effects of an aristocrat of the period, but also their exact appearance, so that their animation by magic would provide efficacious substitutes if the original equipment should decay or be stolen. By the end of the Third Dynasty, when the stela had been moved into the niche at the southern end of the east side of the mastaba, the owner and his wife were represented in relief, and the figures of servants and relatives bringing offerings were carved on contiguous walls. In the mastabas of Meydum, dating to the end of the Third and the beginning of the Fourth Dynasty, the reliefs in the offering niche were accompanied by pictures painted on plastered walls, showing a more elaborate treatment of the scenes of offering and country pursuits. A damaged painting of work in the fields had already appeared in the tomb of Hesy, and subsequent development was to see a great expansion of this subject. It was from the tomb of Itet at Meydum that the famous painting of geese was found, part of a greater scene showing her sons pulling a clap-net shut over a pool covered with pond fowl in the marshlands, an essential theme of all later representations of country life, especially with its ritual undertones of the destruction of evil manifestations.

26

The decoration of the mastabas of the Fourth Dynasty at Giza, on the other hand, appears to have been more modest, and confined largely to the offering niche. Such mastabas were usually provided by the kings for their families and important officials in the vicinity of their own pyramid tombs. Kheops was particularly lavish in laying out two regular groups of mastaba tombs on the east and west side of the Great Pyramid, so forming veritable cities of the dead, and consolidating a tradition of favoured burial near the king that was to last as an ideal until the end of the New Kingdom. Khephren and Mykerinus, the builders of the other pyramids on the Giza plateau,

25

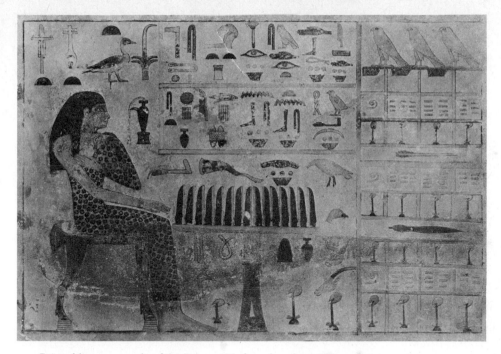

27   Painted limestone stela of the Princess Nofretyabet, from Giza, *c.* 2580 BC.

provided more modest rock-cut tombs for members of their families in the quarries adjacent to their pyramids. One such tomb, that of Queen Meresankh III, contained painted reliefs of articles of furniture, craftsmen at work, agricultural scenes and offering-bearers, showing that the subjects for representation in the Third Dynasty still persisted at the end of the Fourth, with some expansion. Such work, however, lacks the fine finish of earlier reliefs, doubtless because the walls are hewn from coarse nummulitic limestone, faced with plaster, and are not lined with fine blocks from the quarries at Tura.

For the beginning of the Fourth Dynasty, no royal sculpture exists, except in fragments, and private statuary appears to have been generally interdicted. One example, however, has survived in the impressive limestone statue of Hemon, the Vizier of Kheops and, as *30* his Master of Works, doubtless the architect of the Great Pyramid. This statue must be regarded as the masterpiece of the reign, despite the loss of the original eyes. It is in the same tradition as the statue of Rēhotep, with its inlaid inscriptions and what were probably realistic artificial eyes; but the archaic arrangement of the arms has been entirely changed to the same monumental pose of the hands as that in

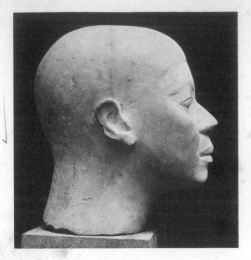
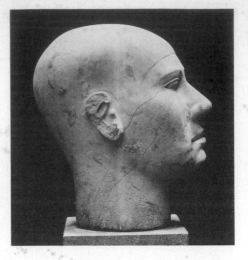

cf. 32 the royal statues of the next reigns. The character of the well-nourished body, as individual as the imperious features, has been rendered with great economy of means.

28, 29 The same bold execution is seen in the so-called 'reserve' heads that in the reign of Kheops, and sporadically for a generation or so afterwards, replaced the tomb statues. They were enclosed in the actual burial chamber, instead of the chapel or serdab. In the treatment of the facial planes, and the suppression of all unnecessary details, they suggest an attempt to reproduce in stone the mask which was summarily modelled in plaster on the linen wrappings over the face of the corpse, if indeed that is not reversing the order of things. The reserve heads are carved in limestone and left unpainted, but adjuncts such as ears are modelled in plaster on some examples, and plaster is also used to cover imperfections in the stone or mistakes in cf. 33, 146 the cutting, a practice that persists thereafter.

These heads are generally thought to be gifts of the king to members of his family, and while the personality of the sitter seems to differ in each case, they bear a generic likeness that may owe much to their style. The statuary of ancient Egypt has appealed to many critics during the past century as recording not only the facial characteristics of the owner, but also something of his mood and underlying character. Such appreciation may, of course, be purely subjective, and the question arises of how far the reserve heads are true portraits, or how far they represent the same ideal type of humanity.

It should cause little surprise that in statuary designed as a substitute for the living model, the face should receive special attention as the prime means of identifying the owner and distinguishing him from

68

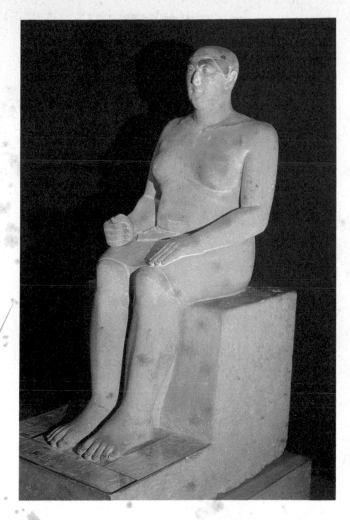

See p. 72

28, 29   Limestone reserve heads of a prince (*right*) and his wife (*left*), from Giza, *c*. 2580 B C.

30   Limestone statue of Prince Hemon, from Giza *c*. 2580 B C.

all others. But as the final means of recognition in Egypt was the name carved upon the statue, the portrait may be no more than a stereotype, as it certainly is in representations of foreigners, where a race of people is portrayed rather than individuals.

There is little doubt, however, that the Egyptian artist, and particularly the sculptor, sought to catch the individuality of some of his sitters, if not their character, by a faithful rendering of their facial structures. A comparison between the mummies of the New Kingdom pharaohs and their statues, reveals that a likeness has been secured in most instances. But it is also evident that royal portraits, with a few exceptions, are cast in an idealistic mould. The sitter is usually shown in the full prime of a successful life, healthy, alert, confident and prosperous. His face is unlined and free from disfigurement. Only for a brief period during the Twelfth Dynasty are signs of age and disillusionment visible in the features of the ruling monarchs, and even they show no deformities or signs of ill health in their sturdy physiques. Crippled or under-nourished persons are rarely represented, and these are mostly peasants, or serfs immortalized in stone by the grace of their employers or owners.

83, 84

cf. 44

While an idealized but distinctive portraiture may be claimed for royalty, it is doubtful whether an individualized likeness was rendered for private owners except in the case of a few important persons. By the Fifth Dynasty, the phrase 'statue after the life' is found in funerary texts, suggesting that, in some instances at least, a conscious effort was made to secure a likeness of the sitter. But in general, private persons tend to be represented by a stereotype of the contemporary royal features, the ideal to which all loyal subjects aspired, and the model with which the sculptors were most familiar through constant copying.

In the Fourth Dynasty, however, men and women who commissioned sculptures were all closely related to the pharaoh, and what we tend to regard as a conventional style may in fact be a family likeness. Later, on the other hand, there are found examples among private statues of the same person represented by differing portraits, and it is only the names and titles upon the statue that provide a means of identification.

The subtle changes that modified the rigid iconography of a royal and religious art throughout the history of ancient Egypt are probably to be accredited to the idiosyncrasies of succeeding master craftsmen. It was doubtless the influence of one such artist which introduced a less austere treatment of the underlying forms and a more plastic rendering of detail in the sculpture of the next two reigns of Djedefrē and Khephren. The statuary of the former king exists only as fragments, though fortunately one piece in the Louvre (no. E. 12627) is sufficiently complete to show his queen on a diminutive scale, squatting at his feet, a design that is known in a relief from the reign of Djoser and which was to persist throughout the Old Kingdom. The best of these fragments, however, is undoubtedly the life-sized head of the king in red quartzite wearing the *nemes* wig-cover with a uraeus. The bony structure of the skull beneath the skin has been modelled in the hard intractable stone with great sympathy and precision. This piece is exceptional in the art of the period, not only for its realistic rendering of an individual physiognomy, but also

cf. 63

31

70

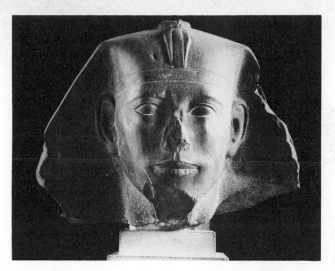

31 Red quartzite head of
King Djedefrē, from Abu
Roash, *c.* 2575 BC.

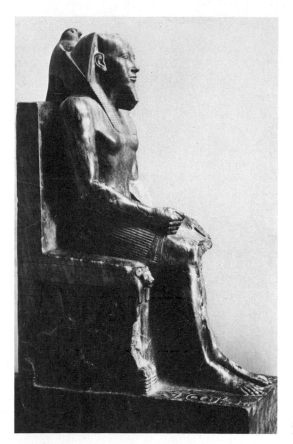

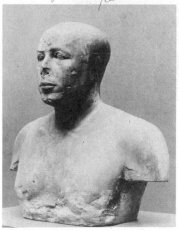

33 Limestone bust of the vizier
Ankh-haf, from Giza, *c.* 2560 BC.

32 Diorite statue of King
Khephren, from Giza, *c.* 2565 BC.

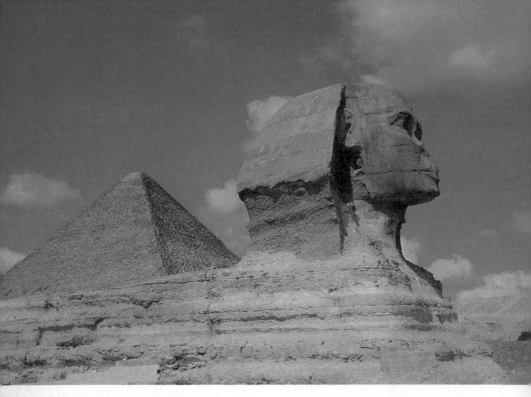

34   The pyramid of King Kheops with the Great Sphinx at Giza, *c.* 2550 BC.

cf. 84 for conveying a certain introspective melancholy, which is not encountered again in royal portraiture until the Middle Kingdom.

32 The supreme masterpiece of this school remains the diorite life-sized statue of Khephren seated upon his lion throne, with the falcon of Horus, of which he is also an incarnation, hovering behind his head. It has been justly famous since its discovery as expressing the apotheosis of divine majesty in ancient Egypt. The gem-hard stone has been worked with consummate skill, the smoothly polished surfaces giving a natural softness to the musculature which is not possible in the more granular quartzite used for the statuary of Djedefrē. In its architectural setting, with the louvred top-lighting reflecting from the alabaster pavement, the effect on the spectator of these monumental statues, representing man the ruler, idealized as Divinity, must have been truly awesome.

33 The same feeling for a restrained realism in portraiture is evident in the bust of Ankh-haf, a development of the reserve heads of the previous reign, where a skin of painted plaster over the limestone core

72

has encouraged the same plastic modelling of the face as is found in the Djedefrē head, though with rather more freedom in a less stubborn medium. This piece transcends the distinctive character of Egyptian art and achieves a timelessness that places it among the world's masterpieces.

The sculpture of the next generation shows the influence of the classic traditions established by the royal craftsmen of Djedefrē and Khephren and is particularly evident in the dyad and triads of Mykerinus. Most of these works are on a smaller scale, but the seated statues of the king in alabaster are larger than life-size. The pair-statue at Boston of Mykerinus and his chief queen is about two-thirds life-size, and though unfinished is a masterpiece of the same order as the Khephren statue. The lonely majesty of the divine king is here shared with his wife, who is shown on a scale equal to that of her husband. She adopts the same male pose, left foot advanced. The association of the two figures is made by their juxtaposition. The left arm of the queen is folded across her body in a posture that recalls the archaic statues of women, but here becomes an embrace, a gesture that appears in the contemporary reliefs. The right hand of her encircling arm achieves an integration which is particularly striking in a side-view, and avoids the disembodied effect of the similar hands of the goddesses on the triads. This pair-statue is the consummation of the idea of man and wife in Egyptian society. It is suffused with a subtle humanity absent in the god-like reserve of the Khephren statue. 35, 36 25

The same feeling pervades the triads of Mykerinus, with the goddess Hathor accompanied by a nome-deity, taking the role of his queen, whose features she bears. In one example, the intimacy of the relationship is indicated by their clasping hands, an innovation in the repertory of poses. In the Boston triad, the seated goddess holds Mykerinus in the same embrace as his queen does in the pair-statue. This particular example is a bold experiment in the conjunction of a standing and a seated figure, and sets the pattern for a number of pair-statues among private statuary as well as royal examples. The triads of Mykerinus are the first complete examples of statues of a king and deities in association, though fragments from the reigns of Djoser, Djedefrē and Khephren show that dyads and group statues had already been designed. All the examples from the valley temple of the Pyramid of Mykerinus at Giza are in schist (greywacke), a stone that allowed the sculptor more scope than the denser diorite of the Khephren statuary. It also encouraged him to develop an interest in rendering the muscles and tendons of the male figure, and the softer forms of the women beneath their close-fitting gowns. In addition, fragments of statues in albaster, some of them over life-size, show a 36 cf. 87

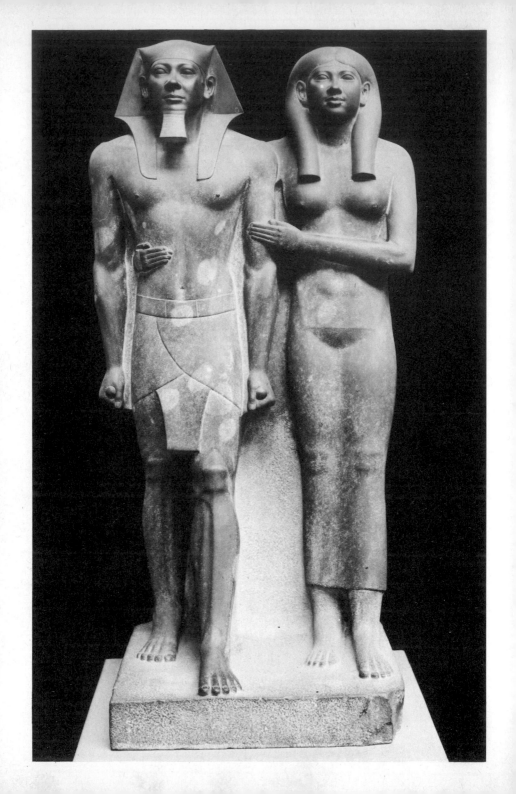

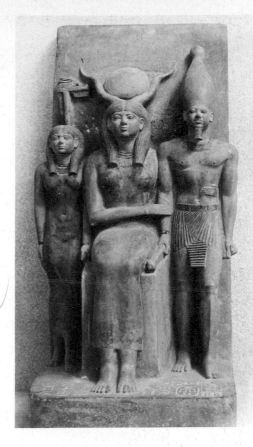

35 Schist pair-statue of King
Mykerinus and Queen Khamerernebty
II, from Giza, *c.* 2530 BC.

36 Schist triad of King Mykerinus
(*right*), Hathor (*centre*) and the personified
Hare nome (*left*), from Giza, *c.* 2530 BC.

more plastic treatment of the human form and features than is evident
in the Khephren examples in this same stone.

Apart from the royal statuary, however, little private sculpture has
survived, perhaps because the corps of trained craftsmen was small
and concerned almost exclusively with work on the monuments of
the kings, and had time to execute commissions only for the most
important of the royal children. Nevertheless, sculptures of the reigns
of Kheops and Djedefrē, though fragmentary, have provided
evidence of the enterprising spirit of these artists in devising new
forms. The statue of the owner squatting cross-legged as a scribe, the
educated man, writing 'the god's words' on a papyrus roll stretched
across his lap, now makes its appearance, the first examples apparently
having been made for Kawab, the eldest son of Kheops. These are
now in the Museum of Fine Arts, Boston (nos. 24.12.1105, 27.11.27
and 34.4.1).

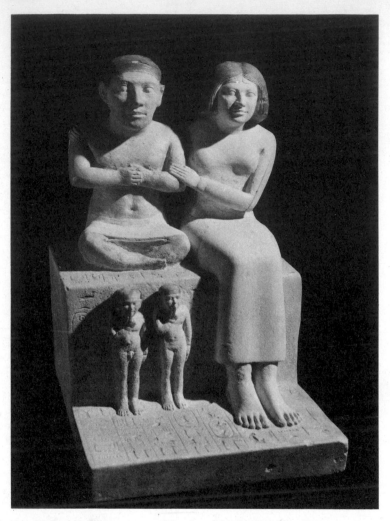

37 Painted limestone group of Seneb and his family, from Giza, *c.* 2530 BC.

In the reign of Mykerinus, private statuary becomes a little more common. The rock-cut tombs of the queens Khamerernebty II and Meresankh III at Giza, have preserved statues half in the round, hewn in niches cut in the coarse native rock, which has had to be supplemented with plaster. One niche shows a group of ten women, comprising figures of Meresankh, her mother and her daughters.

Usually such figures are in the classic standing pose, with feet together and arms by their sides, the fingers extended. There are, however, variations in some of the statues, notably that of a girl on a smaller scale who places one arm round the waist of her neighbour. In another niche two women stand with one arm crossed behind each other's back, the first instance of a pose which was to have a more popular revival at a later period. Similar rock-hewn statues exist in tomb-chapels from this reign onwards, but generally they are of inferior quality, especially where the plaster coating has fallen from the coarse limestone core. A curious feature of the tomb of Meresankh is the rock-hewn statue of her steward Kemten as a scribe squatting within his niche, which originally was concealed behind a stone slab forming a box, as though he were sharing in the funerary offerings on the sly.

cf. 102

Free-standing statues of this period have also survived but are on a small scale; the restored pair-statue in the Museum of Fine Arts, Boston (no. 30.1456), of Hetepheres II and her daughter Meresankh III, standing side by side in the classic pose of women, is exceptional for the close embrace of the elder woman, who places her left arm round the neck of her daughter so that the lower arm hangs down vertically, the hand open upon the breast. This posture is more successfully contrived in a later statue of a man and his wife.

64

But perhaps the most surprising statue of this period to have survived is the group of the chief valet and royal tutor, the dwarf Seneb, with his wife and children. Since its discovery this piece has been dated to the Sixth Dynasty but, as Bernard Bothmer of the Brooklyn Museum has pointed out to the writer, the location, layout and texts of the stone mastaba in which it was found all point to an earlier period. There are a number of stylistic details which suggest a date late in the Fourth Dynasty or early in the Fifth, including the absence of a back pillar, the fashion of the bracelets worn by the wife, the character of the reliefs of Seneb in his mastaba and the fact that, like the statue of Kemten in the tomb of Meresankh III, his statues were found sealed in stone boxes. The pose of the wife, seated beside her husband, with her arms flexed front and rear to support him, recalls the disposition of the arms of the queen in the Mykerinus dyad, but in its context, here seems as much protective as affectionate. Seneb's large head and torso, and the arrangement of his limbs, mitigate her disproportionate size which is against the usual convention that the wife should be slighter in build than her husband. The position of the son and daughter, shown as symbolic infants, in the places where the legs of a normal man would have been carved, ingeniously preserves the unity of the composition and the cubic nature of its conception.

37

4th Dynasty

35

cf. 64

CHAPTER SIX

The Pyramid Age

Dynasties V–VI *Relief Sculpture*

The advent of the Fifth Dynasty marks a turning-point in the culture of the Old Kingdom. The change of dynasty seems to have been occasioned by the extinction of the male line of Snoferu and not through any political challenge to the kingship. The divine might of the pharaoh remained unquestioned, but he now controlled a less centralized state in which all the chief offices were no longer filled by members of his family. He had become less remote and less powerful than in the days of Djoser and Kheops, and could now allow a favoured courtier to kiss his foot instead of the ground it had trodden upon. He was now addressed as the Son of the sun-god, a title that was from this moment added permanently to the titulary of the pharaoh, though Khephren had previously claimed the affiliation. The influence of the cult of the sun-god, Rē of Heliopolis, in fact, is paramount during the remainder of the Old Kingdom, and had a profound effect upon the subject-matter of art and the style of the architecture of the age. The pharaohs built more modest pyramids for themselves at Abusir and Saqqara, reflecting their diminished stature, and they abandoned the grandiose proportions of the mighty Giza monuments; although even there the Pyramid of Mykerinus is but a third of the size of its two earlier rivals.

By the beginning of the Fifth Dynasty, the legend was firmly established that the birth of the pharaoh was the result of a union between the sun-god and the queen who had borne him; but by the end of the dynasty the rival cult of Osiris, a god who had suffered death and resurrection, had emerged. The Osiris religion claimed that on death the pharaoh was assimilated to him, while the royal heir, the new Horus incarnate, was identified with Horus the son of Osiris, who had vindicated his murdered father before the tribunal of the gods, and ruled in his stead. A dichotomy thus arose in the royal destiny: on his death, the pharaoh was not only mingled with the sun-god who had begotten him, but was also the new Osiris, king of the dead, while his son sat upon his throne as the ruler of the living.

The influence of the sun-cult is seen in a number of ways, but its effect upon architecture is perhaps the most significant from an artistic point of view. Unlike the other cults of Egypt, the sun-god did not inhabit the dark primordial shrine of the First Time, the focus of

78

temple observances elsewhere, but was worshipped under an open sky in a cloistered court containing his emblem or fetish, the *ben-ben* stone, raised upon a pillar to form an obelisk. This is presumed to be the basic design of the temple of Rē at Heliopolis, because although that site is almost completely obliterated, six kings of the Fifth Dynasty built copies of it as adjuncts to their funerary monuments. Two such edifices have been located and excavated, although only the sun-temple of Niuserrē at Abu Gurab, near Abusir, has provided *38* enough data to give some idea of its plan and details. Its architect has made ingenious use of the configuration of the ground to build a temple at a high level on the desert escarpment, linked obliquely by a covered causeway to a small portal, or valley temple, at a lower level on the verge of the cultivation. The upper sanctuary consisted of a rectangular walled enclosure 330 feet long and 250 feet wide (100 by 76 metres), within which rose a squat obelisk on a podium near the western end. In the centre of the court before this podium, was a large alabaster altar, open to the sky and lying on the south side of an enclave in which the sacrificial animals were slaughtered. Between this enclave and the north enclosure-wall was a suite of twelve store-rooms.

The most important feature of the temple, however, from an artistic point of view, was the corridor that opened from the entrance hall and ran along the east and south sides of the court. The walls of this covered way were adorned with raised reliefs mostly concerned

38 Reconstruction of the sun-temple of King Niuserrē at Abu Gurab near Abusir, *c.* 2470 BC. *1* enclosure wall; *2* obelisk; *3* podium; *4* open altar; *5* entrance hall; *6* causeway; *7* valley sanctuary; *8* mud-brick solar barque.

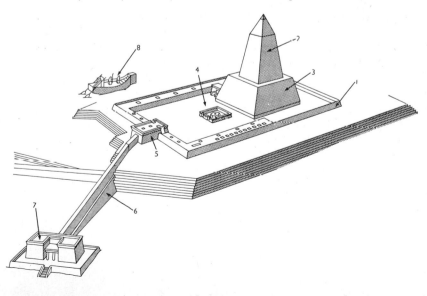

with rites performed by the king and his officials at his jubilee. The south corridor turned northwards at its distal end to open into two narrow chambers lying parallel to each other. The first chapel was decorated with reliefs illustrating ceremonies performed by the king at the founding of a temple and at his jubilee.

The second chamber, however, was the more remarkable, and has come to be known as the 'Room of the Seasons' from the subject of its reliefs which portray activities during the Egyptian agricultural year, as a kind of visual paean to the sun-god for all his bounty. Only disjointed fragments of these scenes remain, like others from the site, but they can be supplemented from versions in the private mastaba tombs of the dynasty. In addition to representations of the Nile and the gods of the nomes of Egypt, bringing their produce to the king, there are large-scale personifications of but two of the three seasons, Spring and Summer, each accompanied by appropriate plants and animals, and displaying the occupations of man at each division of the year. The great seasonal migration of birds and fish are recorded, the ploughing and sowing in spring, the water sports, the hunt in the desert wadis and the harvest in summer.

The almost complete ruin of these sun-temples makes it difficult to assess the significance of the positioning of the various schemes of decoration. A little more information is forthcoming from the remains of the pyramid complexes of the kings, particularly those of Sahurē of the Fifth and Phiops II of the Sixth Dynasty. Here we can see that the valley temple was decorated with scenes of the pharaoh as a sphinx or gryphon trampling the enemies of Egypt; and as a huntsman in the marshy verges, casting his throw-stick into flocks of birds and harpooning the hippopotamus, and so magically protecting the entrance from any evil incursion by air or water. This same theme is continued on the inner walls of the causeway corridor at its lower end, where captive Libyans and Asiatics are shown being led by the gods before the king. If one is to judge by blocks from the causeway of Unas, however, other subjects were represented on the upper end, such as the gathering of figs, the harvesting of corn, the collection of honey, the raising of domestic animals, the hunting of desert fauna, the making of various objects in stone and metal by craftsmen and the transport from the granite quarries at Aswan of the monolithic columns and architraves used in the building. The theme is thus changed to the arrival at the mortuary temple of all the things used in its construction and daily functioning.

The actual mortuary temple at the upper end of the causeway is a development from the Fourth Dynasty examples, and consists essentially of four main parts. An entrance hall leads into a peristyle

80

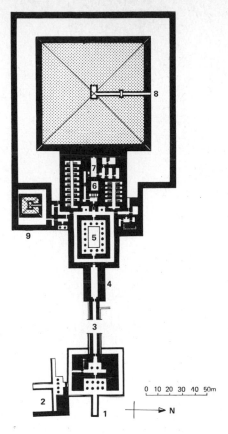

39 Plan of the mortuary temple of King Sahurē at Abusir, *c.* 2510 BC. *1, 2* landing stages; *3* causeway; *4* entrance hall; *5* colonnaded open court; *6* chamber with five statue-niches; *7* sanctuary; *8* pyramid; *9* subsidiary pyramid court.

colonnaded court open to the sky with an altar in its middle. A transverse corridor separates this front half from the rear portion, with another hall containing niches for five statues of the king, leading into the sanctuary with its false door for funerary offerings at its western end, against the east face of the pyramid. Magazines on two levels flanked the inner part in the early temples, and both halves in the later examples.

The entrance hall was probably covered by a ceiling of corbelled slabs, hollowed on their underside to form a barrel-vaulted roof. The walls were decorated with reliefs which appear again to have had a protective function, showing the king harpooning the hippopotamus. This theme is continued on the four walls of the colonnaded court and the corridors that ran behind it. The king with his officials and retinue hunts the animals of the desert or indulges in the marsh sports of fowling and spearing fish; or he makes to slay a

wall
relief
decoration

protective
function

41

81

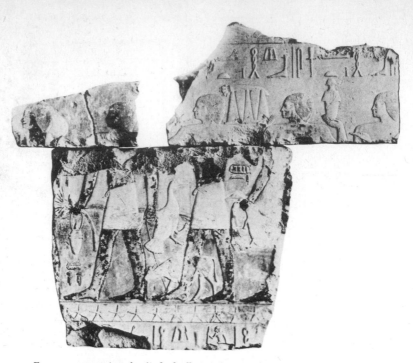

40   Fragmentary painted relief of offering-bearers from the pyramid temple of King Phiops II at Saqqara, *c.* 2280 B C.

Libyan chief before a god, while his wife and children beg for mercy, and the booty is paraded before him. This last theme is probably only symbolic, for in the temple of Phiops II there is an exact replica of the scene, even to a repetition of the names of the protagonists. The subject probably dates back even earlier to some heroic event at the dawn of history: and it is noteworthy that a fragment of an early dynastic palette in Cairo illustrates a cognate theme.

The transverse corridor usually marks a change in the character and direction of the reliefs. The king performs rites connected with his coronation and jubilee; he distributes gifts to his officials and is greeted by the gods of Egypt, and by his high officers of state, as he enters the temple by way of the sanctuary. The chapel, like the entrance hall, was vaulted and was decorated with a scene of the king seated at a table of offerings, to which comes a procession of his funerary priests, courtiers, provincial governors and other high officials bearing provisions of every kind, including cattle, antelopes, gazelles and goats hauled by ropes, and pigeons and quails in cages.

cf. 43, 44

82

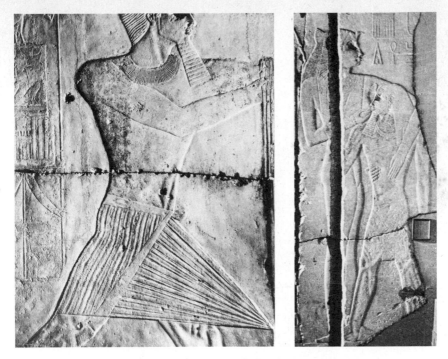

41 Limestone relief of King Sahurē hunting, from Abusir, *c.* 2510 BC.

42 Limestone relief of the goddess of Upper Egypt suckling King Sahurē, from Abusir, *c.* 2510 BC.

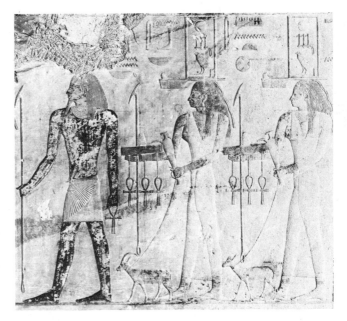

43 Limestone relief of the personified Lower Egyptian estates of King Sahurē, from Abusir, *c.* 2510 BC.

The craftsmanship expended upon these solar temples and pyramid complexes, especially at the beginning of the Fifth Dynasty, was of a very high order. The reliefs of Userkaf and Sahurē are drawn by supremely assured artists and carved with exquisite precision in a very low relief. In subsequent dynasties there is a decline from this high standard, but the reliefs of Phiops II at the end of the Old Kingdom, while reverting to the deeper relief of the Fourth Dynasty, are scarcely inferior and served as a pattern for artists in later ages.

42, 43

cf. 40, 75, 111

In addition to the variety of subject-matter and the fertility of invention displayed by the reliefs, what is remarkable about the mortuary buildings of the Pyramid Age is the beauty of the materials used in their construction. The pavements of open courts were often of polished black basalt which under an Egyptian sky can assume the deep blue colour of the primordial waters of Chaos from which the temple arose at the First Time: or they can be of alabaster, which also in certain lights reflects a limpid blue. Other internal rooms were paved with banded alabaster, and this same rich stone was used in great monolithic blocks from which entire magazines were hollowed out. Red granite was used for columns that imitated palm trees, clustered papyrus stalks or lotus buds. Black basalt or red granite was selected for the dados below the painted reliefs carved in fine Tura limestone. Names and titles were elegantly drawn and crisply carved on columns and architraves, and often inlaid in green paste. The ceilings, whether flat, as over the colonnades, or vaulted, as in the sanctuary and entrance halls, were painted blue and sown with yellow five-pointed stars in relief. The appearance of these buildings in their pristine state, harmonious in their colours and proportions and rich in the beauty of their materials, must have been deeply impressive. It is a heavy loss to art that all that now exists of their glory are random scraps of relief and plundered ruins half covered in blown sand.

The reliefs in the private tombs of some of the high officials of these kings, principally at Saqqara, have suffered less grievously, and some notable examples have been preserved. The practice of building the superstructure of such mastaba tombs in stone instead of mud brick had arisen during the reign of Kheops; but it is only from the beginning of the Fifth Dynasty that they show a progressive increase in the size of the chapel. From being a small cruciform chamber it eventually becomes one or more suites of rooms, some of them large enough to have ceilings supported by piers or columns, occupying the greater part of the mass above the burial shaft. The decoration of this greatly expanded wall-space, clad with Tura limestone, did not become possible until the reserves of labour, trained and organized in the building of the mighty monuments of Giza, were released for

49

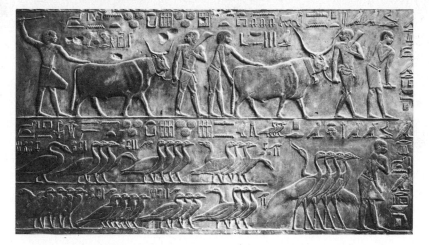

44 Painted limestone relief of the presentation of cranes, geese and cattle, tomb of Ptah-hotep at Saqqara, c. 2450 BC.

private commissions by the more modest ambitions of later pharaohs. Nevertheless, many of these private tombs were gifts of the king to relatives or favoured courtiers. The focal point of the chapels was still the false door, as it was in the mortuary temples of the kings, with the owner seated before a table, or represented half in the round as though coming forth to receive the offerings brought to the altar by relatives or retainers, carved in relief on the adjacent walls and orientated in such a way that the direction of their procession is towards him.

The fact that Egypt enjoyed a predominantly agricultural economy, and the life of these magnates was concerned almost entirely with the management of their estates, is evident from the decoration of their chapels with scenes of the country pursuits which provided them with their funerary offerings. In this respect, the reliefs of the Fifth Dynasty resumed a tradition that evolved in the Third, but had been somewhat in suspense in the chapels of the Fourth Dynasty. Such offerings are often symbolized by the estates of the owner represented as market women bearing their produce in baskets cf. 74 upon their heads, and holding birds in their hands or leading animals by their halters. These are, of course, private versions of the 43 personified districts which attend the king in royal reliefs.

Other offerings, which are enumerated in the essential prayer on the stela, or specified in the accompanying offering-list, are given the same elaborate treatment. The representation of the prescribed cuts of

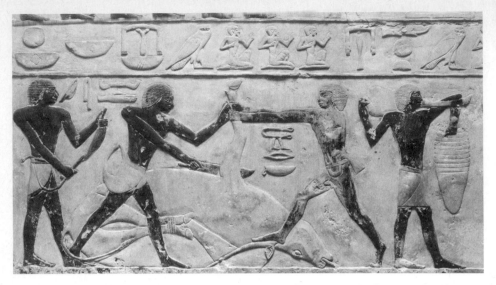

45 Painted relief of butchers cutting up the sacrificial ox, tomb of the Princess Idut at Saqqara, c. 2410 BC.

46 Painted limestone relief of the treading in of seed grain by goats, and cattle fording a canal, tomb of Ti at Saqqara, c. 2450 BC.

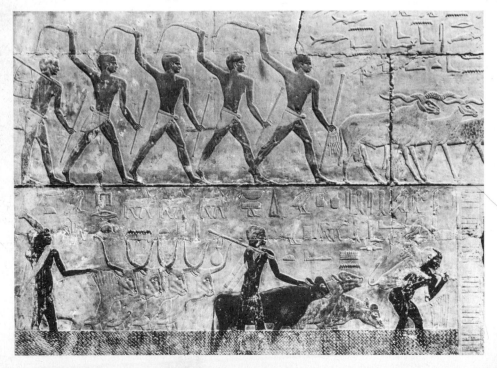

meat for the funerary meal develops into scenes of the raising of cattle, the procession of prize oxen, the lassooing of the sacrificial steer, and its butchering. The loaf of bread and the jug of beer are expanded into the sowing of the corn and barley crops in the new-ploughed fields, their harvesting, threshing and storage, and the preparations in bakehouse and brewery. The jar of wine becomes the growing of grapes on espaliers, and the treading and bottling of the vintage. The scenes of snaring and fowling, or the raising of geese, cranes, pigeons and ducks in the poultry-yard are to provide the offering of a bird. The flax harvest and the weavers busy at their looms supply not only the clothing of the owner, but the bed-linen, which after death will be torn into strips to bandage his corpse. Similarly, craftsmen are shown making the boats for the pilgrimage to Buto, or the last journey across the Nile to the West. Others carve the statues, or prepare the jewels, furniture, stone vessels and other worldly goods that may accompany their owner to his tomb. All the components are represented for a full life in the Hereafter, similar to the one he passed on earth, attended by his family and servants, his wife and children, his friends and household pets, his scribes and valets, his musicians and dwarf jesters, and his bearers with their master's carrying-chair.

    This magic re-creation, however, stops short of vigorous participation: the dignified owner merely 'observes' with a benevolent eye the activities of the life passed on earth. It is the ferrymen at their water-jousts, the butchers pulling down the ox for sacrifice, the ploughmen turning in the seed-corn, the reapers in the

44–6

44

44

47, 45

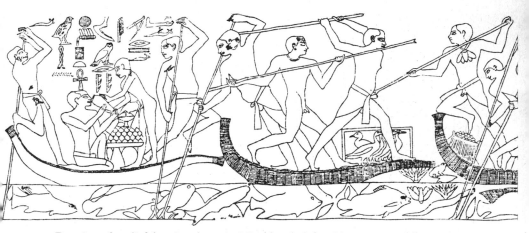

47   Drawing of a relief showing the artist Niankhptah, left, taking a repast while boatmen fight on the water, tomb of Ptah-hotep at Saqqara, *c.* 2450 BC.

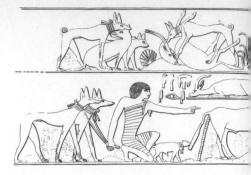

48 Drawing of a relief of the hunt in the desert, tomb of Ptah-hotep at Saqqara, c. 2450 BC.

harvest field, the various craftsmen at their tasks, the children at their games, who are shown in active movement. In these pictures of the good life passed on the country estates, the decoration of the private tombs appears to have been influenced by the scenes in the sun-temples, particularly the cycle of the agricultural year as represented in the 'Room of the Seasons', under the beneficence of the sun-god. Only in the royal sports of harpooning the hippopotamus, spearing fish with the leister and fowling with the throw-stick, was the owner shown in an active role, and such postures were copied after designs in the mortuary temple of his king.

48   In addition to such scenes, which included the hunt in the desert and the entertainment of the owner with music and dancing, there also appear representations of the cult of the dead, such as the funerary cortège with mourners, the censing and dragging of the statue of the deceased to the tomb and the journey by boat to the West or the holy city of Buto. Throughout all these scenes, there runs the connective thread of the life of man in all its aspects, from his nursing at his mother's breast, through the games of his childhood, the pride of his youth, the corpulence of a prosperous maturity, to the final farewell at the tomb door.

The artistic quality of the reliefs during the entire period maintains a fair standard, but certain tombs have long been celebrated for the excellence of their craftsmanship. In particular, the tomb of Ti represents the high-water mark of the Fifth Dynasty style, with its exquisite carving of the finely drawn scenes, remarkable for the
46   variety and scope of their subject-matter, and the precision of their detail. The proportions are graceful, but the very perfection of the carving tends to give a somewhat prim character to the reliefs.

Much of the same quality is evident in the reliefs of the slightly later
45   tombs of Nefer-her-ptah and the Princess Idut near the Unas causeway; but the first was unfinished, though some of its careful preliminary drawings were completed in colour and the second has

88

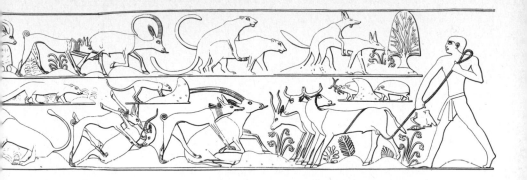

lost the upper courses of its walls. The tomb of Idut, however, still retains some impressive aquatic scenes, with the bird and fish life carefully observed, and faultlessly carved and painted.

The tomb of Nufer, hewn into a quarry-face lower down the Unas causeway, is of a less exalted owner, but despite its more recent discovery, is now celebrated for the excellent condition of its single oblong offering-chamber. The reliefs still hold their colour, but are more deeply carved, and lack the subtlety of the reliefs in the mastaba of his near contemporary, Ti. Nevertheless, they exhibit some unusual features, such as the figure of the baboon assisting at the wine-press, sufficient to show that however closely the scenes in these tombs may copy standard patterns, there are variations in the details that betray the caprices of an individual artist or craftsman.

The demands for 'a good burial in the West' among an ever-increasing class of patrons, outran the resources of the available labour force. It is exceptional for the decoration of a tomb to be found complete. Already, even in the sun-temple of King Niuserrē, a quick and bastard form of raised relief was being used which, however, would be difficult to distinguish from the more elaborate kind when the final painting had been added. Such economies and short-cuts are more evident at the end of the dynasty, and during the Sixth Dynasty, when they were allied to an increasing formalism as less competent and less inspired workmen were brought into service, especially for the less wealthy clients. The important officials, some of whom, like Mereruka, were related to the royal house, were still able to command craftsmen of skill and originality who introduced more movement into the traditional iconography. In the tombs of Ptah-hotep and Akhet-hotep, and of Mahu, Kagemni and Ankhmahor, the *44, 47, 48* relief reverts to a more deeply cut style and the shadows that this casts lend a boldness and solidarity to the figures of men and animals. The calves in the procession of cattle gambol and leap over one another, and no longer move sedately to the sacrifice. The heads of the goats in

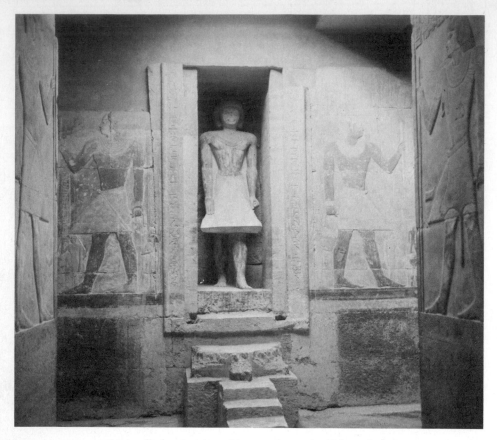

49   Main offering chamber of the mastaba tomb of Mereruka at Saqqara, *c.* 2390 BC.

a flock may be turned in opposite directions, and in a herd of cattle, one breaks the pattern of horns to toss its head. The sacrificial steer is overthrown only by the most strenuous action, and dancers sway backwards with abandon, balanced on one leg.

The tombs that show these features belong to the entourage of the earlier kings, Teti and Phiops I, of the Sixth Dynasty, and represent the full bloom of the Memphite style. In the latter half of the dynasty, the monuments of Phiops II, whose long reign of ninety-four years ended in the twilight of the Old Kingdom, show no decline in the standards of the royal craftsmen; but the innovations of the age are found in the local centres, the residence towns of provincial governors, whose artists introduced a number of modifications to the Memphite iconography which will be noted in a later chapter.

40

CHAPTER SEVEN

The Pyramid Age
Dynasties V–VI *Statuary*

4th Dynasty. Archaic Style >

The achievement of the sculptors of the Fourth Dynasty had been to transform the heavy mass of the Archaic style into lighter and more naturalistic proportions, the heads set proudly upon ample necks, the shoulders squared and the bodies of an athletic build. The search for an underlying simplification of form achieved its canon in the reserve heads and the statue of Hemon. This proved too austere an ideal for the sensibilities of the artists or their patrons, and by the reign of Mykerinus the statuary is characterized by a freer and more plastic rendering of the human form. The classic sculpture that filled the monuments of the period bequeathed a repertoire of poses, an authoritative style and a faultless technique which served as an inspiration to Egyptian sculptors and a point of reference during later ages.

Hemon & Mykerinus

28-30

cf. 87

The transition to the Fifth Dynasty wrought no great changes in the style of royal statuary. A number of fragmentary heads surviving from this period show that the traditions of the Mykerinus school of sculpture were well maintained. The schist head in Washington of a king wearing the White Crown (who may be Shepseskaf or his successor) and the head found in the sun-temple of Userkaf, now in Cairo (no. J. 90220), are of outstanding quality, and in no way inferior to the Mykerinus examples, though the latter head shows a trend towards formalism which is more marked as the Old Kingdom progresses. Nevertheless, as in most Egyptian statuary during a period of high culture, innovations are not lacking. The eyebrow and the cosmetic line at the outer corner of the eye are now generally indicated in raised relief in royal statuary in hard stones, though private sculpture does not show the cosmetic line during the Old Kingdom.

50

1

Another introduction during the Fifth Dynasty is the development of the back pillar, first apparent on a standing statue of Niuserrē from Karnak, shared between the museums of Cairo (no. C. 42003) and Rochester, New York State (no. 42.54). This feature is probably derived from the back-slab, but it may have arisen in statues of women in the classic stance with feet together. Such statues, especially those carved in limestone, would have been liable to break at the ankles without some reinforcement. It is found principally in standing figures but it becomes so integral a part of the statue that it is adopted

2

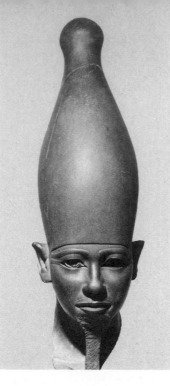

50 Diabase head of a king wearing the White Crown, *c.* 2525 BC.

51 Colossal granite head of King Userkaf, from Saqqara, *c.* 2520 BC.

for figures of seated and even squatting persons. It also achieves eventual importance, despite its obscure location, as an area for inscribing prayers on behalf of the owner together with his name and title. Its upper extremity is also prolonged to support tall headgear such as the crowns of kings and deities.

A third innovation is the emergence of statuary carved on a colossal scale, the first surviving example of which is a head of King Userkaf in red granite. Colossal statuary appears in the reign of Khephren with the figure of the Great Sphinx, carved with the features of the king from a knoll of rock left in a local quarry near his valley temple at Giza. But this gigantic figure is less of a work of art than a landmark, the terrifying guardian of the Giza necropolis. The head of Userkaf is the first example known to come from a free-standing statue which greatly exceeded life-size, and was doubtless shown seated upon a throne. It dominated the colonnaded court of the mortuary temple of the king's small pyramid at Saqqara. The simplified planes of the face, probably determined by the coarse crystalline nature of the stone, and the large scale of the work, convey a powerful impression of the might and majesty of kingship in ancient Egypt. Even in its ruin it is one of the great masterpieces of the age.

92

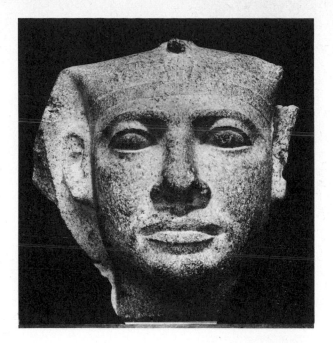

Unfortunately, there is no great range of work in the Old Kingdom with which to compare it. The paucity, especially of high-quality pieces, may be partly due to the modest scale of the mortuary buildings, but it may also, one suspects, owe much to the fact that most of the sculpture was carved in limestone which has not survived the extreme dilapidation of the royal monuments so well as the hard-stone statuary of the Fourth Dynasty. Certainly a limestone head, probably of Userkaf, has survived, and a base from the niches in the inner hall of the mortuary temple of Phiops II shows that the statues were of painted limestone. A diorite seated statue of Sahurē, attended by the personification of the Koptos Nome, is almost intact, thanks to the hard stone from which it is carved. Now in New York (MMA no. 18.2.4) it is expertly fashioned in the tradition of the Mykerinus archetypes, but lacks their inner vitality. There is also a group of small votive statues in the Cairo Museum (nos. C. 38–40, 42), in granite and alabaster, evidently from the temple of Ptah at Memphis, which are mediocre in execution and give the impression of having been produced at the one time, perhaps by a later king who wished to honour those whom he claimed as his ancestors.

From the Sixth Dynasty has survived the upper part of an

93

undistinguished life-sized granite statue of a king found near the Pyramid of Teti, and usually taken to represent him. It is now in the Cairo Museum (no. J.39103). The parts of a life-sized copper statue of Phiops I and another on a smaller scale have been excavated at Hierakonpolis, and represent examples of a kind of statue known from the Palermo Stone to have been made as early as the Second Dynasty. It has been presumed that the metal was hammered in plates over a wooden core, and such adjuncts as crown and kilt were added in gilded plaster. If this is so, the life-sized statue and its smaller companion are technical *tours de force*, but the corrosion that they have suffered gives an imperfect idea of their original quality.

Four statuettes, one in Cairo, the others in Brooklyn, although on too small a scale to reveal fully the true character of art at the end of the Old Kingdom, are expertly carved, three of them in a warm translucent alabaster which, however, makes the effective lighting of such pieces a difficult and fortuitous business. Nevertheless, they do give precious glimpses of the scope and variety of royal statuary at this period, as, since they are presumably *ex votos*, they probably copy larger examples in a soft stone. All have unusual features. The schist figure of Phiops I, kneeling to offer a libation vessel held in each hand,

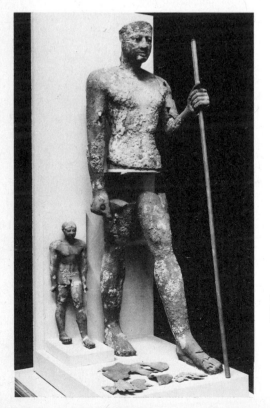

52   Copper sheathed standing statues
of King Phiops I, from
Hierakonpolis, *c.* 2380 BC.

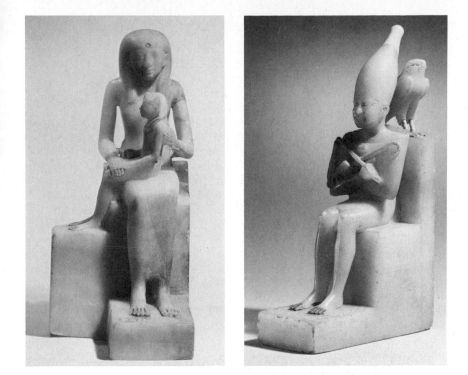

53   Alabaster statue of King Phiops II seated in the lap of his mother. *c.* 2350 BC.

54   Alabaster statuette of King Phiops I seated in jubilee attire, *c.* 2380 BC.

is the first known example of a type of statue which was to have a long tradition in pharaonic sculpture. Despite its small scale, it has been carved so as to release all its limbs from stone fillings; and such details as the nails on the grasping fingers and the splayed-out toes have been faithfully rendered. The portrait is alert and emphatic, the vitality of the smiling features being enhanced by the inlaid eyes. *cf. 131*

The larger alabaster statue of the same king, seated on a throne in his jubilee robe and holding sceptres, is of a kind which goes back to the Second Dynasty, although the pose of the arms has achieved more of a monumental equilibrium, first recorded on a statue of King Menkauhor in the group from Memphis, mentioned above, but which may be later in date. The limbs are again shown fully in the round. The falcon perched on the throne is part of the design of the Horus-name inscribed on the throne-back, but inevitably recalls the falcon of the Khephren statue. *54* *cf. 12* *32*

The third of this remarkable group, all in the Brooklyn Museum, is the still larger alabaster statue of Queen Ankhnesmeryrē, holding her
53 son, Phiops II, on her lap. In this example, too, the limbs have for the most part been released from their fillings. The two figures have been independently conceived on axes at right angles to each other, and assembled by juxtaposition rather than by integration. The infant son is represented as a fully adult king on a miniature scale, with his separate, though conjoined, footstool. This, also, is the first known example of a rare kind of royal statue, of which a few fragmentary or unfinished congeners have survived from subsequent periods.

The last statue in this group, in the Cairo Museum (no. J.50616), is also of Phiops II as a naked child, squatting, knees and feet wide apart, his right forefinger to his lips in a pose that probably equates him with the new-born sun, of which he is the offspring. It is damaged and the work is mediocre, but it is the first in a series of statuettes that appear sporadically throughout the remainder of pharaonic history, though subsequent examples maintain the volumetric form of Egyptian sculpture more successfully by bringing the knees and feet together.

In contrast to royal work, the private statuary of the Old Kingdom has survived in greater quantity, though it can be only a small proportion of what was made. The reduction in the size of the monuments of the kings of the Fifth and Sixth Dynasties released a reserve of skilled craftsmen for work on the tomb-chapels of their courtiers and officials, who were frequently honoured by the royal gift of a tomb or statue. As the Old Kingdom advanced, the size and number of such private chambers and serdabs gave greater scope to the craftsmen of the Memphite studios. A wealth of sculpture in wood, limestone and granite has survived, though it, too, shows a steady progression from the high quality of such pieces as the large
56, 57 statues of Rēnofer, to the generally smaller and less inspired statuary of the end of the period. It was, of course, the royal models that provided the main source of inspiration to sculptor and patron alike. Pair-statues, showing the owner with his wife beside him, follow the
63, 64 pattern of the earlier models of Djedefrē and Mykerinus. The dignity of the king demanded that he should be seated upon a throne, or standing upright, wearing his crowns and carrying his sceptres. Squatting poses belong to infants, or lesser orders of men, though the kneeling pose, which first appears in the statue of a funerary priest of the late Second Dynasty in the Cairo Museum (no. C. 1), is adopted
55 by Phiops I in the Brooklyn statuette. The owner in a squatting pose is first known from the fragmentary statues of Prince Kawab in Boston,
cf. 58 where he is represented as a scribe, seated cross-legged. This type of statue became popular during the Fifth Dynasty, when the variant

96

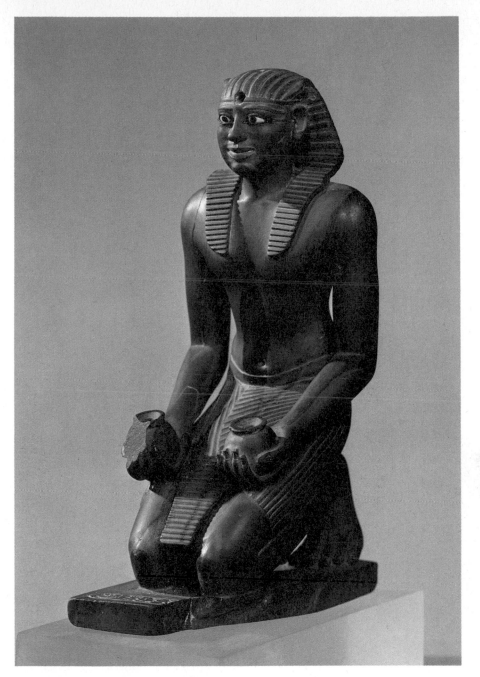

55 Schist statuette of King Phiops I kneeling to offer libation vessels, *c.* 2380 BC.

showing the scribe reading his papyrus roll instead of writing upon it made its appearance.

56, 57   The two large painted limestone statues of Rēnofer, wearing different styles of kilt and coiffure, represent the climax of the private statue in the Old Kingdom; and as the owner was the High Priest of Ptah, he was doubtless responsible for the design, and for commissioning royal craftsmen to carve them. Subsequent examples are usually less than half their size and reveal a less searching attempt to achieve an individual portrait. Where more than one tomb-statue of a person was provided, it was usual to represent the owner in different fashions of dress, just as he would appear in relief on the false door of his tomb.

From the Fifth Dynasty onwards, wood sculpture has often escaped the attentions of the white ant and much has survived, perhaps because it was sealed in the serdab. Wooden statuary has a long tradition in Egypt, the most complete examples being overlaid
59   in gesso, painted and set with realistic artificial eyes in copper frames. The majority of wooden figures show the owner in a walking or

56, 57   Painted limestone statues of Rēnofer, from Saqqara, *c.* 2520 BC.

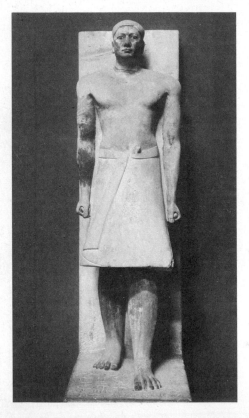
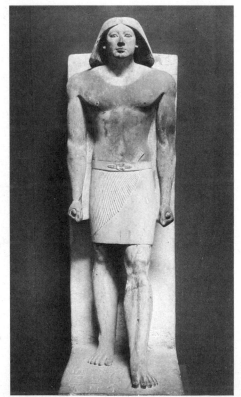

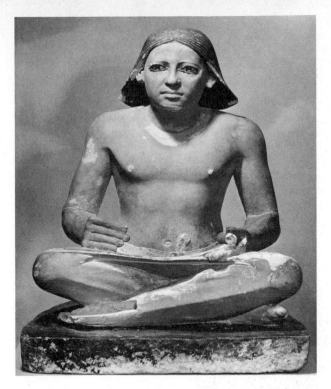

58 Painted limestone statue
of a scribe writing, from
Saqqara, *c.* 2500 BC.

standing attitude, but some half-dozen examples exist of men seated.
In one case in the Pelizaeus Museum at Hildesheim (no. 1572) he reads
a papyrus roll held on his lap. A statue in Cairo of a scribe in the more
orthodox squatting pose is painted in vivid colours, conveying an
exceptionally lively impression of the owner, despite the great
damage it has suffered (no. J.93165). The statue in Brooklyn of   *60*
Methethy in the costume of a mature man, with its inlaid eyes,
individual portrait and restrained modelling of the limbs and torso,
shows that the wood-carver was still able to produce masterpieces in
the earlier half of the Sixth Dynasty, before formalism overtook his
art and a decline in technical standards ensued in the First Intermediate
Period.

The late Jacques Vandier distinguished over 120 different poses in
stone statuary alone during the Old Kingdom, an eloquent comment
on the view that Egyptian statuary is limited to a few stereotypes.
Such a detailed analysis is out of place here; it must suffice to say that a
statue at this period may represent a man or a woman, standing,
sitting, squatting or kneeling. For each pose there is a classic version.
Thus the standing statues of men should have the left foot thrust

99

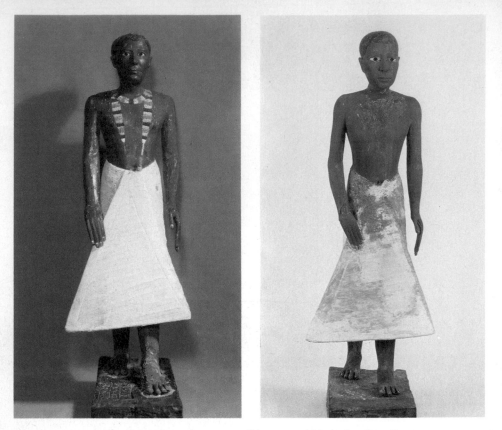

59, 60   Painted wooden statues of the steward Methethy, from Saqqara, *c.* 2370 BC.

forward, whereas those of women should show both feet together. Yet there are many exceptions to these general rules. Pair-statues may represent a man and woman both standing or sitting, or the one seated and the other standing, or the wife kneeling. Group statues may in addition show standing children, though in some cases the child may
37   be seated or squatting.

   The large family groups hewn in the living rock, such as appear in the tomb of Meresankh III, continue to be carved throughout the period and show no variation on the frontal aspect of the deceased and his relatives standing within a niche or doorway. Such groups could also be produced as free-standing units carved in very high relief. The
61   family of Penmeru at Boston is one of the most complete and successful of such compositions. In these groups, multiple figures of

the same person may appear; the phrase 'pseudo-group' has been coined to describe statuary of this sort. Their true purpose is conjectural: they are probably related to the multiplicity of the rock-hewn statues of the deceased that appear in certain tombs, forming a decorative architectural feature, and ensuring that if one of the tomb-statues should suffer damage, the rest may escape. Like their rock-hewn archetypes, the pseudo-groups also usually show the owner in a standing pose, though seated examples are known, and in some cases standing and seated figures appear together. The statues in the Penmeru group, with their simplified modelling of the limbs and pectoral muscles, and their stylized portraiture, reveal an increasing reliance by the sculptor on formalization to achieve his ends, perhaps the result of an increasing demand from a wider clientele.

This tendency grows steadily during the later Old Kingdom, but the genius of an individual sculptor could infuse a routine piece with

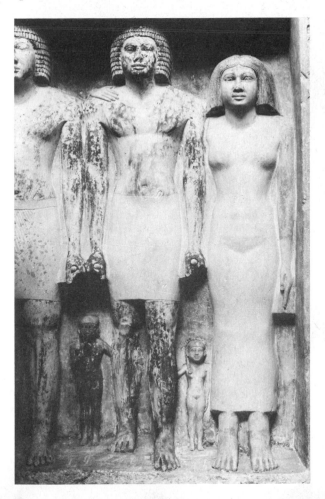

61　Painted limestone group of Penmeru and family, from Giza, c. 2410 BC.

more lively and sensitive qualities. The squatting statue of the chief physician Niankhrē is unique in its disposition of the legs, an example perhaps of a fresh approach by the sculptor or his sitter that tends to subvert the frontal aspect of the subject. The diagonal thrust of the right leg and the position of the right hand upon the kilt, as though the owner is adjusting his limbs to the squatting posture, create a sense of movement which finds its echo in the contemporary reliefs. The portrait of Niankhrē, with its calm but intelligent expression, and the naturalistic modelling of the body, betray the hand of a confident and original craftsman.

As an example of the best work in a more classic style, the Fifth Dynasty group of Iruka-ptah, in Brooklyn, harks back to a model created in statuary in the reign of Djedefrē, in which the wife on a much smaller scale kneels at her husband's feet (though in the archetype the contrast in size is moderated by the fact that Djedefrē is seated). The unnamed wife of Iruka-ptah adopts the usual pose in compositions of this character, kneeling and sitting upon her heels with her feet turned, in her case, to her right, a posture that is also found at a later period in statues of women alone. The son, shown naked and with the symbols of infancy (the side-lock, and forefinger to mouth) balances the figure of his mother on the opposite side.

Another pair-statue, showing Memi-sabu and his wife, to be dated to the early Sixth Dynasty, gives a different version of the theme of conjugal harmony. The man embraces his wife in a posture which had already appeared in a statue of Queen Hetepheres II and her daughter, and like them, the man stands with his feet together, against a back-slab. The convention that a woman should generally be shorter and slighter than her husband has here assisted the sculptor to achieve a more natural pose and an integration of the two figures.

The varied and lively statuary of this later phase of the Old Kingdom has bequeathed us a composite portrait of a somewhat complacent élite, calmly looking into the face of eternity; but another stratum of Egyptian society is represented in the servant statues that appear at the end of the Fourth Dynasty and which increase in number and complexity in the later serdabs of the period. Eventually wood replaces stone in their manufacture and the decline in quality is rapid. Such figures were designed to work by magic for their owners in the Hereafter, and are often dynamic in conception and rather aberrant in their proportions and execution, conveying the same sense of movement and industry that is found in the relief scenes of men and women at work, such as brewers, bakers, butchers, cooks, potters, musicians and women grinding corn. It may be that such relatively unimportant commissions were delegated to the

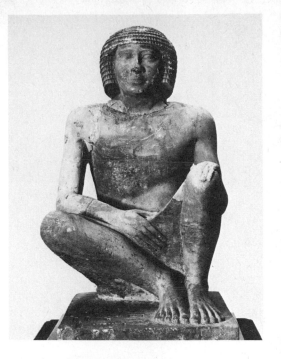

62 Limestone statues of the physician Niankhrē, from Giza, *c.* 2370 BC.

63 Limestone statue of Irukaptah and family, from Saqqara, *c.* 2500 BC.

64 Limestone pair-statue of the steward Memi-sabu and his wife, from Giza, *c.* 2370 BC.

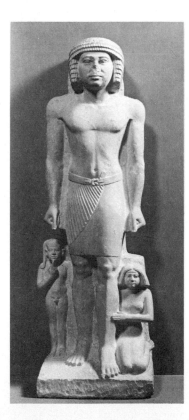

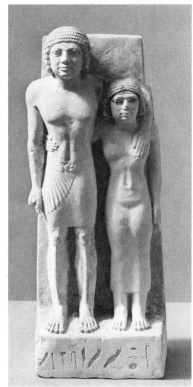

apprentices, not yet fully trained in the mystique and traditions of their craft.

The grandee, Uriren, however, secured the services of an exceptionally able sculptor for the models deposited in his tomb, 65 including the statuette of his funerary priest, Ka'emked, who is represented kneeling, his hands clasped before his midriff in a suppliant attitude. The eyes are inlaid, giving an alert and intelligent expression to the face. The detailed carving of the apron, the hands and the splayed-out feet is in effective contrast to the broad modelling of the arms and torso. Despite its small size, this is one of the masterpieces of Old Kingdom sculpture.

A servant statuette of a man straining mash through a sieve during 66 the preparation of beer is another example, but in a different mood and a more impressionistic style. The effect of muscular pressure being vigorously exercised is derived from the reduction of the various volumes of the body to their essentials in a strong zigzag arrangement, the globular mass of the head being connected to the globular mass of the vat by the downward thrust of the arms. A zigzag counterpoint is thus created on another axis by the contours of the vat upon its conical base and the arms bent outwards at the elbows. There are several examples of this type of design which show that this particular example was not created by the carver of the piece; but whoever first devised this composition succeeded in producing one of the most brilliant essays in the sculptural management of form.

The high civilization of the Old Kingdom suffered a precipitous fall after the long reign of Phiops II, when a period of stress and impoverishment ensued. Under the rule of the pharaoh, Egypt during the Old Kingdom achieved a vigorous and self-assured culture, untroubled by doubts about its destiny and unfaltering in its belief that prosperity depended upon completing a practical education, doing right for the king, respecting superiors and exercising moderation in all things. The ideal of the golden mean is as much in evidence in the calm and disciplined art as in the books that the sages wrote for their posterity.

Such a civilization was essentially aristocratic. In the beginning, only the king mattered, but as his divinity came to be shared to a lesser degree by his children and descendants, his exclusive powers, like the centralized authority of the state, began to be dispersed among a privileged class who boasted of their acquaintance with the king, and partook in some degree of his immortality. It was for them that all the economic and artistic activities were created. It was they whose hopes of eternal life were satisfied with tombs and endowments, at first near the king they had served, but later in the districts they had governed

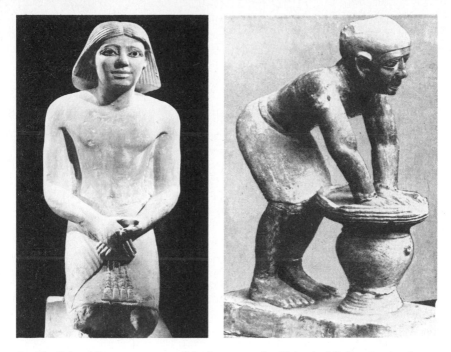

65, 66 Painted limestone statue of the funerary priest Ka'emked (*left*) and painted statuette of a brewer straining mash (*right*), both from Saqqara, *c.* 2410 BC.

on his behalf. They formed, however, no idle court nobility. The political system of the Egyptian state may have been founded by warrior kings, bearing such significant names as Scorpion, Fighter and Serpent, but Egyptian high culture was the creation of a sage, Imhotep, to whom at the end of its long history a Greek pharaoh kneels in supplication on the walls of the temple of Kom Ombo.

The aristocracy who organized and directed the agricultural wealth of Egypt, produced by a toiling peasantry, were the architects, mathematicians, engineers, thinkers and master craftsmen of the day. In later years, the Egyptians looked back upon the Old Kingdom as a Golden Age, in which superhuman deeds were done by wise men for mighty kings. In particular, they instinctively recognized the art of its monuments as the true and characteristic utterance of the Egyptian psyche, and they returned to it again and again as a source of inspiration and a point of departure, even in times when different conditions prevailed.

CHAPTER EIGHT

The First Intermediate Period
Dynasties VII–X

The fall of the Old Kingdom at the end of the Sixth Dynasty appears to have been sudden and complete. This collapse has been attributed by Egyptologists to the progressive decline of the authority of the pharaoh after the Fourth Dynasty, when provincial governorships and other offices came to be regarded as hereditary appointments, though each new incumbent had to be confirmed in his post by the king. A growing independence among these potentates posed a challenge to the supreme power of the pharaoh.

The resources of the state treasury, too, were eroded by gifts of land, exemptions from taxation, often in perpetuity, and alienation of income or property, mostly for the privileged occupants of cities of the dead clustered around the silent pyramids of their former lords. The emergence of a dominant feudal system becomes apparent when the long rule of Phiops II was followed by the brief reigns of a number of ephemeral pharaohs who form the Seventh and Eighth Dynasties. In a few troubled decades, the central authority became too weak to hold back the rising tide of anarchy, and Egypt split up into a number of rival principalities, no one of which was sufficiently strong to overawe the rest.

Recent research, however, has equated this collapse with widespread changes in the climate of Africa and the Near East at this period, in particular with the gradual cessation of the Neolithic Wet Phase about 2350 BC. The spectre of famine began to haunt the area. A relief on the Unas causeway showing a group of horribly emaciated people, weakened by privation and dying of hunger, is an early portent. Egypt was cushioned against the worst of such calamities by its unique irrigation system and the centralized control of its grain stores. It is presumed, however, that a change in the pattern of the monsoon rains falling on the Abyssinian plateau led to a series of low Niles. Egypt's system of basin irrigation and regional granaries would not have been able to cope with protracted disaster on such a scale.

Climatic changes evidently resulted in high winds producing dust storms, the denudation of cultivated land and the creation of shifting sand dunes, exacerbating the droughts. The whole political and economic system of Egypt, developed over the centuries, whereby a god incarnate had controlled by magic the inundations of the Nile for the benefit of mankind, was discredited in a few years. The kingship suffered eclipse. The king-lists refer to many pharaohs during the Seventh and Eighth Dynasties, each ruling for a year or two, before presumably they paid the penalty of being unable to make the Nile flow copiously, and disappeared without trace.

In these conditions, Egypt broke up into a number of feudal states, each governed by a petty ruler who tried to promote the welfare of his own region without much concern for that of his neighbours. There are veiled references, in the meagre records that have survived, to marauding bands of starving people searching for food in more favoured regions, and in at least one instance there is an explicit account of cannibalism. Local governors took measures to protect what they could in their own districts, conserving water supplies, and driving out famine-stricken invaders, whether natives, Libyans or Asiatics. This internecine strife further decreased the areas of cultivation, and the misery of these lean years is reflected in a new, pessimistic literature, and in the boasts of the local rulers that only by their organizing ability and their strong right arms had they been able to preserve their people, their crops and their herds alive.

There is no mention of the king in such texts, and with the eventual passing of the period of severe drought the feudal magnates began to vie with one another for supremacy. The pharaonate was eventually restored under one of their number, Mentuhotep (II) of Thebes, but the office never recovered the universal prestige it had enjoyed in the Old Kingdom. Instead, veneration was directed more to the god Osiris, that personification of kingship who was associated with the rising Nile and the sustenance and the fertility that it brought to the crops and all living things in Egypt.

The steady growth of feudalism in the Fifth and especially the Sixth Dynasty had promoted the rise of a number of provincial centres. The district governors had no longer sought burial near the pyramid of their lord in the Memphite necropolis, but had established their own family burial grounds at their capital towns. A widespread demand thus was created for the funerary arts, including sculpture and painting.

It can safely be assumed that provincial art centres had been formed to meet local needs, and had been greatly influenced by Memphite craftsmen, attracted by the opportunities offered by a new kind of patron. They in their turn would have trained the local workmen to carry on the traditions they had transplanted, though the chief court artists would hardly have been tempted away from their studios in Memphis, even if they had been allowed to migrate. Much provincial art in the Sixth Dynasty bears the stamp of the uninspired journeyman; and where work of more than average ability has survived, it is to be suspected that it was imported from a Memphite studio.

What this local art lacks in quality, however, it often redeems in liveliness and originality. The scenes in which herds of domestic animals are paraded under the eye of the owner include a variety of beasts shown together, instead of in segregated groups. The solemn procession is enlivened by a paucity of herdsmen with their halters, and a freer movement among the animals, with combats between pairs of bulls interrupting the pattern. At Mo'alla, a train of donkeys, which are rarely represented in the Memphite tombs except in harvest scenes, pauses while one of their number rolls on his back in the dust. Dancers, too, are more vigorous and less sedate in their movements, and execute complicated figures. On the whole, the provincial tombs tend to interpolate features of local life as soon as the sophisticated Memphite archetypes are forgotten by a new generation of artists. The roping of the bull may be represented at the moment when it kicks out to send a herdsman reeling back into the arms of his companions. The fisherman dives into the water to free the snagged net only to land head first on a lurking crocodile. The classic metropolitan style is tempered by rustic humour.

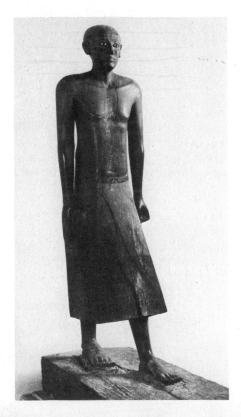

67   Wooden statue of the chancellor Nakhti, from Asyut, *c.* 2050 BC.

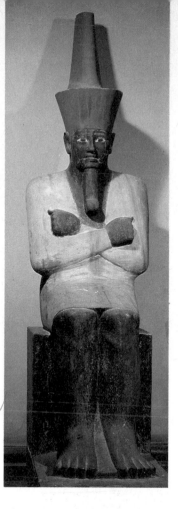

68　Painted sandstone statue of King Mentuhotep II, from Deir el-Bahri, *c.* 2030 B C.

In the earlier years of the First Intermediate Period, abject poverty reduced considerably the patronage of art and the opportunities for craftsmen to exercise their skills. It is probable that except in Memphis, where some kind of activity was maintained at a rather feeble level, the provincial art centres completely ceased to function and tradition was broken. But with a returning prosperity, as the worst of the droughts receded, demand for the funerary arts revived among the various feudal lords who now governed Egypt. The rulers of Heracleopolis fell heir to the Memphite workshops, while rival princes at Thinis, Dendera, Mo'alla, Asyut and Thebes developed their own versions of Sixth Dynasty traditions in splendid isolation.

Unfortunately, hardly any work in stone has survived from this

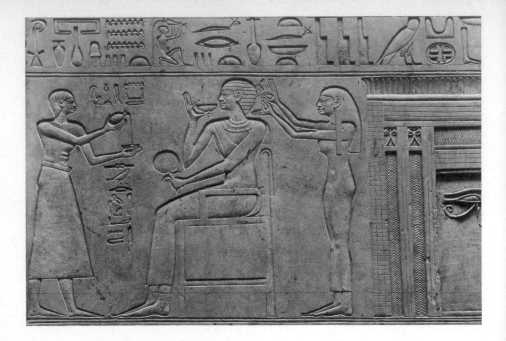

troubled period, but from the few fragments that remain and are attributed to the Heracleopolitan kings, the presumption is that they fell not far short of maintaining the standard of the Old Kingdom. In other places, the poverty of the times dictated changes in burial customs, which persisted into the ensuing period of the Middle Kingdom. Where the grandees could still afford to hew tombs in the rock, scenes were usually painted upon plastered walls. Elsewhere rectangular wooden coffins received texts that had previously been carved on tomb walls, or pictures of funerary equipment that had been buried with the dead, or painted or drawn in burial chambers. The number of servant figures increased and these were now hacked out of wood and crudely painted. Groups of these figures appear in models of brew- and bakehouses, slaughter-yards, granaries and the like, replacing the two-dimensional representations that had enlivened the walls of Old Kingdom tomb chapels.

Statuary in local wood replaced work in granite or in the fine limestone of Tura. The necropolis of Asyut has yielded the works of a distinctive school of wood sculptors extending over this period and into the Middle Kingdom. The most remarkable of such pieces is the life-sized statue of Nakhti in the Louvre. The pose and costume recall those of the mature Methethy at Brooklyn, and to this extent the

67
60

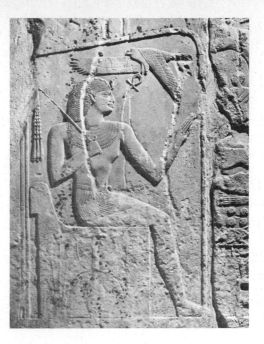

69   Relief on the limestone sarcophagus of the Princess Kawit, from Deir el-Bahri, *c.* 2030 BC, showing her drinking beer poured out by an attendant while a handmaiden dresses her hair.

70   Relief on the limestone shrine of King Mentuhotep II, from Dendera, *c.* 2030 BC.

work is in the tradition of the wood sculpture of the Sixth Dynasty; but it is distinguished from it by its greater size, the simplified planes, the large extremities and the aggressive mien, enhanced by the wide-open, inlaid eyes. The total effect is of savage force, typical of the harsh and disturbed age in which the owner lived.

A similar expression of brutal power is found in the work of a contemporary school of sculptors at Thebes, well exemplified by the sandstone statues erected in the mortuary temple of Mentuhotep II at Deir el-Bahri, with their squat proportions and massive limbs. Of these, the most complete is the seated example found in a subterranean chamber of the temple, representing the king clad in a jubilee robe and wearing the Red Crown of Lower Egypt. The wide staring eyes with their long inner canthi and outer paint stripe, the eyebrows in relief, and the thick lips with edges defined by sharp ridges, the heavy chin and the muscles emphasized round the corners of the mouth and nose, are derived from the mannerisms of late Sixth Dynasty portraiture, but are infused with a barbaric force that in effect creates a new archaism, a point of departure for the statuary of the Middle Kingdom.

The same qualities are found in the contemporary reliefs which decorated the tomb of Queen Nofru, and the chapels and sarcophagi

68

III

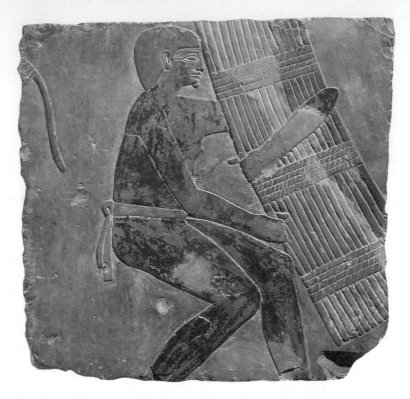

71   Painted limestone relief of a papyrus bearer, from Deir el-Bahri, *c.* 2010 BC.

69   of ladies of the king's court also buried at Deir el-Bahri. The sunk
reliefs of these latter are carved in a hard white limestone which lends
itself to the crisp cutting of details. The drawing is precise, and a little
geometrical, lacking subtlety in its contours, but clear in its design and
elegant in its proportions, with a recall of the works of Phiops II in the
elongated lobes of the ears.

The scenes of the king before Hathor, Min and other Theban
deities, in the little chapel that Mentuhotep erected at Dendera in the
early years of his reign, are in raised relief, deeply cut but showing the
70   same elegant proportions and careful attention to detail. A shallower
relief and less elongated figures appear in the fragmentary scenes,
71   which are all that remain from his own mortuary temple at Deir el-
Bahri. With these later representations, the Middle Kingdom makes
its appearance, both as a political reality and as an artistic revelation.

112

CHAPTER NINE

The Middle Kingdom
Dynasties XI–XIII

During his long reign, the Theban prince Mentuhotep II succeeded in overcoming the opposition of his rivals, and his eventual defeat of the Heracleopolitan power in the north united Egypt once more under the rule of a pharaoh. The Mentuhoteps of the Eleventh Dynasty at first wielded the absolute power of conquerors, but troubled times near the beginning of the second millennium BC, with a possible return of low Niles and years of want, brought about a change of dynasty and a shift in political power.

The king now found himself in a feudal state in which he was little more than the first among equals. He had to share his authority with provincial lords who dated events to their own years of rule, maintained their own armed forces and fleets of ships, and quarried stone for their own monuments, some of which were of a considerable size. He now claimed that God had appointed him 'the Herdsman of the land', to keep his people in health and prosperity as a good shepherd looked after his flocks. The form of benevolent despotism that had sustained some provinces in times of famine and distress was now carried over into the principles of government during the Middle Kingdom. The pharaohs of the Twelfth Dynasty promoted widespread economic development by irrigation works and land reclamation, particularly in the Faiyum, the most easterly of the string of fertile oases that lay in depressions in the Nile water-table in the Libyan desert. Trading posts were established in the Sudan, and mines and quarries reopened in Sinai and Nubia. Fortifications were raised on the northern and southern frontiers to protect Egypt from the incursions of famine-stricken marauders. Trade was also re-established with Byblos and the timber-bearing regions of the Lebanon.

The victories of Mentuhotep II must have brought the rustic Thebans into sustained contact with the traditions of Memphis; and, indeed, the king's chief sculptor in his later years had evidently served under the last of the Heracleopolitan kings. A more sophisticated influence is apparent in the later work of the reign and is to be discerned in the inner parts of his mortuary temple and particularly in *71* reliefs from Tod, and in the works of his successor S'ankh-ka-rē *72* (Mentuhotep III) at Tod and Armant. A somewhat austere but *73* delicate raised relief, more elegant in its proportions, emerges, which while it is obviously in the Theban manner of rather prim drawing, is carved with a more assured and flexible hand. This is the classic Theban style, to which local artists had recourse for inspiration after breaks in the continuity of their traditions, as for instance during the sixteenth century BC (see Chapter Eleven).

cf. 105

110 The tomb of Mentuhotep II, in the amphitheatre of the Theban cliffs at Deir el-Bahri on the western bank of the Nile, underwent four changes of plan, and occupied architects, sculptors and painters for some twenty-five years of the king's reign; it must have given ample opportunities for the training of a whole generation of artists.

It was an unusual structure, combining the portico rock tombs of the Upper Egyptian princes with the pyramid complexes of the Old Kingdom pharaohs, though its orientation was different. Its main features were a burial chamber below a sanctuary hewn into the mountainside, and a stepped mastaba rising in three stages within the forecourt. Between them lay a colonnaded court leading to a hypostyle hall with an altar. The lower stage of the mastaba was surrounded on three sides by a double colonnade of square pillars. A ramp led along the main axis of the court to the second stage which was surrounded on three sides by a triple colonnade, and on the western side by a double colonnade, all of octagonal columns. The temple lay within a large shield-shaped forecourt planted with a grove of tamarisks and sycamore-figs, from which a causeway led to a valley temple at the edge of the cultivation.

The decoration of this great monument saw the transition from the provincial mannerisms of the earliest phase to the full classic style of

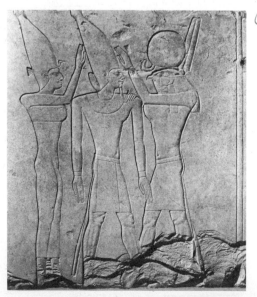

72 Limestone relief of King Mentuhotep II and deities, from Tod, *c.* 2010 BC.

73 Limestone relief of King Mentuhotep III being crowned by the goddesses of Upper and Lower Egypt (one missing), from Tod, *c.* 2000 BC.

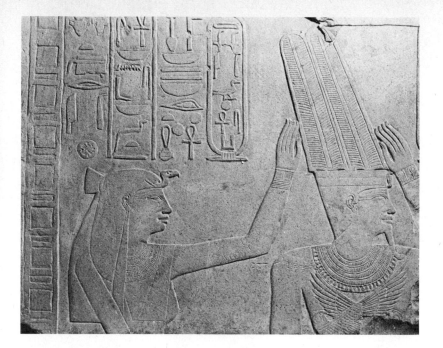

the Middle Kingdom; but the painted limestone reliefs exist only in cf. 71 widely dispersed fragments, mostly unpublished, and until their study has been completed the true character of the building will not be revealed. Already, however, it would appear that it served not only the cult of the dead king, but also those of Osiris, to whom the dead king was assimilated, Hathor the goddess of this hilly area of western Thebes, Amun, the god of Karnak on the river opposite, and Mentu, the falcon-headed god of the entire Thebaid.

The contemporary statuary is sparse and fragmentary, and still shows the new archaic features which are visible to an exaggerated extent in the seated statue of Mentuhotep II belonging to the earlier 68 years of his reign. The tomb-models of Meket-rē, however, are among the best of their kind to have survived. In particular, two figures of offering-bearers, carved on a much larger scale, reveal an 74 assured but restrained handling of the material, and a certain delicacy in their colouring. The same tradition of fine craftsmanship in wood-carving is found in the later group of servant figures from Bershah, 76 where a greater elegance has been achieved with some small loss of vigour. It was the provision of such servant figures and groups in the burials of the earlier half of the Twelfth Dynasty that is probably responsible for a paucity of carved reliefs in many of the

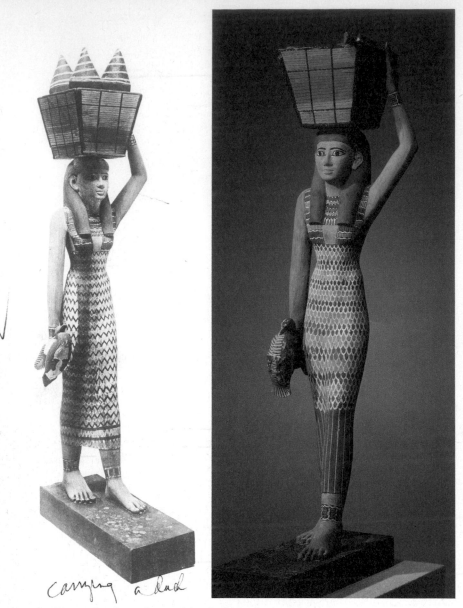

carrying a duck

74   Two painted wooden models of offering-bearers, from the tomb of Meket-rē at Deir el-Bahri, *c.* 2000 BC.

75   (*Right, above*) Limestone relief of offering-bearers from the pyramid temple of Sesostris I at Lisht, *c.* 1930 BC.

76   (*Right, below*) Painted wooden model of offering-bearers, from Bershah, *c.* 1900 BC.

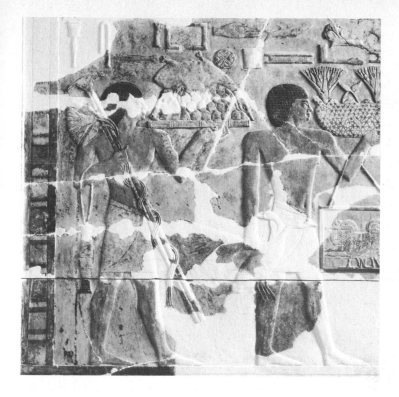

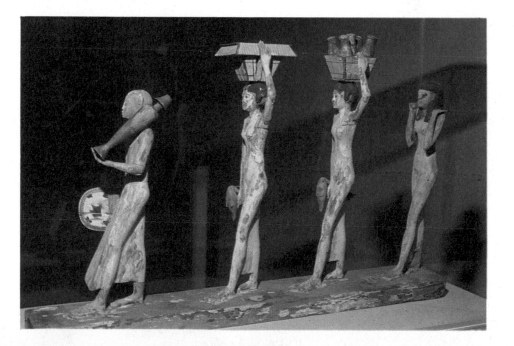

contemporary tomb chapels. especially the rarity of scenes of baking, brewing and butchery.

The new features of the Middle Kingdom style, however, are not fully revealed until the reigns of Ammenemes I, and more particularly his son Sesostris I, of the Twelfth Dynasty. Much sculpture in hard stone and limestone has survived from this period from various sites in Upper and Lower Egypt, and it shows a range of subjects, from sphinxes and standing or seated colossi to statuary of a more natural size. The contemporary literature is often concerned with a nostalgic recall of the glories of the Fourth Dynasty as a time of great achievement, just as the classic form of the pyramid was revived for the royal tomb in place of the rock-hewn hypogeum. Three kings of the Twelfth Dynasty built pyramids at Dahshur, the hallowed site of the great stone monuments of Snoferu. Sesostris I copied the plan and decoration of the mortuary temple of Phiops II for his pyramid complex at Lisht. The fragments of relief from the entrance hall of his pyramid, showing offering-bearers, are greatly influenced by similar scenes from the sanctuary of Phiops II at Saqqara. Like his father, who used pieces of Old Kingdom monuments in the construction of his tomb complex, also at Lisht, Sesostris I copied the style and proportions of Old Kingdom reliefs so successfully that it has sometimes proved difficult to date isolated fragments found at the sites of the Lisht pyramids.

75, 40

At Thebes, on the other hand, the local style which had developed during the construction of the monuments of Mentuhotep II and III in the later Eleventh Dynasty, was sufficiently well established to determine the character of the raised reliefs in the region during the ensuing dynasties. The little peripteral kiosk which was built at Karnak, in the precincts of the local god Amun, for the jubilee of Sesostris I, shows this style in a greatly developed form with rather deeper cutting. As usual in such buildings, sunk relief is employed on those parts which receive the full glare of the daylight, and raised relief for architraves and pillars that are in partial shade. This kiosk, modest in its dimensions, is of an austere perfection in its proportions and in the expert carving of its carefully arranged texts and scenes. It is one of the few non-funerary temples to have survived from the period. Another, at Medinet Madi in the Faiyum and dating to the end of the dynasty, is less impressive in its dilapidated state and is of even smaller size. It consists of a tiny hypostyle hall, with the ceiling upheld by two papyrus columns, leading to a vestibule from which opens three sanctuaries in the rear wall. The ruins of a gateway to a temple at Hermopolis, rebuilt by Ammenemes II, is of greater importance, since the ground-plan reveals that it was flanked by the

77, 78

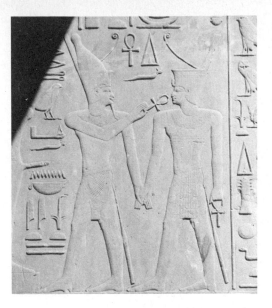

77   Relief on the limestone jubilee kiosk of Sesostris I at Karnak, c. 1940 BC, showing the primordial god Atum introducing the king to Amun.

78   Rebuilt limestone jubilee kiosk of Sesostris I at Karnak, c. 1940 BC.

east and west towers of a pylon, a new architectural feature to appear on the Egyptian scene that is best discussed later.

The decoration of such a temple can only be conjectural, but it is doubtful whether it included such scenes as appear for instance in the 'Room of the Seasons' in the sun-temples of the Old Kingdom. To judge from the Karnak kiosk and from a pillar from a similar

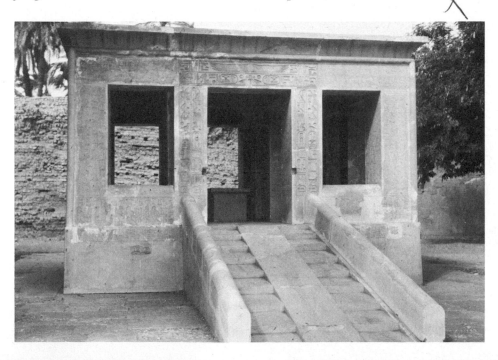

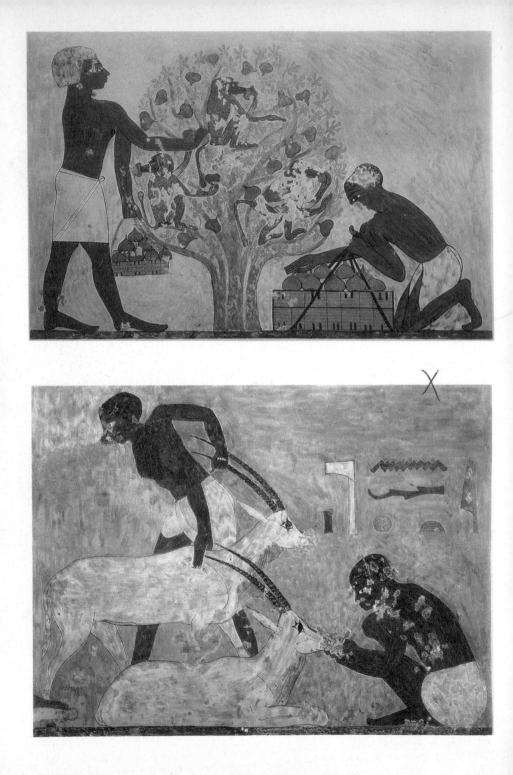

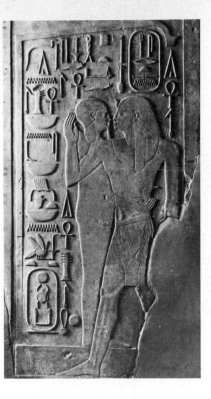

MIDDLE K.
Pepi II
Mentuhotep II
Sesostris
Kiosk-karnak

79   Copy of a wall-painting in the tomb of Khnum-hotep at Beni Hasan, with men gathering figs, *c.* 1890 BC.

80   Copy of a wall-painting in the tomb of Khnum-hotep at Beni Hasan, with men feeding oryxes, *c.* 1890 BC.

81   Relief on a limestone pillar of King Sesostris I embraced by Ptah, from Karnak, *c.* 1940 BC.

structure excavated at Karnak, the reliefs are concerned chiefly with the reception of the king by the gods of the temple, who lead him into the shrine where he presents offerings to them, and they in turn hold the symbol of life to his nostrils or embrace him as their son.

81

77, 81

Reliefs of a less formal character, illustrating most of the subjects that are found in the mastabas of the Old Kingdom, appear in some of the rock-cut chapels at Meir, Thebes and elsewhere. They are generally in poor condition and lack the technical excellence of the best of the earlier examples, making use of the rapid method of cutting bastard raised relief in stone that is inferior to the incomparable Tura limestone. Instead of the suites of rooms found in the mastabas, the rock tombs are generally restricted to a portico leading to a single, large, but usually well-cut chamber hewn into the hillside of the necropolis. Nevertheless, the reliefs of such chapels frequently show new departures, not only in the development of unusual features that appear in the provincial tombs of the Sixth Dynasty, but also in the reinterpretations of standard scenes of the Old Kingdom. Thus at Meir, the tomb of Senbi has a damaged but

121

82 dynamic Upper Egyptian version of the hunt in the desert, with the owner in huntsman's garb standing in a realistic tensed pose to fire his arrows at game within a netted reserve. The various animals, however, are not represented in a single file on a flat baseline, or in static poses on a rocky ground, but in brisk movement over the whole field, which is indicated by undulating lines defining pebbly hillocks. Some of the predators and their quarry confront one another, such as a dog who pulls down an ibex, or a lion who seizes a bull by the muzzle, a feature which appears in the late Fifth Dynasty tomb of 48 Ptah-hotep, but with less realism. The Senbi relief, however, is the work of a lone master in the early years of the Twelfth Dynasty. The next generation of artists at Meir shows no such inspiration.

Tomb decoration in relief is, however, rare in the Middle Kingdom and tends to be replaced by painting as at Meir and Bershah. At the latter site, a school of painters flourished whose work is seen in the wooden sarcophagi, painted in delicate enamel-like colours with figures, objects and hieroglyphs minutely detailed. Similar taste and skill are shown in contemporary wall painting at Meir, some twenty miles upstream, where artists practised who had a particular ability to represent animal life, birds in gay plumage, fish with gorgeous iridescent scales, the hippopotamus wallowing in mud and the tangled plants of the marshes.

The most celebrated of tomb paintings, however, are found at Beni Hasan, the burial place of a powerful family who ruled in Middle Egypt during the Eleventh and much of the Twelfth Dynasty. They cut their tomb-chapels into a terrace of the cliffs flanking the east bank of the Nile and commanding a magnificent view of the river in both directions. Some of these chambers are very spacious with arched roofs supported on slender lotus-bud columns hewn out of the living rock. The painted decoration, however, has been largely obscured by a limy exudation from the surface of the plastered walls, though the tomb of Khnumhotep II has recently been partly cleaned with startling results, largely restoring the original brilliance of the colours. For the most part, the paintings in these tombs are inferior in quality, the proportions of the figures being erratic and the drawing poor. The various subjects are crowded on the walls without much regard for layout and coherence. The hunt in the desert, for instance, is usually skied in the uppermost register, and consists of a tame procession of walking animals with one or two fantastic creatures not seen cf. 5 previously except on the carved predynastic palettes.

The paintings do, however, give vivid pictures of everyday life in all its bustle, Middle Kingdom versions of most of the scenes that decorate Old Kingdom mastabas, with some new introductions of

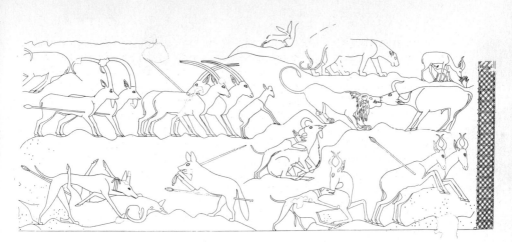

82 Detail from a drawing of a relief of Senbi hunting in the desert, from his tomb at Meir, *c.* 1900 BC.

dress, pose and accoutrements. Scenes of wrestling, battle and siege warfare appear commonly, whereas they are very rare in the Old Kingdom. The pilgrimage by boat to and from the holy cities of Osiris at Busiris and Abydos replaces the journey to the West or to Buto. Children's games, some with hand-balls, are more complicated. Dancing is also more elaborate, sometimes resembling ballet or mime, as in the religious Dance of the Four Winds. The oryx, one of the wild animals captured in the desert hunts and fattened up in captivity, is shown being restrained only by force. Apes may appear in the fig harvest helping themselves to the ripe fruit. A scene of Semites in their multicoloured garb coming to trade their minerals with the Egyptians is no longer seen to be a forerunner of the story of Joseph and his brethren, but gives a glimpse of the owner's responsibilities for policing the frontiers in the Eastern Desert. The local grandee may be shown *preceded* by his wife, who is often represented on the same scale as himself, and he takes more of an active part in certain exploits, such as the wild beast hunt and the netting of birds. The old royal sports of fishing with the spear, fowling in the marshes and hunting the hippopotamus, are now arrogated by every princeling without the royal sanction.

The tombs of Khnumhotep and Amenemhēt (nos. 2 and 3), dating from the middle reigns of the Twelfth Dynasty, are superior to the rest in their dignified 'proto-Doric' porticoes, their accurately cut and nicely proportioned halls, with two rows of sixteen-sided columns upholding a slightly barrel-vaulted roof with two side-aisles, and in the finer quality of their painted decoration. This is best studied in extracts, those of the later tomb (no. 3) being the most celebrated for their assured drawing and strict proportions.

79, 80

All such work, whether at Meir, Bershah, Beni Hasan, Aswan or elsewhere, however, is provincial and fails to give a true indication of the court art with its Memphite traditions, but of this latter style very little has survived. The kings of the Eleventh Dynasty were of Theban origin, and though the last of them and their successors found it convenient to move their capital to a fortress city, It-tawi, at the junction of Upper and Lower Egypt near modern Lisht, the cultural pre-eminence of Memphis and near-by Heliopolis remained unchallenged.

The progress of art during the Middle Kingdom can be most satisfactorily studied in its statuary, of which a fair amount has survived. The earlier kings of the Twelfth Dynasty had evidently enlisted the aid of publicists to justify their seizure of the crown from the last of the Mentuhoteps, and to promote their claims *vis-à-vis* their feudal rivals. In the contemporary literature they are represented as powerful terrestrial rulers, as well as beneficent gods. The Good Shepherd rules his flock with a firm but just hand. He will tolerate no insurrection, and trusts no one. It would appear that the skill of sculptors was also enlisted to serve such propaganda, so that in the local shrine the statue of the pharaoh, as intermediary between man and the god, would express a latent force and brooding power designed to overawe all who beheld it. The huge granite statues of Ammenemes I and Sesostris I, found on Delta sites and now in the Cairo Museum (nos. J. 37470, C. 384), impress not only by their size but by their grim appearance, and simplified planes and prominent masses expressing the concept' of the king as ruthless overlord. This tendency, springing from the traditions already apparent in the earlier statuary of Mentuhotep II, gives an intimidating character to most Middle Kingdom portraiture.

89

68

Such statuary may be defined as 'official', and the new uses to which it could be put are seen in the statue which Sesostris III set up on his southern frontier at Semna in the Second Cataract to overawe his Nubian subjects, and in the 40-foot (12-metre) seated colossi that Ammenemes III erected on pedestals at Biyahmu in the Faiyum. Most of this official sculpture was designed for the temples raised to local gods all over Egypt, and in the building of which the Middle Kingdom pharaohs appear to have been more active than their predecessors.

Of such statuary, the granite colossi of Sesostris I from Karnak, now in the Cairo Museum (nos. J. 38286–7), express in their size and

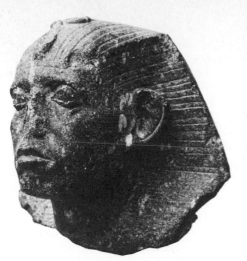 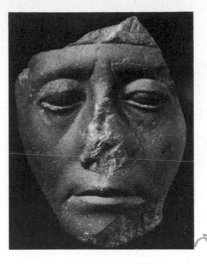

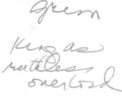

83　Grey granite head of King Sesostris III, from Medamud, *c.* 1850 BC.

84　Brown quartzite head from a statue of King Sesostris III, *c.* 1850 BC.

85　Red granite sphinx of King Ammenemes II, from Tanis, *c.* 1900 BC.

green

King as ruthless overlord

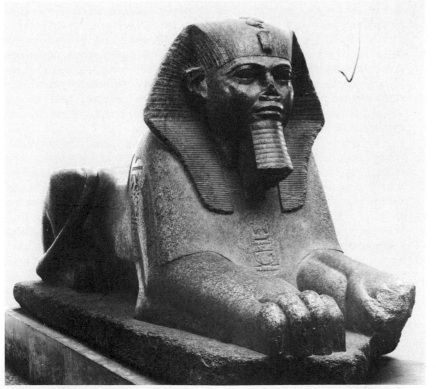

muscular tension the alert power of the pharaoh, ready to spring into action against all rivals. The massive sphinx of Ammenemes II, one of the great masterpieces of its kind, shows a similar majestic but watchful gaze in the human head, and a latent power in the recumbent lion body. It is, however, with the statuary of Sesostris III that the portrait of the pharaoh achieves an introspective grandeur, expressed by the realism in the carving of the face, with its heavy-lidded eyes, severe mouth, firm chin and the lines and folds of flesh between the brows and at the corners of nose and mouth. Sesostris III extended the royal authority in Egypt and Nubia, breaking the power of the feudal governors and reducing them to the status of local mayors. The diorite sphinx of Sesostris III and the fragment of a head, both in New York, as well as a number of fragments from Medamud in the Cairo Museum (nos. C.486, J.32639), are the most haunting of the many impressive portraits of this world-weary autocrat, and among the supreme masterpieces of Middle Kingdom art.

During the long reign of his successor, Ammenemes III, the last great king of the period, a slight but appreciable modification in such realism is apparent. There is a tendency for the treatment to become formalized, the torso to be modelled only summarily, the pectoral muscles to be joined together in a merely decorative gadroon, and the navel to be placed at the base of a deep ventral furrow. The sternal notch disappears, and the corners of the *nemes* headdress rise into prominent peaks.

This stylization reflects the changes that were taking place in the social structure and political system. The pharaoh had secured once more a lonely eminence and the machinery of government was again under his sole control. The estates of the former provincial governors must have been parcelled out among the temples of chief gods, as well as the palace administrators. Their expert staffs, including artists, had doubtless to find employment elsewhere.

Though the Middle Kingdom temple of Amun at Thebes is too ruined for much evidence to have survived, it was clearly wealthy and received generous patronage from the rulers of the Twelfth Dynasty, particularly the last two kings. Doubtless the workshops of Amun would have accepted the duty of carving statues of the king, as was the practice later. It was such studios that were called into requisition whenever a great quantity of sculpture was suddenly required, as when a new building was planned, especially at the beginning of a reign or for a jubilee. Such a supplementation of the royal ateliers, especially in the late Middle Kingdom, probably accounts for the varied styles of statuary that have led some observers to speak of different regional schools of sculpture.

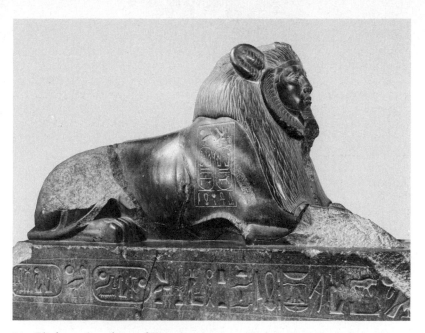

86   Black granite sphinx of King Ammenemes III, from Tanis, *c.* 1800 BC.

The long reign of Ammenemes III must also have seen two or more generations of artists working for the king, and they would have introduced changes in portraiture and iconography. The sphinxes of Ammenemes III from Tanis are virtually recumbent lions with the *86* bearded masks of the king. The bodies lack the muscular tension of the Louvre sphinx, and in such details as the hair, ribs, paws and *85* haunches, they show a stylization on the way to becoming a formula. The powerful modelling of the savage faces, however, is admirably in harmony with the carving of the lion bodies, and produces a rare integration of the human and animal aspects. It was the style of the sculptures of Ammenemes III, given great authority during the half century of his reign, that set the pattern for royal statuary for much of *cf. 101* the remaining Middle Kingdom.

During the Twelfth Dynasty, however, there was another tradition of sculpture existing side by side with the 'official' style. This was the mortuary sculpture designed for the funerary monuments of the pharaohs, which reveals a calmer, more idealized portraiture and a rather more subtle modelling of the body. As such statuary is in the softer limestones, it may be claimed that it represents the traditional style of the Memphite studios. In the idealistic manner of Old Kingdom art the dead king is represented as an immortal. The influence of Fourth Dynasty models is clear. The pose of the hands reverts under Sesostris II to that of the Khephren statues, the clenched right hand being held upright, and not flat, on the thigh. A fragmentary dyad of Sesostris I and the goddess Hathor seated recalls the Mykerinus triad of the king, Hathor and the Hare Nome in Boston. Sometimes in this idealized aspect the king is shown swathed in the shroud of the resurrected god Osiris, whose cult had now risen to great importance in the state, and with whom the dead king was identified – as in Osiride statues from the Cairo Museum (nos. C.401, J.38230, 48851).

36, 87

Apart from fragmentary sculptures, the mortuary style is well represented in the ten unfinished seated statues of Sesostris I from his pyramid complex at Lisht, in which the characteristic portrait of the king with his bilobed chin has lost its moroseness, and achieved a bland expression with the loss of the horizontal eyebrows carved in relief. Individual statues in this group of ten are undoubted masterpieces, though *en masse* they tend to dull the appreciation of the modern spectator.

88

The sole mortuary statue of Ammenemes III to have survived largely intact, shows a similar idealization of the formidable features of this monarch, the eyes achieving a flatter effect than was the

92

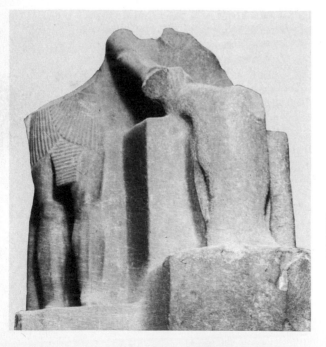

87　Fragment of a black basalt dyad of Hathor and King Sesostris I, from Karnak, *c.* 1930 BC.

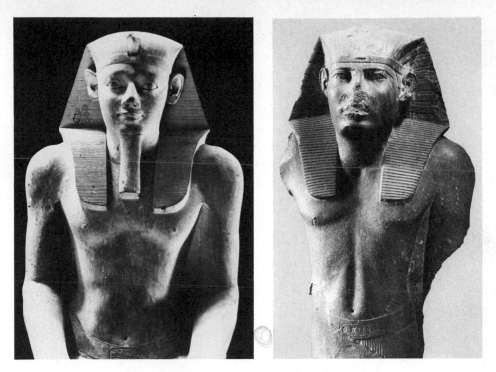

88   Limestone statue of King Sesostris I, from his pyramid temple at Lisht, *c.* 1930 BC.

89   Grey granite statue of King Sesostris I, from Memphis, *c.* 1930 BC.

convention in his father's reign, and the lips, though unsmiling, having lost the severe cast of the mouth of Sesostris III. Complete monumentality is attained by resting the palms of both hands flat upon the upper thighs, a pose that had been *de rigueur* for the seated statues of women since the early Old Kingdom, but which was now adopted for men, becoming obligatory for seated pharaohs in this costume.

The idealistic style is also seen in a number of quartzite and granite heads which may be attributed to Ammenemes III, where an incipient smile plays about the relaxed mouth, similar to the expression on the features of the statue of this king in the Hermitage Museum (no. 729). This smile, indeed, becomes unequivocal in the schist head of a king in Vienna, which the writer identifies as of Ammenemes III.   *90*

Pair-statues of men and women in the poses of the Old Kingdom are extremely rare during the Middle Kingdom, since the burials of private persons were generally much more modest, and the serdab for

129

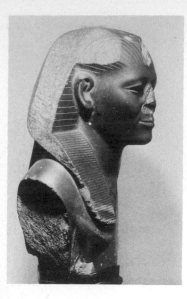

90 Green schist head of King
Ammenemes III(?), c. 1800 B.C.

91 Black granite statue of Sennu, from
Kerma, c. 1920 B.C.

92 Yellow limestone statue of King
Ammenemes III, from Hawara, c. 1800 B.C.

93 Chlorite(?) head of a female sphinx,
c. 1890 B.C.

94 Grey granite group of Ukh-hotep
with his wives and daughter, from Meir,
c. 1870 B.C.

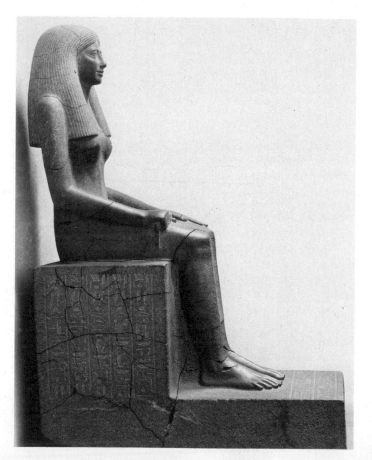

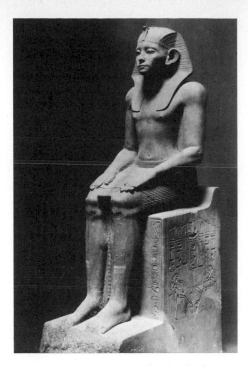

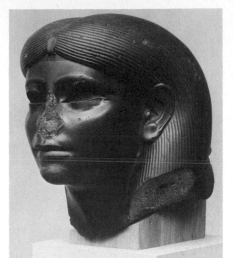

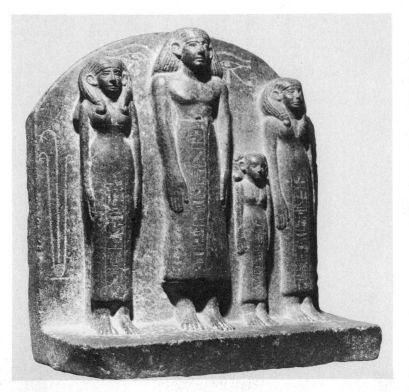

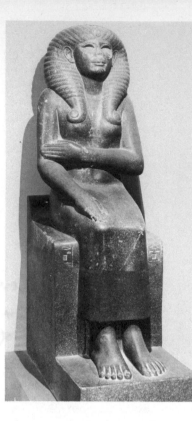

95 Black granite statue of Queen Nofret, from Tanis, c. 1890 BC.

the housing of tomb-statues had disappeared. Only the great feudal lords made provision for statue niches in their tomb-chapels, and of the larger examples hewn *in situ*, as in tomb no. 2 at Beni Hasan, little has survived, the plaster coating of the core having disappeared.

94 The group statue of the district governor Ukh-hotep, from his tomb chapel at Meir, shows him standing with two of his wives and a daughter against a stela-shaped back-slab, all in passive formal poses and enveloped in long garments that emphasize the monumental character of the piece. Despite its small size this is a tomb-statue, and shows to what insignificance the feudal lords were being reduced in the reign of Sesostris III, when this group was carved.

91 On the other hand, individual statues of queens and women are commoner than in the Old Kingdom; and of these the life-sized granite statue of the Lady Sennu is outstanding for its quality and condition. As the wife of an influential provincial governor, she could be represented in a seated pose more usual for men, with her right hand grasping a folded cloth on her upper thigh. It has been carved by a

132

sculptor who has agreeably softened the official style of such hard-stone statuary. By dispensing with the back pillar he has achieved a more feminine grace in the figure of a woman, and a greater release from the stone matrix.

The same relaxation of the rigours of the official style is also to be discerned in the head of a female sphinx, recognized in Roman times *93* as a masterpiece and removed to adorn the art gallery attached to an imperial villa at Tivoli. The statues of queens as sphinxes are known only from the middle of the Twelfth Dynasty and are extremely rare. This example is worked from what must have been a block of green stone of impressive size and beauty. Its style and craftsmanship recall *85* those of the Louvre sphinx, revealing a feminine version of the same majestic and aloof repose.

The granite statues of Queen Nofret in Cairo are in the severe classic style of the middle reigns of the Twelfth Dynasty, when the *95* inspiration of the royal sculptures of the Fourth Dynasty seems more dominant. The large bouffant wigs of the goddess Hathor, worn by the royal ladies at this period, lend themselves to the same treatment as the simplified corporeal masses of these hard stone sculptures, and are elegantly contrasted with the precision of the details of jewellery and inscriptions brilliantly incised. In this example, the arm bent at the elbow in a pose recalling that of the queen in the Mykerinus dyad, *35* suggests that it was probably associated with a separate statue of her husband, Sesostris II, also in a seated pose.

Private sculpture, by contrast, is often of mediocre quality and medium size; and though the grey-speckled granite statue of Amenemhēt in the British Museum is by a superior sculptor, its excellence cannot be appreciated in this medium without favourable *96* lighting. The bared upper torso and pose of the hands indicate that it belongs to the earlier half of the dynasty. As the age wears on, the owner tends to be represented wrapped in cloaks or long kilts squatting or sitting in postures that reduced the body to summary volumes. *98, 99*

The type of statue *par excellence* in which the body is reduced to its most simplified form, so accentuating the features of the head, is the 'block statue', showing the owner sitting on the ground with his arms folded on his drawn-up knees, and wrapped in a cloak that leaves only the head and hands, and sometimes the feet exposed. Such statues first appear at the end of the Sixth Dynasty, in the wooden figurines sitting under the awnings of model funerary boats that enabled the deceased to make the pilgrimage to Abydos, or other holy cities, by magical proxy. It would seem that the block statue symbolized the dead man as a *hesy*, or sanctified being, perhaps as a result of the pilgrimage, and it is particularly associated with the many monuments found at

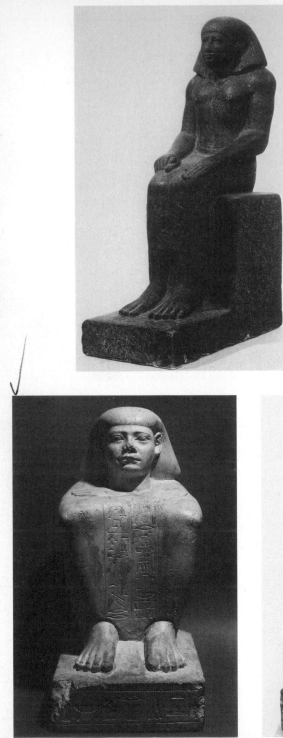

96   Grey granite statue of the court
official Amenemhēt, c. 1890 BC.

97   Painted limestone block-statue
of the treasurer Si–Hathor, from
Abydos, c. 1900 BC.

98   Black granite squatting statue
of the chancellor Gebu, from
Karnak, c. 1750 BC.

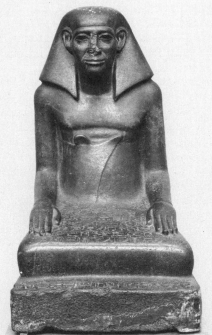

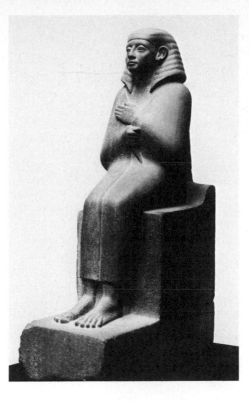

99 Brown quartzite statue of Kherti-hotep, from the Asyut region, *c.* 1780 BC.

Abydos, the great cult centre of Osiris during the Middle Kingdom. The earliest dated example from this site is the block statue of Si-Hathor in the British Museum, which belongs to the middle years of the Twelfth Dynasty. It comes from a niche in a stela that the owner erected at Abydos, which would ensure his spiritual presence at the annual mystery play of the death and resurrection of Osiris re-enacted in the temple. Similar *ex votos* have been found in other temple ruins. The simplified form of the body and the conventional portraiture of the heads, recalling the features of the contemporary monarch, allowed such statuettes to be mass-produced by journeymen for sale to visitors to the shrines of popular gods during the great annual festivals. Many of these devotees were of limited means, well content to acquire a piece of shop-work on which their names could be roughly inscribed in places left blank for the purpose, and deposited as votive offerings in the temple precincts. Occasionally the sculptor achieved a certain harmony between the stylized portraiture and the simplified masses of the body, but much of this statuary is on a very small scale and of deplorable mediocrity, even crudity.

97

No such criticism can be levelled against larger examples in quartzite, dating mostly to the earlier years of the Thirteenth Dynasty, when for a brief interlude private patrons seem to have been able to command sculptors of experience and ability. Among such masterpieces are the seated statues of Si-kahika in Cairo (no. J. 43928),

99 Rehemu-ankh in London (BM no. 1785) and Kherti-hotep in Berlin. All are distinguished by the reduction of the body to an integration of simplified volumes by means of the long kilt or enveloping cloak, thus throwing into prominence the passive pose and the careworn

98 portraits with their signs of age and their calm introspective gaze.

During the Thirteenth Dynasty, royal sculpture developed on different lines. The age was one of increasing troubles, exacerbated by a recrudescence of erratic Niles. Once more the king-lists reveal a multitude of rulers within a comparatively short space of time. There is another decline in the prestige of the pharaoh, to be witnessed in the wholesale usurpation of the trappings of royal burial for the interments of private citizens, including even the protective uraeus. The kings of this dynasty, with one or two exceptions, could not command the resources to build the pyramid tombs that had been

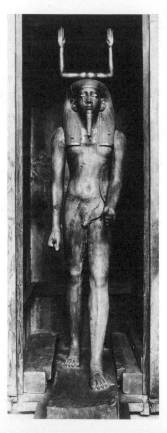

100   Wooden *ka*-statue of King Hor Awibrē standing within the shrine in which it was found, from Dahshur, *c.* 1760 BC, the glyph for *ka* borne on its head.

101   Wooden cult statues of an unknown king, from Lisht, *c.* 1780 BC.

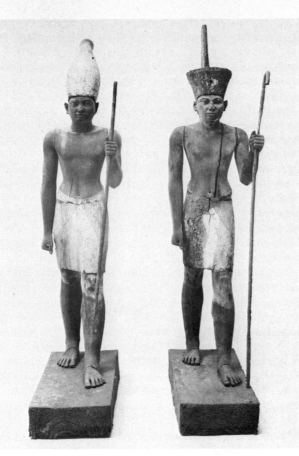

revived for royal sepulchres in the Twelfth Dynasty. They now often sought burial for themselves and their families in or near the pyramid precincts of their great ancestors of the preceding dynasty at Lisht and Dahshur. Thus a wooden *ka*-statue of Awibrē Hor, the fourteenth *100* king of the Thirteenth Dynasty, was found enclosed in a wooden shrine within the enclosure of the pyramid complex of Ammenemes III at Dahshur. Similarly uninscribed statues buried near the pyramid enclosure of Sesostris I at Lisht have been accredited until recently to *101* that king. They are, in fact, statues of gods with the features of the ruling pharaoh, like the cult statues found in the tomb of Tutankhamun, and on stylistic grounds appear to belong to the first *Frontispiece* two or three reigns of the Thirteenth Dynasty, when the portraiture of Ammenemes III was the ideal to which his immediate successors aspired.

This tradition was enfeebled as the dynasty advanced and the later royal statues tend to be mannerist, with their elongated proportions, heavy shoulders, narrow waists and wig-covers with wide wings or rising in exaggerated peaks at the upper corners. By the end of the period, the statuary had declined in size and quality to the vapidity of the standing Meryankhrē in London (BM no. 65429) or the Neferhotep in Bologna (no. 1799).

The royal statuary of the Middle Kingdom differs markedly from the work of the Old Kingdom, however much it may have been influenced by the classical archetypes. The majestic reserve of the Fourth and early Fifth Dynasty sculptures was replaced by a compelling minacity which is transmuted by the end of the Twelfth Dynasty, in its official aspects at least, to a watchful, though somewhat weary passivity.

In private statuary the deceased is no longer shown optimistically stepping into the daylight in all the eager pride of an ideal physique. The sculptured form seems to shrink into a bleaker introspection. The athletic, semi-nude body of the Old Kingdom is now concealed beneath long kilts, cloaks and heavy wigs. As the age proceeds, back pillars, infills and the postures adopted seem designed to accentuate the brooding immobility of the statue. At the same time inscriptions that had been confined to plinths now tend to be incised on the flesh and clothing, finally destroying any illusion of naturalism.

This change in style echoes a distinct social cleavage that arose between the two cultures. In the Old Kingdom, private statuary had been produced for the relatives and officials of the pharaoh, whose persistence near them after death was their hope of immortality. The traumatic collapse of the Old Kingdom, reflected in the pessimistic literature of the First Intermediate Period, turned men's minds to the promise of eternal life by the side of a resurrected god. The pilgrimage to Abydos, and the erection of a stela or votive statuette to Osiris there, became of more importance for many Egyptians than burial near their lord, especially after the disappearance of the great feudal magnates. Statues even of a modest kind could achieve this end by magic, and were, therefore, carved in the form of the contemplative suppliant, content to assist at the funeral festival of the god by proxy. It is significant that by the end of the period the prayer for funerary offerings is no longer recited for the benefit of the person of the deceased but for his spirit (ka).

cf. 100

138

CHAPTER TEN

The Second Intermediate Period; the Character of the New Kingdom

Dynasties XIV–XX

At the end of the Twelfth Dynasty, fluctuating climatic conditions seem to have returned to Egypt and were responsible for the wayward behaviour of the Nile. High floods, slow to fall and allow seed to be sown at the proper time, were as disastrous in their effects as feeble inundations. The patent inability of the divine king to control the Nile may have been the chief reason for another slump in the prestige of the kingship which is evident throughout the Thirteenth Dynasty, with a host of pharaohs each ruling in obscurity for a short time, and leaving few memorials behind him. During interludes when more stable conditions prevailed, some kings were able to erect monuments, including large statues and even a small pyramid tomb, but the general picture is of the protracted decline of the royal power. Unlike the similar crisis at the end of the Old Kingdom, however, the climatic changes were not so severe; and though the feudal nobility had been suppressed in the reign of Sesostris III, the bureaucracy established by the last two kings of the Twelfth Dynasty was able to carry on the government of the country under the direction of powerful viziers and chancellors who held office for long periods.

During the First Intermediate Period Asiatics, mostly Western Semites, had begun to infiltrate into the Delta, driven by famine and ethnic displacements in lands to their north and east. These newcomers sold themselves into slavery to exchange a penurious and uncertain existence for a modest livelihood, or offered themselves as cooks, brewers, seamstresses, vine dressers and the like, in return for food and shelter. Many of them earned their manumission and assumed positions of importance and trust. Others acquired Egyptian names and disappear from our view.

The Egyptians referred to the tribal leaders of these Asiatics as *Hikau Khasut*, or 'Princes of Foreign Uplands', a term which Manetho wrongly transcribed as *Hyk-sos*, and translated as 'Shepherd kings'. This name has since been applied, erroneously but tenaciously, to the whole race of immigrant peoples, rather than to their rulers. During the Eleventh Dynasty the Egyptians built a string of fortresses on their northeastern frontier to regulate the entry of these incomers into the Delta; but in times of trouble and decline this control

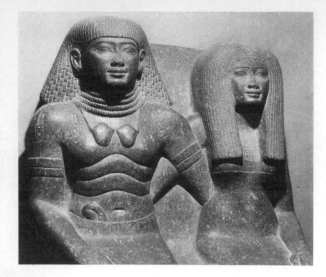

102 Upper part of a black granite seated statue of Sennufer and his wife, with their daughter standing between them, from Karnak, *c.* 1395 BC.

weakened, and the immigrations increased in volume and insolence. It is assumed that groups of Asiatics established themselves under their sheikhs in different localities in the Delta, until one of their number was sufficiently powerful and ambitious to unite them, seize Memphis and proclaim himself the ruler of Lower Egypt. Later, as the Thirteenth Dynasty at its centres in It-tawi and Thebes vanished in confusion, the Hyksos were recognized as a new family of pharaohs, and formed the Fifteenth and Sixteenth of Manetho's list of dynasties.

Although of Asiatic origin, the Hyksos kings accepted Egyptian manners and customs, writing their outlandish names in hieroglyphs, as well as adopting Egyptian personal names and embracing the worship of Egyptian gods, whom they equated with their own Asiatic divinities. They also patronized Egyptian learning, and showed their veneration for the monuments of their Middle Kingdom precursors by carving their names upon them. But apart from such usurpations, it is difficult to assess their original contributions to Egyptian art and architecture, as most of their monuments were probably destroyed in the campaigns that the Thebans mounted against them. The Hyksos, however, were always regarded as legitimate rulers by the Lower Egyptian compilers of king-lists.

It was a line of vassal princes in Thebes, forming Manetho's Seventeenth Dynasty, who in the sixteenth century BC felt themselves strong enough to challenge their Hyksos overlords, and eventually under the leadership of Amosis, to overthrow them and reunite Egypt and Nubia. Amosis, the first king of the Eighteenth Dynasty, ushered in the era of the New Kingdom, a period which saw Egypt rise to unparalleled prosperity and imperial expansion in Palestine and Syria, until checked by the Hittite Kingdom in the fourteenth century B C. Thereafter both states declined in power.

All this, however, was in the future. The reign of Amosis was the beginning of a brave new world. The Hyksos invasions had destroyed for ever the Egyptians' former belief in their uniqueness and superiority. The more intimate contacts that were now established with the high civilizations of western Asia and the Aegean world brought home to them that their pharaoh, traditionally the incarnation of the god who had created their universe, and ruled its extent as far as the circuit of the sun, in practice shared his sovereignty with brother monarchs in other lands. The triumph of Amosis on the field of battle introduced a new concept of the pharaoh as national hero, a personification of Egypt itself, and the leader of a military machine and a social system created by the introduction of the horse-drawn chariot and new weaponry from Asia in the closing phases of the struggle between the Thebans and the Hyksos. The pharaoh was now regarded as the incarnation of some warrior-god, Baal or Seth or Mentu, at the head of a caste of professional military leaders, accomplished in athletic sports and the management of horses, besides all the skills of a new mobile warfare.

The second legacy of the Hyksos rulers was the pharaoh's inheritance of a kingdom which included northern Sinai and much of Palestine. While Amosis continued his war against the Hyksos by the destruction of their power in southern Palestine, he also adopted the suzerainty that they had previously enjoyed over that region. Long campaigns were to be fought by his successors to consolidate and extend this supremacy over Asiatic vassals. The Asiatic component in the civilization of the New Kingdom is considerable, extending even to an alteration in the racial type of the Egyptian ruling class. The men and women of the New Kingdom have lost the heavy physiques of their Old Kingdom counterparts and the morose solemnity of their Middle Kingdom forerunners. The countenances of the men are bland, often smiling. The women are slight and pretty with great gala wigs, *102, 124, 128,* tip-tilted noses and long almond eyes fringed with thick lashes. An *133* exotic element enters the art of the Eighteenth Dynasty, perhaps as a result of the introduction of nude goddess cults from Asia. The luxury of the age is seen in the rich jewels adorning both men and women. *141*

Asiatics played a great part in the chariot arm of pharaoh's forces; and the parts of the chariot retained their Canaanite names and their Asiatic style of decoration, influenced by motifs from the Aegean world. Asiatic princesses entered into the harems of the pharaohs as part of the diplomacy of the age, and at the end of the Eighteenth

Dynasty Queen Ankhesenamun could offer herself in marriage to a Hittite prince in order to make him pharaoh in the absence of a legitimate heir.

The New Kingdom idea of the pharaoh as a Homeric champion is expressed in representations of him on a heroic scale. Colossal statues of kings, and sometimes their queens, dominate the ancient sites. The wealth and grandeur of these monarchs and the taste of the age stimulated a great demand for luxurious possessions, including statuary, not only for themselves but also for their retainers, who were sufficiently influential to act as the patrons of artists, or to be favoured with tombs and gifts of statuary from kings, to whom they were frequently related. The ambitions of these kings and their courts instigated the building of great temples to the gods in the main cities and to their own funerary cults at Thebes. All had to be richly furnished with equipment of every kind. The mortuary temple of Hatshepsut at Deir el-Bahri was supplied with over 200 statues of different sizes and materials. More than 500 statues of the goddess Sekhmet were installed in the temple of Mut in Ashru at Thebes by Amenophis III, who was also responsible for similar lavish provision at Luxor, Medinet Habu and elsewhere.

A taste for the colossal and the opulent had existed in Egypt since the advent of the Old Kingdom, when mighty monuments had been raised at Giza and Saqqara. In a period of consolidation and prosperity during the Twelfth Dynasty, Ammenemes III had revived such ambitions with his extensive funerary temple, the so-called 'Labyrinth', at Hawara; but during the New Kingdom colossal building schemes were the aim of every ruler.

There were two prime reasons for this growth in the size and volume of works of art, apart from the increase in wealth and ambition that had resulted from greatly expanded frontiers and a wider interchange of goods and people over the Eastern Mediterranean. The reorganization of the government of Egypt as a military autocracy, with its bureaucracy reshaped to deal with the logistics of a military state, meant that a large disciplined standing army, with its intake of conscripts, could be employed at home as a labour force when field operations were not in season. Reinforced with criminals and prisoners captured in the imperial wars, it provided the means of exploiting new gold mines in the Eastern Desert and increasing the supplies of precious metals on which so much of the prosperity of the new Egyptian state depended. In the reign of Ramesses IV it was the army that formed the backbone of the expedition that quarried greywacke in the quarries of the Wadi Hammamat; and army personnel are seen working on the constructions of Akhenaten. The

Margin notes: 155; 102, 120, 136; 167; 110, 113, 115

use of the army could ensure that a well-organized and constant supply of building materials, and a labour corps for massive constructional schemes, could function without affecting the vital agricultural operations that went on for most of the year, and included hydraulic works during the season of inundation.

The second factor was the opening of quarries on the banks of the Nile at Gebel es-Silsileh, where fine-quality sandstone could be easily extracted and transported in great quantities and sizes with comparatively little effort. Access to this plentiful building material made it possible to span wider spaces and to raise enormous buildings in a relatively short time. Such huge constructions had to be furnished with painted reliefs and statues comparable in size and numbers. The erection of both seated and standing statues rising to a fair height necessitated the use of hard stones such as granites, quartzites, basalts and indurated limestone, and much of the work of the period is in such materials, even the private statuary. Sculpture of more than life-size, however, was generally appropriate only for kings and their chief wives, though in the reign of Amenophis III, the statues of Kha'emhet, carved in the living rock of his tomb (no. 57 at Thebes), are very large.

A feature of the new and extensive temples that were now built is the increased number of private statues allowed to stand in the precincts by the grace and favour of the king. Many of them were evidently made in the royal ateliers as gifts from the pharaoh to a *120, 137* favourite official. Such statues had a mortuary purpose, receiving part of the reversion of daily offerings within the temple, but they were not hidden away in remote shrines or chapels accessible only to a few privileged priests – they now stood in places where they could receive the petitions of suppliants, anxious for their intervention with the god. Funerary sculpture, however, was only supplemented, not superseded by such votives. Tomb-chapels continued to be furnished with statues of the deceased and his wife, frequently of life-size and carved in the living rock as at Thebes, Amarna and Gebel es-Silsileh. Sometimes, however, the funerary statue was of small size and made of hard stone. In the royal tombs at Thebes, only the two life-sized statues of the king in black varnished wood, and one or two cult statuettes, represented the old tradition of the funerary *ka*-statue. It was in the mortuary temple associated with the royal tomb that the great stone statues of the king were housed, both as the living ruler *104* and as the Osirified king of the dead.

It is, in fact, the great temples of the New Kingdom that reveal the full extent of the wealth and might of the reformed state, whether it be the additions that each pharaoh made to earlier shrines such as those of Amun, Khons and Osiris, or the complete temples he built on new sites as at Sulb, Amarna and Abu Simbel, or for his mortuary cult at Western Thebes. Though most of these edifices are now in a ruinous state, enough remains to give a fair picture of their former glory.

The Egyptian temple, 'the god's house', had its origins in the prehistoric reed or palm-leaf booth, similar to the maize-stalk shelter that the peasant even today erects in his fields to shield his beasts and himself from the cold winds of winter and the burning heat of summer. In the beginning, the god had arisen on the primeval mound above the waters of Chaos, and by magic the shrine was built round him, with a fence to keep off intruders, and a rag of cloth on a pole to show that the place was taboo. As the work of creation continued and light appeared on the face of the waters, the god of the Void lifted the sky from the new marshy earth, and kept it in position on its four pole-like supports. Thus the temple as the abode of the god grew to its final form, not as an architectural concept so much as myth made tangible in stone. This finite model of the universe at its beginning is visible in the primal Egyptian temple, and determines its decoration.

cf. 81, 100

The sanctuary, housing the image of the god, is built on the highest point of the ground, on a sort of hillock representing the primeval mound, and is a stone interpretation of the prehistoric reed hut, which is clearly discernible as a small house within a larger dwelling. Except when the doors of this shrine are opened at certain times of day, the god lives here in the elemental darkness prevailing before the First Time.

The adjacent hypostyle hall, separated by a vestibule from the shrine, is the abode of the subsidiary gods who continued the work of

103   Towers flanking the eastern gateway to the mortuary temple of King Ramesses III at Medinet Habu, Western Thebes, c. 1175 BC.

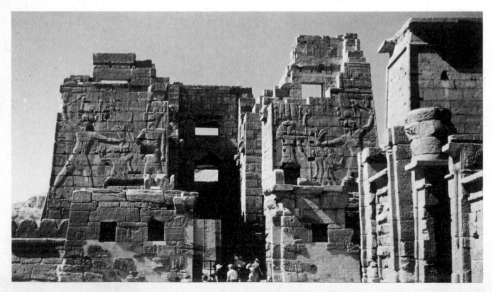

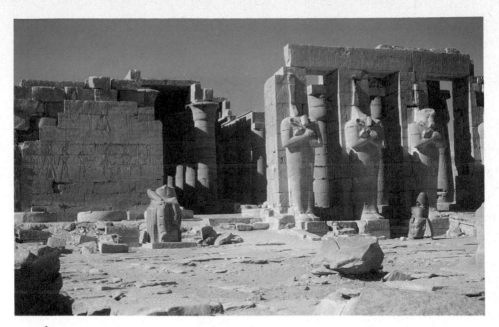

104   The Ramesseum – the mortuary temple of King Ramesses II at Western Thebes, *c.* 1250 BC – showing the Second Court with Osiride pillars and the hypostyle hall beyond.

creation. It symbolizes the primordial marsh, with its floor imitating water, and the supports of its roof rising usually in vegetable form as palm trees or bundles of papyrus or lotus stalks, with their capitals as feathery fronds or umbels or buds. Occasionally a plain sky-pole or pillar upholds the ceiling, which is decorated with flying vultures, or stars or constellations, to represent the day and night sky. The hypostyle hall is in half light, for the darkness on the face of the waters has been dispelled. This is the primal Egyptian temple, carefully orientated in its scheme of decoration, to which all designs conform, though elaborate examples may increase the number of vestibules and halls and enlarge the size of the flanking magazines that store the apparatus of the cult.

104, 132
23, 109

By the New Kingdom, most of the local divinities had become solarized under the influence of the theologians of Heliopolis, and had attached to themselves the name of Rē-Herakhty, the active aspect of the sun-god, so that forms like Amun-rē, Sobek-rē and Mentu-rē are now found. The sun-god, however, was worshipped at an altar set in a colonnaded court under the open sky where he was lord. This structure was, therefore, joined to the hypostyle hall, with the addition of a great entrance pylon, consisting of a portal between two

145

massive towers, representing the two mountains between which the
sun rose daily to shine upon the temple and bring it to life.

The Egyptian temple in its fully developed form in the New
Kingdom combines all these architectural elements within a great
estate circumscribed by a mud-brick temenos wall, often built on
alternate concave and convex beds to represent the waves of watery
Chaos from which it arose at the First Time. It is fully protected from
assault by the forces of evil. Guardian lions or sphinxes flank the
approach, and lion gargoyles tame any sudden downpour that might
threaten the roof. The figure of the pharaoh slaughtering the
northern and southern foes decorates the towers of the pylon, and his
defeat of the animal and human predators of the Egyptians and their
domestic beasts and crops are represented on the external walls. The
winged disc of the triumphant Horus protects every doorway. The
pole with its piece of cloth, signifying that the holy place is taboo, has
become one of four or more great flag-staves with long pennons at
their summits. The shrine may be hewn from a monolithic block of
hard stone and its floor could be of silver or gold. The colonnade may
have several rows of columns. The furnishing of such temples was on
the same lavish and opulent scale, and the endowments for their
upkeep matched the great wealth that the warrior-pharaohs now
commanded at home and abroad.

The resources that had formerly been devoted to the building of
the kings' pyramid complexes now went into their mortuary temples,
built along the desert margin of the western riverbank at Thebes, the
birthplace of their founder Amosis. These were separated from their
actual burial places, which from the reign of Tuthmosis I were hewn
into the rocky walls of a wadi, now known as the Valley of the Kings,
about a mile to the west, beneath the dominating peak of a natural
pyramid. The tombs themselves were decorated in painted relief, or
with wall and ceiling paintings, of scenes from the sacred books that,
under the influence of Heliopolis, now governed ideas on the royal
destiny. The tomb corridors and chambers became the passageway of
the sleeping night-sun through the caverns of the Underworld to his
resurrection at dawn in the burial chamber; and obscure texts and
weird pictures illustrate this magical progress.

Besides representation of kings, figures of the gods are commonly
found. The age also saw a growth in the idea of divinities grouped
into triads consisting of a god, his consort and their child. The concept
of a Holy Family with the child member in the guise of the king is not
given plastic expression until the reign of Tuthmosis III, but by
Ramesside times a king and his son can be incorporated in a family or
group of gods as at Abydos and Abu Simbel.

146

CHAPTER ELEVEN

The Early New Kingdom
Dynasty XVIII

- a Return to inspiration of the early Middle Kingdom -

The reunification of Egypt under a native pharaoh had been the work of aggressive Theban princes whose revolt against their Hyksos overlords developed into a patriotic war of 'liberation' only because it was successful. The nationalistic fervour that was awakened in the Upper Egyptians by this uprising also found expression in the local pride of the Theban craftsmen who in seeking to restore the highest standards to match the new patriotism naturally looked to their own past for guidance. The monuments of earlier Theban kings who had also established a unified state by warring in Lower Egypt were still standing as eloquent examples of the classic works produced by illustrious ancestors of the Theban line.

The scanty remains of buildings and their furniture, surviving from the first reigns of the Eighteenth Dynasty, reveal a faithful reversion to past traditions, rather than a conscious attempt to express new ideas. The reliefs of Amosis and Amenophis I at Karnak show a departure from the style of their immediate predecessors, who were still working in the traditions of the late Thirteenth Dynasty, and a return to the inspiration of the early Middle Kingdom. The great stela of Amosis from Abydos copies the style and proportions of work by Mentuhotep II at Tod. The reliefs of Amenophis I in the alabaster shrine of Karnak take their inspiration from the monuments of Mentuhotep III and Sesostris I, which at that time were still standing at various sites in the Thebaid. Only new fashions of dress, such as the Blue Crown worn by the pharaoh, and the 'lily' sceptre carried by the queen, distinguish the work of the later from that of the earlier period. *105* *72* *73, 77, 81* *cf. 122, 130, 105*

The limestone sphinx, now accredited on stylistic grounds and by its portraiture to Amenophis I, was previously dated to the Middle Kingdom. The front upper part of a statue of a queen in hard limestone is carved in the same restrained style that prevailed in the late Eleventh and early Twelfth Dynasties, with the subtle modelling of the face, the sharp edges to the lips and the faint folds of flesh at the corners of the mouth and wings of the nose. Only the incised details of the braids introduce a new fashion of representing the wig worn by women at this time. *106* *107* *new style*

In the later reign of Amenophis I, however, there is a relaxation of this austere style. A relief of the king in Edinburgh shows an early *108*

147

new fashion
Blue Crown - Pharaoh
lily sceptre - Queen
Early New Kingdom

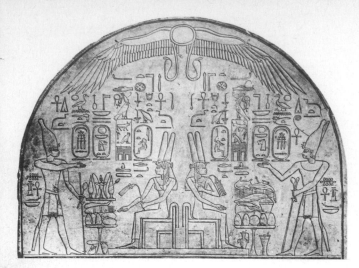

105 Upper part of a limestone stela of King Amosis invoking his mother Queen Teti-shery, from Abydos, *c.* 1540 BC.

example of that benign face that the New Kingdom pharaohs turn to their subjects for the first half of the period. The same expression is found on a statue head in Cairo (no. J.52364), and on the great sphinx from Badrashein (near Memphis), both dated to the reign of this same king or his successor, Tuthmosis I. In them, the stern, square-jawed appearance of the early Middle Kingdom heads with their horizontal eyebrows and flat-topped headcloth has been replaced by a rounded chin, fleshy cheeks, eyebrows lifted in elegant curves, headdress rising in a high arch and lips suffused with an incipient smile. These features are fully developed in the early statuary of Tuthmosis III and his co-regent Queen Hatshepsut.

[margin: 114, 116]

[margin: Theban / Memphite]

The Theban style derived from its early Middle Kingdom heritage, the influence of which can be seen in the return to the pose of the hands flat on the upper thighs in standing and seated figures, as in the reign of Ammenemes III; or the statues and sphinxes of queens wearing the same bouffant Hathorian headdress as Middle Kingdom models; or the recumbent guardian lion with the face of the pharaoh. Nevertheless, this tradition was modified by a more sophisticated urbanity which may be accredited to a reassertion of Memphite influence. The first two kings of the Eighteenth Dynasty, no less than their masterful queens, were staunch Thebans; but they must have found it impossible to govern their new empire from so remote a seat, and inevitably shifted their residence to the northern capital. A beginning is perhaps to be seen in the founding at Memphis of a vast palace complex by Tuthmosis I, which was still flourishing by the end of the dynasty. It was also in his reign that the first of the new

[margin: 92, 114 / 95 / 86, 115]

148

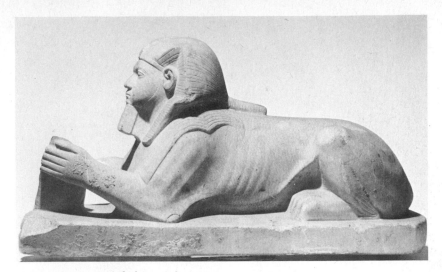

Hathorian headdress

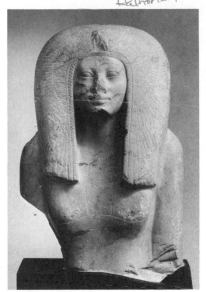

106   Alabaster human-handed
sphinx of King Amenophis I
making an offering of a libation jar,
from Karnak, *c.* 1500 BC.

107   Upper part of an indurated
limestone statue of a queen, from
Deir el-Bahri, *c.* 1520 BC.

108   Painted limestone relief of
King Amenophis I making an
offering of milk, *c.* 1520 BC.

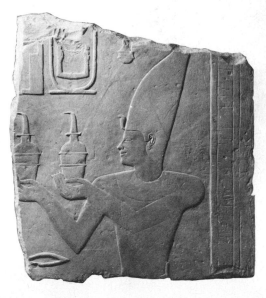

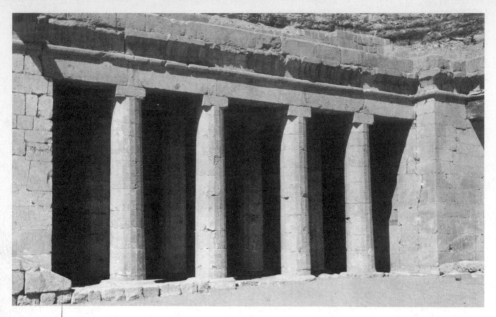

109 'Proto-Doric' colonnade of the Anubis Chapel, in the mortuary temple of Queen Hatshepsut at Deir el-Bahri, c. 1470 BC.

Heliopolitan sacred books was drafted on limestone slabs destined for the lining of his tomb at Thebes.

THEBEN

This northern influence becomes more marked in the reign of his daughter Hatshepsut, who claims to have repaired buildings in Middle Egypt left in ruins since the wars with the Hyksos; and presumably similar restorations were made to the monuments of Lower Egypt. During the course of such work a close acquaintance must have been made with the Old Kingdom style still visible in the Memphite region. A profound antiquarian study of the past clearly emerges in the reign of Amenophis III, but similar researches must have been made earlier. A heavily damaged kneeling statue of Amenophis II, found in his mortuary temple at Thebes and now at University College, London (no. U.C. 14665), reveals that the head of the king was protected by the hovering falcon of Horus in the same way as the seated Khephren. Amenophis II also decorated the Eighth Pylon at Karnak with scenes greatly influenced by reliefs in the mortuary temple of Phiops II. Graffiti disclose that the Step Pyramid of Djoser, besides other famous monuments, was being visited by learned scribes as early as the reign of Amenophis I, and this study increased in intensity during the reign of Hatshepsut. The influence of Old Kingdom models is seen not only in the copying of reliefs, but

32

also in the softer treatment of the torso and limbs of royal statues, the athletic ideal that they revive and the beneficent expression of their countenances that dispels the intimidating Middle Kingdom chill.

The first great enterprise to stimulate new artistic activity at Thebes was the building of Hatshepsut's great mortuary temple at Deir el-Bahri, in which she associates herself with her 'father', Amun of Thebes. The site was already dominated by the earlier monument of Mentuhotep II, which provided a challenge as well as an inspiration to her architect in planning a colonnaded structure on three levels built with the white Theban limestone. Whoever he was, he soon surpassed the example of his predecessor and produced a more ambitious and grander conception as the building progressed. Essentially, his structure is the New Kingdom temple arranged on three levels, consisting of a sanctuary within the mountainside, a hypostyle hall leading from it on an upper terrace, and two colonnaded courts, connected by ramps along the central axis, at a middle and lower level. There are also several subsidiary chapels, including one to Anubis, the god of embalming, and another to Hathor, the local goddess of this desert necropolis. An altar for the worship of Rē-Herakhty is sited in a court on the upper terrace. The line of approach was planted with trees and guarded by sphinxes facing each other in pairs. A T-shaped papyrus pool flanked each side of the bottom ramp.

The decoration of this edifice with painted reliefs on the walls behind the colonnades immortalized the great deeds of the queen, including the hewing of two huge obelisks in the granite quarries at

110 General view of the mortuary temple of Queen Hatshepsut at Deir el-Bahri, c. 1470 BC, with the earlier monument of Mentuhotep II on the left.

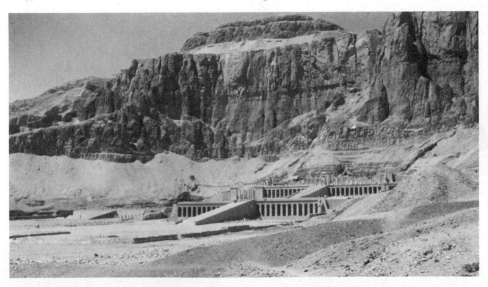

Aswan, and their transport to Thebes, and the expedition to procure myrrh and incense trees from the land of Punt. In addition, there were represented the traditional protective icons of the ruler snaring the birds of evil with the clap-net and as a sphinx treading down the foes of Egypt. There also appeared the first known version of the divine conception and birth of the queen, and her recognition by Amun of Thebes as his legitimate offspring. The drawing and carving of these reliefs are precise and unfaltering in the best early Theban manner, but they show the influence of the reliefs of Phiops II, the last great utterance of the now hallowed Old Kingdom, especially in the *111, 40* decoration of the hypostyle hall and its offering chambers. Unfortunately, the temple has suffered grievously from the hands of several groups of iconoclasts over the centuries, and it is only in the Hathor chapel that some idea of the pristine quality of these coloured *112* reliefs can be obtained.

The present plain appearance of the façades, particularly the uppermost colonnade, was originally mitigated by twenty-eight colossal standing statues of the queen in the mummiform guise of Osiris. As they were built up in courses with the walls and pillars in which they were engaged, they represent the earliest style of statuary on the site. The later free-standing statues of the queen, as a pharaoh and as a sphinx, lined the processional way from the entrance gateway to the sanctuary. Some of this statuary was on a colossal scale such as the six sphinxes in the middle terrace and the eight kneeling figures of *113* the queen in the hypostyle hall; but most of it was life-size, and some

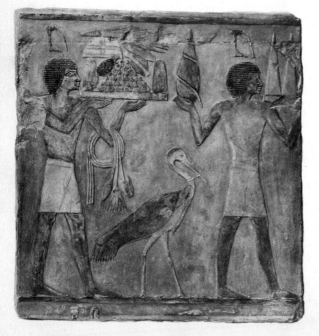

111   Painted limestone relief of offering-bearers, from the cult chapel of Queen Hatshepsut in her mortuary temple at Deir el-Bahri, *c.* 1470 BC.

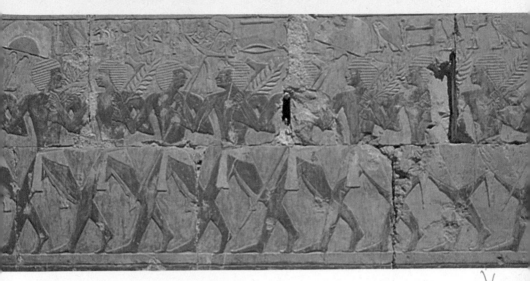

112 Painted limestone relief of soldiers rejoicing, from the Hathor chapel in the mortuary temple of Queen Hatshepsut at Deir el-Bahri, *c.* 1470 BC.

was half-size depending very much on where it was located, whether in the open or in various shrines and chapels.

The smaller pieces included a pair of guardian lions in painted limestone with the faces of the queen in place of the leonine mask, a *115* type which in design recalls the ferocious and menacing lions of Ammenemes III. They are, however, wholly feminine in their softer *86* musculature and smooth surfaces. There is a difference of treatment between the various groups of statuary from the temple site, which appears to have much to do with the different technique of carving statues in hard stones from that used for soft stones. The hard stones included a coarse-grained, crystalline, pink granite, chosen for the colossi, which required a more summary treatment of the underlying *113* masses.

Such limitations are less evident in the indurated limestone statue of Hatshepsut, which is believed to have come from the queen's own *114* funerary chapel in the uppermost terrace. This seated statue, slightly over life-size, represents the queen in the male costume of a pharaoh, yet its slender limbs and waist, its unmistakable breasts and delicate features, give an idealization of feminine elegance. Hatshepsut is represented as a male in the costume of a pharaoh throughout the decoration of the temple, yet there is often ambiguity in the gender of the epithets applied to her in the texts. Such an epicene fusion, evident particularly in the smaller seated statues of the queen, may have been

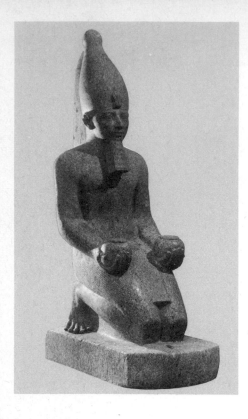

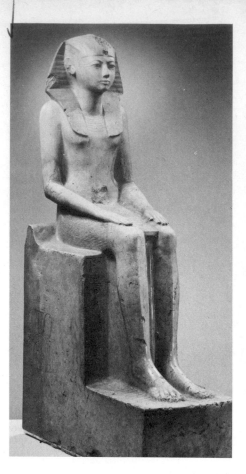

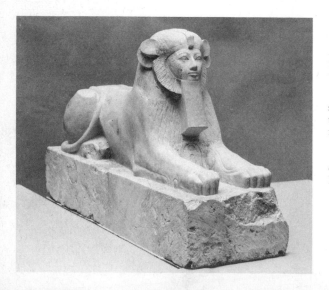

113   Kneeling granite colossus of Queen Hatshepsut wearing the White Crown and offering libation vessels, from Deir el-Bahri, c. 1460 BC.

114   Indurated limestone statue of Queen Hatshepsut in the costume of a pharaoh, from Deir el-Bahri, c. 1460 BC.

115   Painted limestone sphinx of Queen Hatshepsut, from Deir el-Bahri, c. 1470 BC.

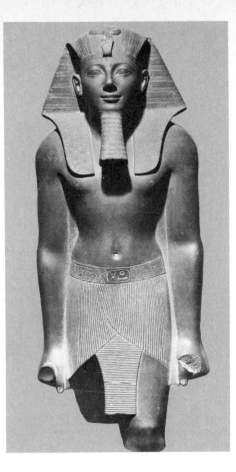

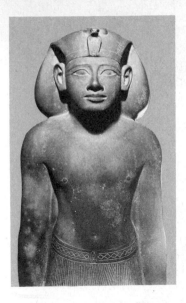

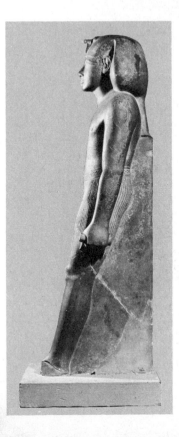

116 Schist statue of King Tuthmosis III wearing the *nemes* headdress and *shendyt* kilt, from Karnak, c. 1460 B.C.

117 Green schist statue of King Amenophis II wearing the *afnet* headdress and *shendyt* kilt, from Karnak, c. 1425 B.C.

118 Green schist statue of King Amenophis II, showing left-hand side, with left leg advanced, from Karnak, c. 1425 B.C.

responsible for giving a <u>feminine bias</u> in the idealistic royal sculpture of the reign.

Cairo no.
C. 42053

Such an influence can be detected in the life-sized schist statue of the co-regent Tuthmosis III. Judging from the soft juvenile forms and the arched eyebrows, this piece dates to his earliest years as king. The material and pose recall the classic statues of the earlier Old Kingdom, a period which is suggested by the design of the belt. The same combination of youthful, faintly smiling features, and a smooth lissom body persists as the ideal of the heroic king throughout the long reign of Tuthmosis III and is still in force in the reign of his successor. Slight modifications are introduced; the eyebrows are lowered to assume a more natural position, the physique becomes a little more robust, but no effect of advancing years is indicated in the many royal statues produced during these two long reigns.

116–118

The contemporary private sculpture also shows its point of departure in its devotion to Middle Kingdom models and in its preference for summary figures hidden beneath long cloaks in either the seated or squatting pose. Such sculpture aspires to the condition of the block-like matrix, probably because a monumental effect was the

120

119   Black granite statue of Senenmut holding the Princess Nofrurē, from Karnak(?), *c.* 1470 BC.

120   Black granite statue of Senenmut nursing the Princess Nofrurē within his cloak, from Karnak(?), *c.* 1470 BC.

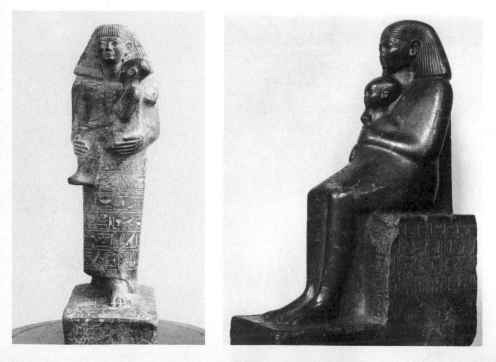

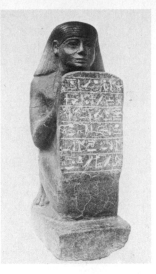

121   Black granite statue of
Pehsukher kneeling and raising his
hands in a hymn to the sun-god,
inscribed on the stela before him,
from Karnak(?), c. 1425 BC.

aim in designing statuary to be exhibited in strong sunlight in temple
courts. Thus the block statue, evolved in the Middle Kingdom, was
particularly favoured as providing a number of plane surfaces on
which prayers and dedications could be inscribed. Such texts become
longer and more complex as the age advances. But however bold and
uncompromising the underlying masses of such statuary may be, the
face is carved in the youthful idealistic pattern of the contemporary
ruler, and lacks the brooding introspection of its Middle Kingdom
counterpart.

To a great extent, the full range of masculine statuary during the
early Eighteenth Dynasty has to be sought in the many quasi-royal
statues produced for Senenmut, the favourite of Queen Hatshepsut,
who was the tutor of her daughter, Nofrurē, and the Master of Works
at Deir el-Bahri. A score of hard-stone statues of Senenmut have
survived. Some show him sitting or squatting in the manner of
Middle Kingdom archetypes, yet embracing within the folds of his
cloak the infant form of Nofrurē. This is a novel solution of the   120
problem of rendering an adult and a child together in Egyptian
statuary, and it was copied by two of his near contemporaries.
Another example, which shows Senenmut with the princess in his lap,
is also similar to Middle Kingdom statuettes of women or queens
nursing children. A standing statue of the same pair, however, is an
entirely new departure. It shows an adult standing figure holding the
child and is unique in Egyptian private sculpture. Other statues of   119
Senenmut reveal a similar originality. The majority show the owner
kneeling to present an object such as a shrine with an image of a god

157

within it, or a coiled-up surveyor's measuring-cord or the snake-goddess of Armant forming a rebus of the prenomen of Hatshepsut. Five sculptures of various sizes show him kneeling to offer a huge sistrum to the goddess Hathor or Mut, evidently the first of a type of statue that gained in popularity thereafter.

Another sort of private statue, which had appeared at a slightly earlier date under the increasing influence of the sun religion, shows the owner kneeling and lifting his hands to recite a hymn of praise to the sun-god at his rising and setting. The pose went through several developments before the final version, which has the owner peering over the top of a stela behind which he kneels and on which his prayer is inscribed. The block-like shape made such statues particularly suitable for placing in niches on the pyramidion above the private tomb, or even within the shrine of the tomb-chapel, or in temple loculi. The design is limited to private statuary until the reign of Akhenaten, when it was adapted for large standing figures of the king and queen, holding stelae before them. These statues, however, were not used in funerary contexts, but in the temples and at the Boundary Stelae of the City of the Aten at Amarna (see below).

The full repertoire of royal statuary in the middle of the Eighteenth Dynasty is pictured in the tombs at Thebes, notably those of Rekhmirē and Kenamun. The entire range cannot be represented in the actual statues that have survived from the reigns of the kings whom these two officials served, but most of it can be completed by slightly later examples. A number of innovations are to be remarked. Kneeling statuettes of the king presenting a large unguent jar are known from actual examples, perhaps of slightly earlier date (e.g. Cairo nos. C.42060–2). Notable are the statues of the king prostrating himself full length, the palms of his hands either flat on the ground or holding a shrine or emblem. Pair-statues also appear of the royal couple seated side by side, generally on the same scale, but a change of posture, not previously encountered before the Fourth Dynasty, is the crossing of their adjacent arms behind the other's back (e.g. Cairo no. C.42080). The same pose is adopted for private statues of men and their wives, designed for the inner shrines of their tombs or for temple sites. Some kings return to the pattern of earlier ages. The pose of Hatshepsut's hands flat on her thighs in the manner of women, even where she is represented as a pharaoh, has already been remarked. Tuthmosis III varies this pose with the earlier fashion of holding a folded cloth clenched in the right hand. The same king may be shown with one hand holding a crook-sceptre on one shoulder in the style of the Fifth Dynasty. Usually in such cases the sitter wears the Blue Crown as in a fragment in New York (MMA no. 44.4.68). Some of the

121

cf. 163

cf. 102

cf. 91

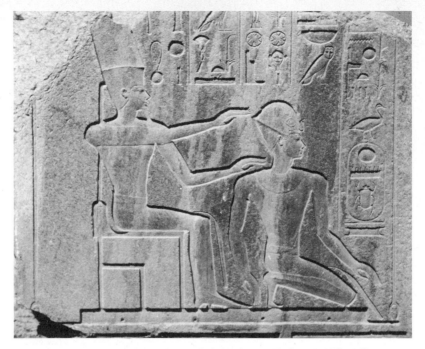

122   Red granite relief from a fallen obelisk of King Tuthmosis III kneeling
to be crowned by the god Amun, in the great temple of Amun at Karnak,
c. 1460 BC.

paintings in the tombs of Rekhmirē and Kenamun are of statues that
could hardly have been carved from monolithic blocks of stone, but
are clearly designed to be made of wood coated with black resin or
gold foil, of which complete examples have come to light among the
funerary statues deposited in the tomb of Tutankhamun.   *Frontispiece*
    The apogee of this first phase of art in the Eighteenth Dynasty was
reached in the later years of the reign of Tuthmosis III. Its features are
to be seen in the raised reliefs in sandstone and the sunk reliefs in
granite or quartzite on various buildings that the king erected at
Karnak. The pure but somewhat hard lines of the drawing are carved
with faultless precision in both the hard and soft stones. The scene of   *122*
the king kneeling to have his crown affixed by Amun is the same
design as was carved on the capstone of a granite obelisk of
Hatshepsut on the same site, but it has escaped the erasure of the figure
of the god by Akhenaten's iconoclasts.

159

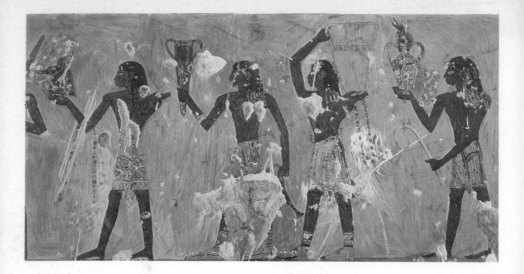

123   Copy of a wall-painting in the tomb of Menkheperrēsoub at Western Thebes (no. 86), showing Aegeans bringing gifts to the pharaoh, *c.* 1430 BC.

124   Copy of a wall-painting in the tomb of Menna at Western Thebes (no. 69), showing the owner and his family fishing and fowling in the marshes, *c.* 1380 BC.

125   Wall-painting in the tomb of Userhet at Western Thebes (no. 56), showing the owner hunting desert game from his chariot, *c.* 1395 BC.

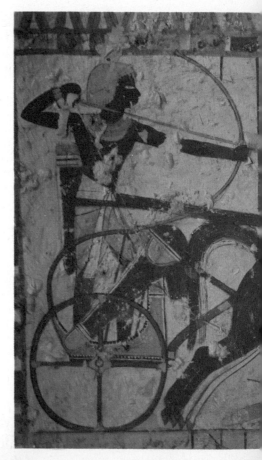

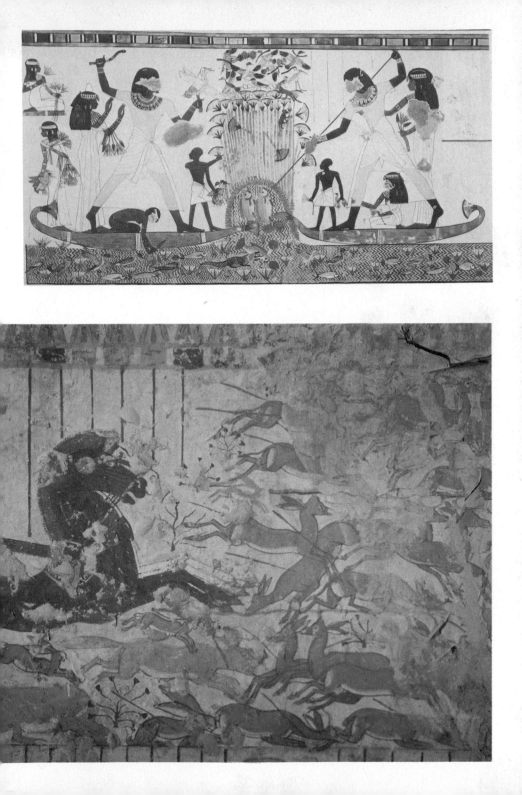

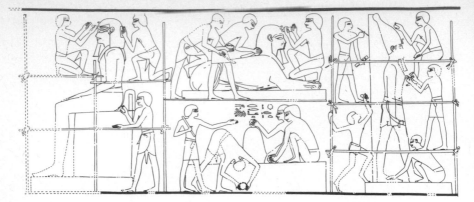

126 Drawing from a wall-painting in the tomb of Rekhmirē at Western Thebes (no. 100), showing sculptors at work carving statues, a sphinx and an altar, c. 1430 BC.

The same careful draughtsmanship is found in the tomb paintings of many of the high officials of Tuthmosis III. The somewhat stiff, faintly archaic, paintings in the Theban tombs of the earlier half of his reign are still in the traditions of the Middle Kingdom, not only in their style, but also in their choice of subject-matter, such as the hippopotamus hunt and the country crafts among the papyrus thickets. By the last years of the reign this old-fashioned, formal treatment had given way to a bravura in the painting that is still within the bounds of discipline, even when new subjects are being tackled, such as the presentation of gifts to the pharaoh by unfamiliar *123* Asiatic and Aegean legates. The false door can still be a focal point, though like every other subject from the traditional repertoire, it assumes new details and the royal sports of fishing and fowling in the *124* marshes are still popular though given an up-to-date look. The hunt *125 cf. 165* in the desert still appears. A novel variant is the chase from a chariot instead of on foot, in imitation of the new sporting pharaoh. The *129, 141* funerary repast, whereby communion was maintained between the dead and their living descendants, becomes ever more elaborate, and the theme of mourners at the tomb door, and the funerary rites, also assume an increasing importance. A new departure is the representation of gods, particularly Osiris to whom offering is made by the owner and his wife.

The masterpieces in this mature style are to be found in paintings in *126, 127, 129* the tomb of Rekhmirē, the last vizier of Tuthmosis III, in which a broad picture of the age, and of the deceased in his many roles, is apparently attempted. The various subjects represented, from the reception of foreign embassies, the operation of the law courts of the

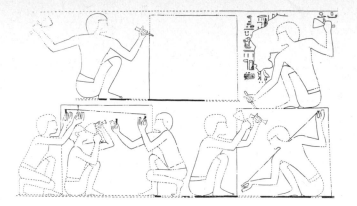

127 Drawing from a wall-painting in the tomb of Rekhmirē
at Western Thebes (no. 100), showing masons using boning
rods on a block of stone, *c.* 1430 BC.

vizier, the collection of taxes and the activities of the craftsmen of the
temple of Amun at Thebes, to the funerary banquet and the musical
accompaniment, appear to be original in their design; even the
traditional themes of the hunt in marsh and desert have novel features.
The scenes are drawn and coloured with devoted skill. Even the
hieroglyphs are masterpieces of miniature painting. The artists of the
Theban tombs were to have many subsequent triumphs, but no one
excelled the unknown artist of Rekhmirē in the fertility of his
invention. Even the few falterings in his style have a naïve charm, and   *129*
become almost virtues.

By the reign of Tuthmosis IV a change had been effected in the
culture of the Eighteenth Dynasty. The Asiatic wars of Tuthmosis III
and Amenophis II, and the reformed Nubian dependencies, brought
new ideas, wealth, peoples and commodities into Egypt. Contacts
with the Aegean and Asiatic worlds were doubtless responsible for the
more opulent use of such materials as glass and black bronze inlaid
with gold and silver, and for the proliferation of such decorative
motifs as the flying gallop, the running spiral and the palmette. An
age of luxury had arrived. Tomb paintings lost their prim formality,
and a more dashing, fluid line, and a more sumptuous use of colour
are evident. An erotic element enters into the life of the sophisticated   *141*
ruling class, clearly expressed in a new form, the love poem, and more
symbolically represented in art. The female nude is the most obvious
aspect of this sensuousness, and it reached a peak in the reign of
Akhenaten when one of the royal women is depicted in a Brooklyn
Museum relief (no. 60.197.9) as a lutenist in a papyrus skiff, a motive
which appears on the toilet spoons of the period. The wealth and

ostentation of the age is visible in the modes of dress. Women's garments become ampler, falling in folds; a cloak is added, and girded by a long sash. In addition to the matron's tripartite wig, a massive gala wig comes into fashion, and the military crop is also favoured for women in the Amarna Period. Men wear a shirt as well as a longer kilt, and a long gown is confined at the waist by a broad sash. Their coiffures tend to be long and to fall in lappets over the clavicles. More elaborate collars, fillets and jewels are worn by both sexes.

In the statuary of this later period, the sensuousness of the age is apparent in the softening of the underlying forms and a tendency towards a tactile quality in the treatment of the surfaces. The most remarkable of such pieces is the head of a large statue of Amenophis III in Brooklyn, one of a series of such heads in which the plump features of the young king have been stylized into a decorative pattern. Such

128 Wooden statuette of the high priestess Tuyu wearing a gala wig and clinging robe, c. 1390 BC.

129 Wall-painting in the tomb of Rekhmirē at Western Thebes (no. 100), showing maidservants waiting upon women guests, c. 1430 BC. Note the three-quarter rear view of the servant, upper right.

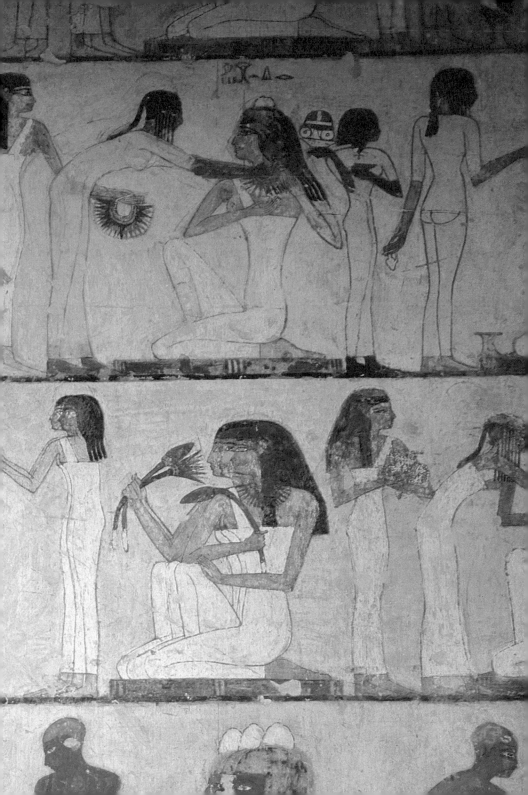

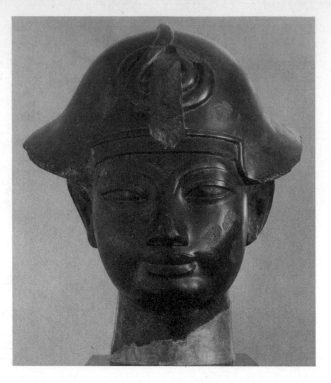

elements as the thick outlines of the long almond eyes, the prominent lips, arched eyebrows and well-defined nose persist in the colossal portraits of this king for most of his long reign. Only the nose changes, attaining a rounded tip with advancing years. Similarly, the treatment of the body shows the same tendency to abstraction, the pectoral muscles, for instance, being joined in a single fold, similar to the tradition prevailing in the late Twelfth and Thirteenth Dynasties. Private portraiture as usual tends to follow the conventions made fashionable by royalty.

cf. 98

In contrast to the monumentality of such pieces, the smaller works of art have a more naturalistic appeal. Prominent among them is the statuette of the Lady Tuyu, probably the mother of the future Queen Tiye, the earliest and the most classically restrained of a number of statuettes of court ladies which appear throughout the later Eighteenth and early Nineteenth Dynasties. All are carved in a hard nut-brown wood (probably boxwood imported from Asia). Later examples exhibit a more voluptuous form beneath their elaborately pleated gowns. Statuettes in such diverse materials as stone, wood and glazed steatite, with details such as eyes and brows inlaid in glass or

128

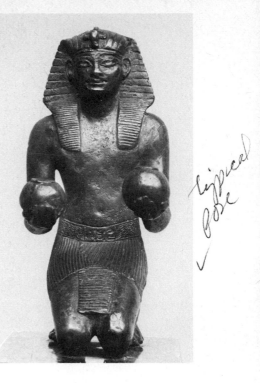

typical pose ✓ (handwritten note)

130 Basalt head of a statue of King Amenophis III wearing the Blue Crown, *c.* 1384 BC.

131 Kneeling bronze statuette inlaid with silver of King Tuthmosis IV offering libation vessels, *c.* 1385 BC.

faience, reveal the ferment of activity in the studios during this prosperous period. A kneeling statuette of Tuthmosis IV offering water-jars, of bronze inlaid with silver, is the first known example in a genre of metal-working which was to become particularly important in Bubastite times. It is appreciably larger than most earlier examples, and is hollow cast, though the core is retained within on chaplets, a notable landmark in the history of bronze casting.

131, 170

Of the great building schemes that Amenophis III promoted, little now remains in Egypt. His vast mortuary temple at Western Thebes has disappeared, apart from the two quartzite colossi (the so-called 'Colossi of Memnon') that once stood before its pylon. The temple he built to Mut, the patron goddess of the family of his chief queen Tiye, at Ashru in Thebes, is but a series of mounds. The huge Third Pylon he raised at Karnak is reduced to a few courses. Other temples at Thebes have vanished almost without trace. Only the temple he began in Luxor survives substantially intact, though it is badly dilapidated. This huge structure was unusual in having two sanctuaries, one as a way-station for the bark of Amun during its journeying from Karnak, the other for housing a colossal statue of

132

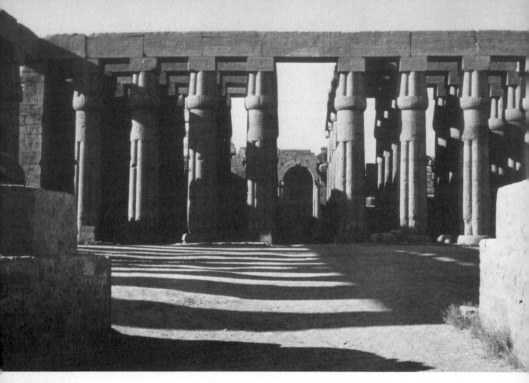

Amun of which nothing now remains. The temple, like his others at Thebes, was handsomely equipped with many statues, some of life-size, others of colossal proportions. Most were unfinished at his death and were completed and usurped by Ramesses II and Merenptah. The surviving examples show that this sculpture in black and in red granite was superbly worked, but in the official style of the reign, making its effect by its omnipresence rather than the impact of an inner vitality. The delicate raised reliefs carved in soft sandstone are sadly damaged but display the sensuous style of the reign, better seen in the reliefs of his high officials in their tombs at Thebes. The scene of the foreign princesses pouring libations at the king's third jubilee in the tomb of Kheruef and the scene of Kha'emhet being honoured before the king at his first jubilee, show the character of this relief sculpture with its elegantly proportioned figures drawn with fine classical precision and carved with a sensuous delight in their modelling.

133
134

There were, however, new forces gathering strength beneath the surface of Egyptian art which seem to emerge in the last decade of the reign of Amenophis III and coincide with his first jubilee. A certain

132　The temple of Amun at
Luxor, the hypostyle hall of
King Amenophis III with
clustered papyrus-bud columns,
c. 1360 BC.

133　Limestone relief in the
tomb of Kheruef at Western
Thebes (no. 192), showing
foreign princesses pouring
libations at the third jubilee of
King Amenophis III, *c.* 1347 BC

134　Limestone relief in the
tomb of Kha'emhet at Western
Thebes (no. 57), showing the
investiture of officials at the first
jubilee of King Amenophis III,
c. 1354 BC.

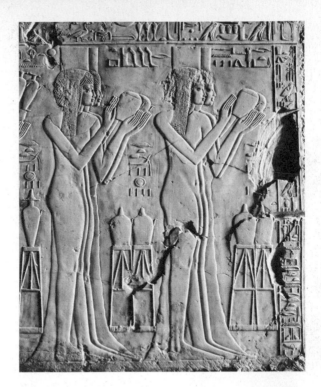

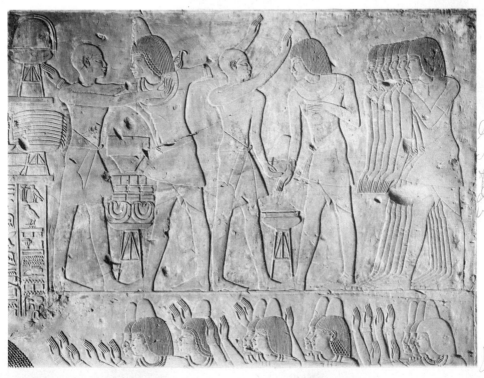

realism comes into the art of the period. Statues of the king frankly reveal him in all the obesity of his later years. The head of a statuette of

135 Queen Tiye found at Sinai may be dated to this same decade. In its lined features and pouting expression it shows a realistic interpretation of imperious royal dignity. A wooden head in Berlin, believed to represent Tiye, reveals the same plastic modelling of the eye within its socket, lines defining wrinkles and folds on the neck and face, an unsmiling mouth with carefully shaped lips and a sombre expression. How far such innovations are to be accredited to a new chief sculptor appointed about the time of the king's first jubilee cannot now be assessed. If, as some scholars claim, there was a long co-regency between Amenophis III and his son, Amenophis IV (Akhenaten), there may have been an interchange of ideas between the artists of the two courts, since Men and Bak, the chief sculptors of these kings, were also father and son. In either case, free expression was given to the tendencies of the time.

These manifestations of a new spirit that was abroad are seen also in the contemporary private statues, which often express an enhanced piety in the attitude of the sitter in the invisible presence of his god. The most notable are those in which the sitter is represented as a scribe with his papyrus roll on his lap and his head bent as though writing or

136 reading under the inspiration of his god. The Old Kingdom examples had shown the deceased in all the pride of his learning, alert and

cf. 58 confidently gazing ahead. In the New Kingdom versions the mood is quite different. The writer or reader humbly bows his head in the divine presence. This type of statue, evidently inspired by the Old Kingdom archetypes, first appears in the reign of Amenophis II, and occurs sporadically thereafter. It was particularly popular for a

136 number of votive statues of the great sage Amenhotep-son-of-Hapu and other high officials of the reign of Amenophis III. Usually the divinity is not represented, though it may be referred to in the inscription. But examples exist in which the deity takes the form of the baboon of Thoth, the god of writing and wisdom, perched on an

167 altar in the presence of the scribe, or even squatting upon his shoulders.

Such statues show the features of the owner in an idealistic cast, devout, tranquil, in communion with his god. But another statue of Amenhotep-son-of-Hapu is in the more realistic style, with its heavy-

137 lidded eyes and wrinkled features, and in its mood recalls the heads of

cf. 135 Queen Tiye. It gives expression, however, to another idea of the age, the antiquarian recall of the past, which is seen, for instance, in the research that was undertaken to enact the rites of the first jubilee of Amenophis III in their ancient and proper form. The statue in its pose

170

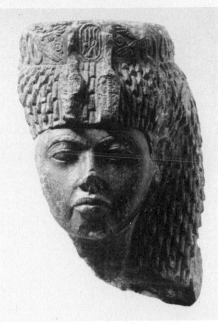

135 Steatite head of a statuette of
Queen Tiye, from Serabit el-Khadim,
Sinai, c. 1358 BC.

136 Grey granite statue of
Amenhotep-son-of-Hapu as a scribe
writing under the inspiration of a god,
from Karnak, c. 1360 BC.

137 Grey granite statue of
Amenhotep-son-of-Hapu carved in the
style of the Thirteenth Dynasty to
represent an aged man, from Karnak,
c. 1358 BC.

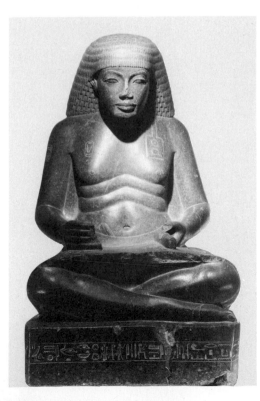

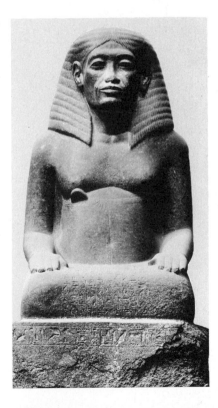

cf. 98

and costume, and to some extent in its portraiture, copies examples dating to the Thirteenth Dynasty.

The realistic tendencies apparent in art during the last years of Amenophis III, with the replacement of the official, benign, style of portraiture with a somewhat careworn expression, has more the appearance of a deviation in the work of his successor, Amenophis IV. This young pharaoh, who later took the name of Akhenaten, introduced ideas which modified the religious beliefs that had guided Egyptian philosophy and shaped its institutions since the advent of Menes. The most important aspect of this ideology, from which all other innovations arose, was a monotheistic and abstract concept of godhead. The teaching of the Heliopolitan theologians had been in the direction of the primacy and supremacy of the sun-god, Rē-Herakhty, who was thought to have absorbed the other gods of Egypt. This deity was now promoted by Akhenaten to pre-eminence, but under a new aspect, that of a heavenly king and father whose power was manifest in the light that streamed from the solar disc, the Aten.

To express his ideas, Akhenaten instigated a novel style of art which has aroused great interest from the time of its impact upon

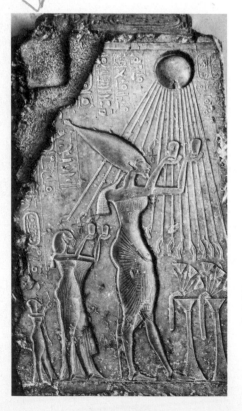

138 Indurated limestone relief of King Akhenaten and Queen Nòfreteti offering libations to the Aten while a daughter shakes her sistrum, from Amarna, c. 1352 BC.

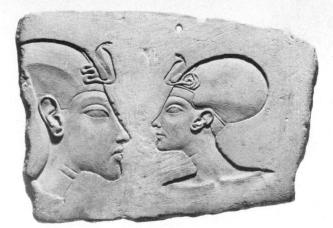

139   Sculptor's model relief in limestone with portraits of
King Akhenaten and Queen Nofreteti, from Amarna, *c.* 1344 BC.

scholars in the nineteenth century, when the first contacts with it were
made in the ruins of the capital city which he built for the Aten. This
township was at modern Tell el-Amarna in Middle Egypt, which has
given its name to the entire period of the seventeen-year reign of
Akhenaten, and also to the characteristic culture which he promoted
during his lifetime. Although Akhenaten encouraged no change in   *138*
the conceptual view of reality that Egyptian artists had cherished since
the Archaic Period, some idiosyncratic distortions were introduced,
undoubtedly at his promptings, in the portrayal of the persons of the
king, his chief queen, Nofreteti, and their daughters; and even these
traits tend to be moderated in the later years of his reign.   *139*

It is in two other important aspects, however, that the art of the
Amarna Period differs more significantly from the traditional art that
preceded it. The first, concerning subject-matter, was deliberate and
sprang from the proscription of all gods except one, who was to be
represented by a symbol, an elaborated hieroglyph for the sunlight in
which Akhenaten's god manifested his power. The second, concerned
with a new idea of representing space, was unconscious and arose out
of the Egyptian artistic psyche, released from conventional restraint.

When Akhenaten proscribed the representation of his sun-god in
the form of a graven image, he banished at a blow nearly all the
traditional subjects that had been reserved for the decoration of
temples since earliest times. Even where he felt obliged to preserve
conventional themes of great antiquity he gave them a new look.
Thus the scene of the pharaoh freeing Egypt from evil forces by

173

dispatching the traditional foes before the god of the temple, was changed to place the slaughtering under the elaborated hieroglyph of the new sun-god in the presence of the queen and the eldest daughter.

This example, however, is almost the only one of the traditional subjects to be retained. In their place appeared incidents from the life of the royal family such as one finds on the house stelae. It would appear that during the reign of Akhenaten, the ancestral busts and similar godlings that protected the Egyptian household were replaced by little shrines built either in the chief room of the house or in the garden. The central feature of these shrines was a stela showing the royal family engaged in what at first sight appears to be purely domestic activities.

One of the most important of such stelae is an example in Berlin. Here Akhenaten sits on a simple stool and raises his eldest daughter in his arms to kiss her while she points to her mother opposite, whose other daughters clamber upon her. It is perhaps worth pointing out that at Amarna the artists abandoned the old symbolic way of representing a child by its hieroglyphic ideograph, a miniature naked adult sucking its forefinger. Here the royal daughters have taken their fingers out of their mouths and use them for the typically childish gesture of pointing. Ankhesenpaaten, standing on her mother's left arm, plays with the queen's ear ornament in much the same way as the child of a peasant woman reaches up to pull her mother's hair, in a painting in the tomb of Menna. The time represented is not eternity but a brief moment in the lives of five beings as they are caught in an act of mutual affection under the daytime disc of their sun-god, the Aten, with the Amarna wind fluttering the streamers on their dress. The world in which they exist is circumscribed by a garden pavilion built of slender reeds and rushes – a pleasure-dome furnished with jars of wine. The royal family are far from being represented as perfect beings existing in an ideal eternity, like the beings depicted in the reliefs of Kha'emhet and Kheruef; but they are very much alive in a transient world of human emotions.

The vernacular and domestic nature of these novel scenes, however, which appear on the house-stelae but which probably copied reliefs and paintings in the destroyed temples and palaces of Amarna, should not obscure their deeper religious import. The family represented is a divine one. As many observers have remarked, Akhenaten was not averse to claiming a considerable share of the Aten's godhead, and for some scholars that share sometimes approaches complete identity. Nofreteti, also, is a great divinity. In the Berlin stela, she sits on a royal stool while her husband is content with a simpler seat. She usually appears in a tall blue crown, which

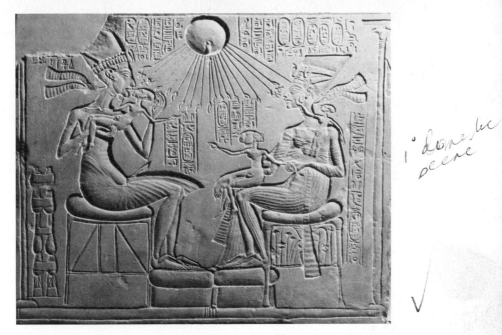

140 Limestone house stela of King Akhenaten, his wife and three of their daughters in a kiosk, from Amarna, c. 1350 BC.

seems to have a connection with the headgear of Tephenis, the daughter of the sun-god. She alone makes offering to the Aten on a par with the king, and it is only such royal couples that the life-giving rays of the Aten sustain. On a fragment of a sarcophagus in Berlin she takes the place of the goddesses who stand at the corners of the example in which Tutankhamun was buried.

Attention has in the past been directed to the subject-matter of these designs, in stressing the domestic and secular aspects of the new icons of the Aten religion, and it has rather been overlooked that they replace the images of the old ruling gods with representations of the new divine rulers. What they illustrate are the significant acts of a Holy Family, the visible intermediaries between man and the godhead supreme, the invisible sun-god whose symbol predominates at the summit of every composition.

There is, however, another characteristic of Amarna art which has been largely ignored but which is even more revolutionary in its implications. This is a new attempt to represent space in two

134   dimensions. A glance at the relief of Kha'emhet will show man as an idealization – as a symbol with both feet seen in their interior aspect and each pair of hands consisting of duplicates of the same hand. They are, in fact, symbols of feet and hands and as such had existed with few exceptions since Egyptian drawing had crystallized into an accepted canon in Archaic times. In the Berlin stela, however, the left and right feet are carefully distinguished and the hands of the children also appear to be differentiated, though the scale is too small for certainty. What is clear, however, is that while the side-lock of Maketaten is shown in detail worn on her right side, those of the other children are obscured since they are facing left. In other words the artist conceived of his figures as existing within the reality of space and not within the two-dimensional confines of the picture area. This is an entirely new vision on the part of the sculptor and is rare in the ancient world before this time. Admittedly, in that vernacular art which is particularly evident in the Theban wall paintings, left and right feet had appeared rarely as an artistic aberration. Thus one scene of guests at meat from the tomb of Nebamun in the British Museum shows left and right feet whereas its companion painting from the same tomb makes no such differentiation.

140

cf. 141

The distinction between left and right feet is not made in the carefully sculptured tombs of Kha'emhet, Surer and Kheruef; nor does it appear in the Theban tombs of Parennefer and Ramose dating

141   Wall-painting from the tomb of Nebamun at Western Thebes, with a scene of musicians entertaining guests at a meal, *c.* 1356 BC.

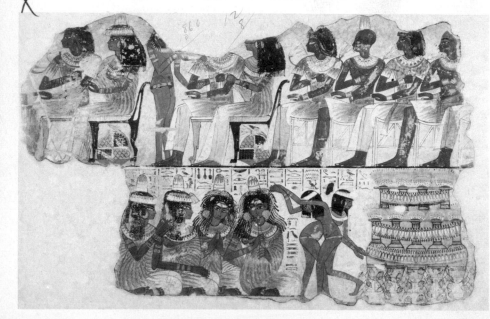

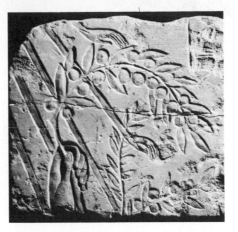

142 Limestone relief fragment of a hand offering an olive branch to the Aten, originally from Amarna, found at Hermopolis, *c.* 1344 B C.

to the first years of Akhenaten's reign, but it was fully established between his sixth and ninth regnal years. It appears to be an innovation of the king's sculptors because it is confined to figures of the royal family. For others, the old conventions prevailed, as is evident on the walls of the private tombs at Amarna.

As with feet, so with hands. It is sometimes difficult to decide whether a left or right hand has been correctly drawn on the same body owing to the fact that a mere line defining the ball of the thumb is all that is required to differentiate one from the other. From the early Old Kingdom, the artist had distinguished a clenched right hand from a clenched left hand, though he did not always correctly represent them on the same figure, especially when it was orientated facing left. In the Amarna Period, however, there is frequently an effort exhibited to look at hands with a fresh vision and to represent them properly in a spatial context. The most striking of a number of examples is a relief in the Schimmel Collection in New York showing a hand, probably that of Akhenaten himself, holding up an olive branch which is bending under the weight of its fruit, to the caressing rays of the Aten. This unique scene is the best testimony to the spatial reality of the new vision. The olive, an exotic tree imported into Egypt in the New Kingdom, has here replaced the traditional bouquets that are offered to the Aten. The novelty of the scene may have induced the artist to draw the branch and the hand that holds it from life rather than according to time-honoured convention. The grasping hand is drawn to show the thumb in relation to the branch and the enclosing fingers in an aspect which as nearly approaches perspective as any Egyptian draughtsman ever

3

142

177

attained. The contrast between the old and the new will be apparent by comparing the hand of the king in this relief with those of the Aten rays.

The idea of such a hand, represented as though operating within a spatial reality, necessarily involved the artist in attempting to give an illusion of depth within the confines of the scene he was representing in relief or painting. There are several examples of this, notably a new way of representing a stand of wheat in an informal arrangement of bearded ears, as though moving in a breeze, and not as an impenetrable wall of straw below a zone of ripened seed, which had been the usual convention in painting and relief since the early Old Kingdom. The new effect gives an illusion of depth, as if the spectator is looking through the waving stalks to what lies beyond.

This novel conception of space in Egyptian art is seen in the reliefs carved on the tomb walls at Amarna, which almost certainly copied designs used in the decoration of the Aten temples. In place of the former extracts, selected from pattern books according to the taste of the patron in a medley of subjects, each wall is considered as a single unit and covered with one complete scene. In a chamber in the Royal Tomb one subject is spread over two contiguous walls, and the same arrangement is used in private tombs such as those of Meryrē I and Mahu. The vertical line, emphasized by block borders and a twisted rope pattern, which defines the corner where two walls meet in Egyptian architecture, has been completely discarded, and the

143

143   Limestone relief fragment of a stand of wheat, originally from Amarna, found at Hermopolis, *c.* 1344 BC.

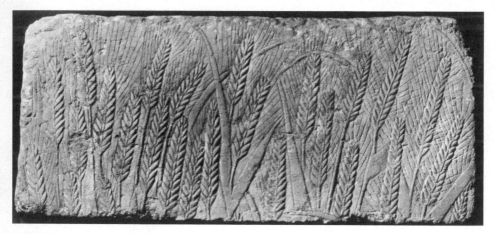

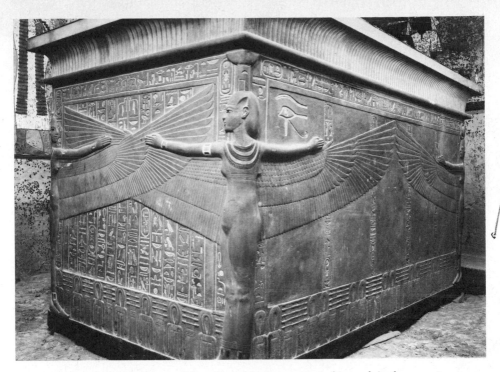

144   Red quartzite sarcophagus of King Tutankhamun, *in situ* in his tomb in the Valley of the Kings, *c.* 1330 BC.

composition spills over from one wall to the other. The Egyptian artist was now conceiving of space as a totality, and not as the contiguity of separate, if adjacent, planes.

The same management of space, but in its external aspects, is seen in the sarcophagi of the period. Tutankhamun had a sarcophagus with *144* one of the goddesses of the four quarters standing at each exterior corner in such a position that half her body falls vertically on the long side, and the other half on the short end. This is the persistence of a design evolved during the Amarna Period. That it was outside the natural instinct of the Egyptian artist is seen in the sarcophagi of Ay and Haremhab, which although a mere five years or so later in date, reveal that the position of the goddesses had been shifted slightly, so that two are fully revealed on each long side, only one of their winged arms being visible at the head and foot ends, and so conforming more comfortably to Egyptian experience.

This new conception of space breaks out of the Egyptian artistic consciousness in these somewhat oblique manifestations. The appearance of depth on a two-dimensional field could only have been

179

achieved by the introduction of perspective and the Egyptian artist drew back from so revolutionary an innovation; for there were other constraints that kept him well within the bounds of tradition. Egyptian art had grown up in the service of its kings and could not be changed fundamentally until a new conception of government prevailed. Akhenaten did not change any of the ideas of kingship. Indeed, he appears to have reverted to some concepts of the divinity of the pharaoh that belong more to the Age of Djoser. Changes were made by Akhenaten in the choice of subjects to be illustrated and the manner in which the royal family should be portrayed, but the age-old conventions in which those subjects were rendered was retained. Nevertheless, when even minor constraints had been removed, the Egyptian artists began to stumble towards a new way of representing the space around them.

Such ideas had little effect upon the statuary of the reign, which was trammelled by technical and architectonic considerations. Even so, it has produced the most dramatic result of Akhenaten's innovations in *149* the colossi that were erected at Karnak at the outset of the reign. These statues must have startled the king's contemporaries by their violent departure from the ideals of representing the god-king. Here realism

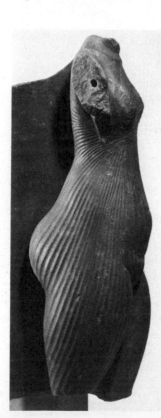

145   Red quartzite torso from a statue of Queen Nofreteti, from Amarna(?), *c.* 1350 BC.

146   Painted limestone master portrait bust of Queen Nofreteti, from Amarna, *c.* 1344 BC.

147   Original plaster cast of a modelled portrait mask of a man, from Amarna, *c.* 1340 BC.

148   Limestone head of Queen Nofreteti in process of being carved, *c.* 1342 BC.

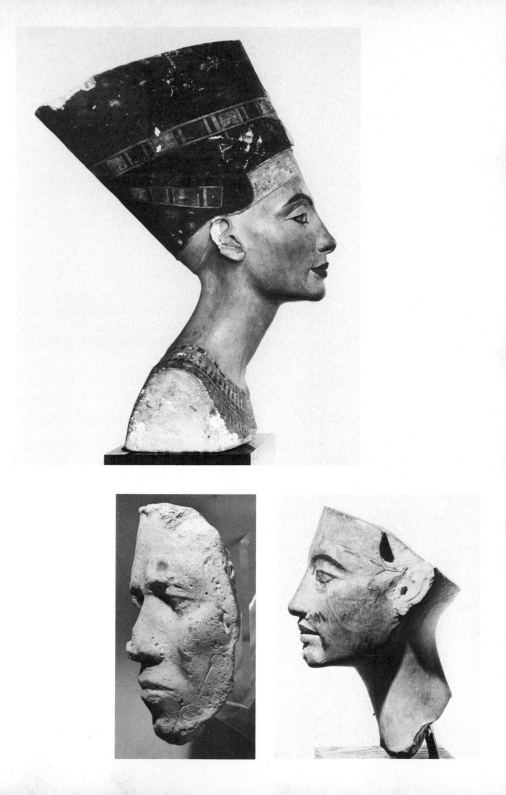

has been transmuted into abnormality, the peculiar physique of Akhenaten being elongated and distorted into a new symbol of godhead. The chief sculptor Bak, doubtless the designer of these statues, claims that he was the pupil whom the king instructed; which suggests that it was Akhenaten who prescribed their exact form. They represent the only conscious attempt in the history of ancient Egyptian art to introduce an entirely new form of expression, and to discard the traditions of the past, even when the innovator could not break entirely with the old conventions. The statues are among the most disturbing works of art that the ancient world has bequeathed us, an outward and visible expression of an inward and spiritual force that has a gleam of fanaticism in its steady gaze. In these colossi, the transcendental quality of the piety immanent in the contemporary votive statues has reached a pitch of ecstasy.

The exaggerations in the king's physique are echoed in the erotic distortions to which the figure of Queen Nofreteti is subjected. She is shown in relief and in the round as a woman of great allure, according to an Oriental ideal of voluptuousness, with a small waist, large thighs and buttocks and a prominent pubic mound, thus stressing the epithets that are often applied to her in the texts: 'Fair of Face, Mistress of Joy, Endowed with Favours, Great of Love'. The torso in the Louvre emphasizes these features to a compelling degree, half concealed beneath pleated draperies. This was an innovation in the statuary of the reign which attained a high degree of technical excellence in suggesting the human form beneath the folds and goffering of thin garments.

The extreme style of this early phase was modified in the second decade of the king's reign, perhaps as the result of the appointment of a new chief sculptor, or an ebbing in the king's religious fervour. Most of the sculpture recovered from the ruins of the studio of his chief sculptor, Tuthmose, at Amarna, is free from the distortions of the Karnak colossi and the destroyed temple statues that have been recovered in fragments from a dump at Amarna. The studio of Tuthmose has bequeathed us a whole series of objects which reveal the full range of the art of the portrait sculptors, such as heads, arms, hands and feet carved in quartzite and jasper for fitting into composite statues of kings, queens and princesses. There are also heads in the process of being carved, and plaster casts made from studies rapidly modelled from the life in clay or wax in order to catch a likeness, for subsequent working over to an acceptable ideal. Among these relics are some half-dozen supreme masterpieces of Egyptian art: but the most celebrated is the painted bust of Queen Nofreteti, plastered in places over a limestone core, and doubtless serving as the official

182

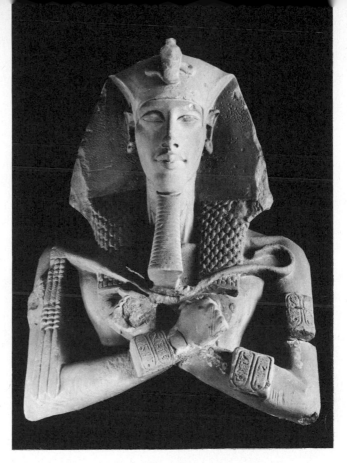

149 Upper portion
of a painted
sandstone colossus of
Amenophis IV
(Akhenaten), from
Karnak, c. 1356 BC.

master portrait for copying by lesser sculptors working on the royal commissions.

The reversion to orthodoxy under Tutankhamun and his two successors, Ay and Haremhab, inspired no return to the classic conventions of the past. There was a new stimulus given to refashioning and repairing images of the gods and to restoring the damage done by Akhenaten's iconoclasm, but the sculptors continued to produce their work in the late Amarna style without much modification. It is probable that Tuthmose remained in office as the chief sculptor under Tutankhamun. The granite statues of the king found at Karnak and now in the Cairo Museum (nos. C.42091–2) show him with a normal physique, lacking the heavy hips and pronounced paunch, breasts and chin of Akhenaten but with the same grave expression. The fashion of showing sandals on the feet, introduced in the reign of Tuthmosis III, is still followed even when

183

the king is represented wearing the more formal kilt and *nemes* headdress. The statues found in his tomb cannot with certainty all be dated to his reign: some of them may have been usurped from his Amarna predecessors, Akhenaten and Smenkhkarē, though they have been inscribed for him. He finished the statue of a guardian lion designed for the temple of Amenophis III at Sulb, which he claimed was still lying unfinished in the quarry, though it was Ay who subsequently moved it into position in the temple. Its companion is too damaged to disclose whether any stylistic differences are detectable between the two statues. What is clear is that the Tutankhamun specimen is one of the great masterpieces of animal sculpture that the ancient world has bequeathed us (as Ruskin was not slow to remark), monumental in its simplified masses yet instinct with latent power, and strangely appealing in its leonine dignity.

Frontispiece

150

The representation of the human form beneath pleated robes changed from a novelty to a convention. The folds became more numerous on the sleeves of shirts and gowns as the age progressed. The classic figures in this genre are the woefully damaged statue of the wife of the general Minnakht in Cairo (no. C.779B), and the figures of the goddesses in gilded wood that protected the canopic shrine of the king.

Throughout Tutankhamun's reign, a number of private statues and reliefs of very high quality were produced, despite the demands

150   Red granite guardian lion of King Tutankhamun, originally from the temple of King Amenophis III, at Sulb, *c.* 1329 BC.

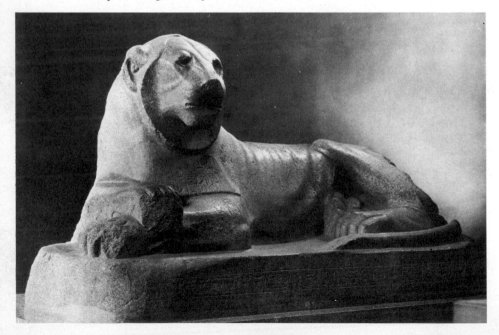

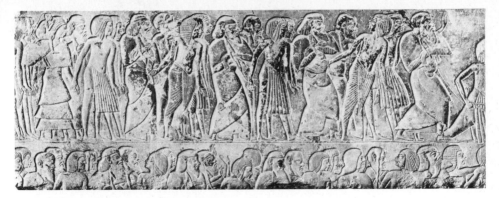

151 Limestone relief of Asiatic rebels being paraded before the king, from the tomb of Haremhab at Saqqara, c. 1338 BC.

made upon the sculptors by the work of repair and replacement. At this time the court had abandoned Amarna and moved to the palace complex at Memphis, where the near-by necropolis of Saqqara has yielded a group of tomb reliefs which, in the verve of their drawing and the sensitivity of their carving, are among the best ever produced in Egypt.

Among these, the limestone reliefs that were carved in the tomb that Haremhab built before he became king are outstanding. Most of them are now scattered among the museums of Europe and America, but the recent discovery of his tomb, south of the Pyramid of Unas, has uncovered more. Having regard to the importance of Haremhab at the court of Tutankhamun and Ay, and to the great extent of his tomb, there is little doubt that he was able to command the services of royal craftsmen in the carving of its decoration. Some features of the Amarna style persisted, such as the use of sunk and raised relief in the same scenes to achieve greater depth. In the crowd scenes, the heads in various poses, each one almost an individual portrait, are particularly *151* striking. The arrangement of the composition imposes order on a mass of crowded forms. Until the restoration of the tomb has been completed it is impossible to say whether the Amarna conception of space prevailed. Although it is significant that there is an avoidance of straight registers in some scenes, only the royal pair are shown with left and right feet. The draughtsmanship of the reliefs is by one of the great anonymous masters of ancient Egypt, a man who could make the blank areas of his design as eloquent as the worked spaces.

The reign of Haremhab as king shows the working out of the Amarna legacy. New generations of artists must have succeeded their

185

fathers; and a certain formalism and hardness of contour replaced the relaxation in poses and the freedom in the handling which are characteristic of the Amarna style. In the scenes painted in the Theban tomb-chapels, the erotic element was expunged from the scenes of feasting and music, and some of the mannerisms of the Ramesside style were anticipated, such as a black dot or line emphasizing the corner of the mouth and a thick black outline to the figure in place of the former thin, sensitive, line in a warm bistre.

During the Eighteenth Dynasty, royal and private statuary also underwent constant stylistic change, the modifications being most marked in the later decade of the reign of Amenophis III. The flat 'hieroglyphic' eye, with its thick outlines and prominent paintstripe, fashionable in Tuthmoside times, was replaced by a more plastically rendered version, with the upper lid modelled to catch the light, and carved to terminate more naturally in an outer fold over the lower lid, except in the case of colossi. Eyebrows ceased to be decorative arched appliqués, and followed instead the more natural line of the brow. The medial line of the lips changed from a straight division under the Tuthmoside kings, to a double curve; and the lips were modelled, transforming a gentle smile into a more pensive moue. Ears became more fleshy, the upper and lower tips curving away from the head, the lobe pitted with a round depression which was later elongated into a slit. The main coils of the uraeus placed near the summit of the brow changed their form and position to become an S-shaped fold behind the hood. Where they were not hidden by the large ceremonial beard, the tendons of the neck were boldly indicated, as were the collar-bones and sternal notch. These innovations of the Amarna sculptors persisted for the next three reigns. The lappets of the *nemes* headcloth revived the Thirteenth Dynasty fashion of an inner border. The Blue Crown became taller and more upright, and acquired streamers that hang down the nape of the neck, eventually assuming a broader shape and a ribbed appearance. Contemporary changes in dress are also reflected both in statuary and relief.

The statue of the male owner holding a stave surmounted by the aegis of a deity is a new design. The earliest example known dates to the reign of Amenophis III, and may be an elaboration of a design known from a statue of Ammenemes III in the Cairo Museum (no. C.395). Statues of this type became more common in the ensuing period, the number of staves being frequently doubled, so that one is held by each arm of the officiant. In a unique example, now in a private collection, Queen Nofretari, the wife of Ramesses II, holds the temple staff of her patron, the goddess Mut.

cf. 117, 137
cf. 114, 117

116, 135

cf. 116, 149

137, 149

CHAPTER TWELVE

The New Kingdom: Ramesside Period

Dynasties XIX–XX

The dynasty of the Ramessides came from the Delta, but although they built their residences and their treasure cities in the north, they continued to embellish Thebes, the holy city of Amun, with great temples, and to cut their tombs in the Valley of the Kings. In their foreign policy they revived the claims to hegemony over the Lebanon and southern Syria which Egypt had exercised before the rise of the Hittite Kingdom in the fourteenth century BC. Their challenge was accepted by the Hittites who dominated the disputed territories, and inconclusive wars between the two powers resulted in the exhaustion of both, and a treaty from which Egypt got very little except a pact of mutual assistance. The truth was that ethnic movements, probably the result of further climatic changes, were already threatening the balance of power in the Near East, and were eventually to overwhelm the Hittite Kingdom, and drive Egypt back behind its borders. The period of the Nineteenth and Twentieth Dynasties was thus one of a fluctuating but decisive decline in the power and prestige of the pharaoh, and in the wealth of the state. Towards the end of the era, low Niles brought famine and internal disorder. The extinction of the unitary state under the sole rule of the pharaoh occurred even before the last of the Ramessides died in his northern residence.

The accession of Sethos I, the virtual founder of the Nineteenth Dynasty, began with high hopes. That it was believed that a new era had dawned can be inferred from the epithet which the king sometimes applied to himself, 'Repeating Births', a title which Ammenemes I had used at the outset of the Twelfth Dynasty to show that he was inaugurating a 'Renaissance'. The vigour of a resurgent Egypt may be seen not only in the campaigns that were fought to win back influence in Palestine and Syria, but also in the building activities of Sethos I and the extension of gold mining and prospecting in the Eastern Desert.

The buildings that the king raised at Thebes and Abydos reveal that his workmen were concerned to maintain the highest traditions of craftsmanship. At Abydos he built in massive granite a subterranean cenotaph to Osiris, beneath a great mound representing the primeval mound. He identified with the dead god all the pharaohs of Egypt whom he recognized as his legitimate precursors. The associated

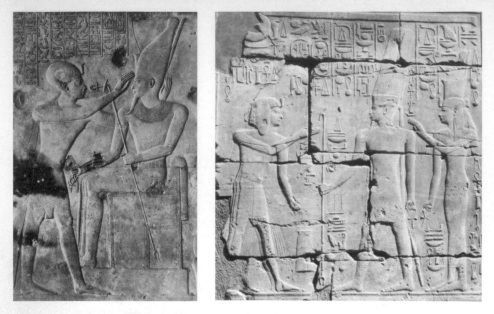

152 Limestone relief of King Sethos I crowning the image of the primordial god Atum in his temple at Abydos, c. 1290 BC.

153 Sandstone relief of King Sethos I worshipping Amun and Mut in the hypostyle hall of the great temple of Amun at Karnak, c. 1280 BC.

154 Sandstone relief of King Ramesses II smiting a Libyan chieftain, in the main temple at Abu Simbel in Nubia, c. 1260 BC.

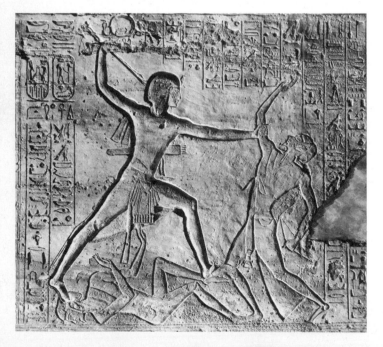

temple nearby was built in a fine hard limestone capable of registering 152
minute detail in its delicate raised reliefs. The very perfection of this
great work, with its exquisite drawing, cannot but arouse admiration,
even though the inner life has an erratic pulse. A similar suavity of
style is found in the sandstone reliefs in the great hypostyle hall which 153
he continued between the Third and Second Pylons at Karnak. The
scenes of warfare with Asiatic and Libyan foes on the northern outer
wall comprise some spirited compositions which are among the first
of the great Ramesside battle pieces. The style probably owes
something to the lost Amarna temple reliefs of battle or hunting
subjects; but the organization of the picture space into strict registers
so as to show various episodes of the engagements in their
chronological order and topographical setting in Palestine and Syria
is new. The old symbolic way of representing the pharaoh in his
chariot on a gigantic scale charging a disordered mass of foes and so
confronting Evil and Chaos with Right and Order, here gives way to
the depiction of incidents in the campaigns of his first regnal year. Still
largely heraldic in their composition, they disclose, nevertheless, a
number of original details of which one, the design of the king
smiting a Libyan chief, was copied at Abu Simbel by the artists of 154
Ramesses II.

Large statuary of Sethos I has not survived except for unpublished
pieces at Memphis and fragments elsewhere. The partly restored
black granite kneeling figure of the king from Abydos, now in New
York (MMA no. 22.2.21), presenting the glyph for 'food' to Osiris,
while accepting all the conventions of the post-Amarna style in such
features as the plastic treatment of eyes and lips, the S-coil of the
uraeus behind its hood and the folds in the neck, has yet infused them
with the hard precision of the Tuthmoside style, evident also in the
revival of the arched eyebrow and the elongated paint stripe at the
outer corner of the eye. An innovation is the benevolent smile,
emphasized by a distinct depression at the corner of the mouth that
replaces the triste expression of the post-Amarna lips and becomes a
dominant characteristic of the Ramesside style, particularly in its cf. 159
official utterances. A large alabaster statue from Karnak, made in
several pieces and designed to be joined by metal ties disguised under
jewels and clothing, appears to have been left unfinished from an
earlier reign and merely inscribed for Sethos I (Cairo no. C. 42139).

Sethos I's reign was the last in which some lingering echo may be
caught of the private Theban tomb painting of the preceding
dynasty. The Amarna interlude had discarded the old subjects for
decoration on tomb walls, and the return to orthodoxy had not
succeeded in recapturing the old delight in the material world. In the

Ramesside tombs, the prime concern is with the scenes of burial in the necropolis, the last judgment before the gods of the Underworld, and vignettes extracted from the *Book of the Dead* enabling the owner by their magic spells to reach eternal bliss. One or two chapels of the reign, however, still recall the pleasures of life on earth, particularly the sitting in the cool of a garden, or fishing in its well-stocked pool. The tomb of Userhet has a celebrated scene of this character with the owner, his wife and mother, seated beside a T-shaped pool in Paradise while their bird-souls drink the cool water, poured by the goddess of the sycamore tree. The scene, although of the Otherworld, is redolent of the joy remembered on earth. For all its charm, however, the bright colours, the busy detail and the careful drawing cannot disguise certain weaknesses in the design, such as the inept positioning of the cup which the nearest woman holds. The artist was happier with the standard icons of purely funerary import.

156

In contrast to the relative paucity of works surviving from the reign of Sethos I, the monuments of his son, Ramesses II, abound, a great many having been produced during his long reign of sixty-seven years, in all sizes and materials, and in different styles and qualities. The king proved to be the most industrious builder to occupy the throne of Egypt. Not only were great new constructions raised at Thebes, Memphis, Hermopolis and other large towns in Egypt, and in Nubia, but many of the temples still standing

155 Façade of the main rock-hewn temple of King Ramesses II at Abu Simbel in Nubia, *c*. 1260 BC.

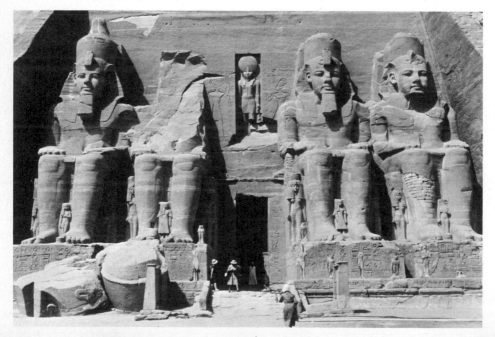

Colossi

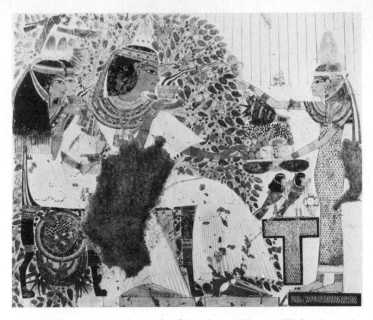

156 Wall-painting in the tomb of Userhet at Western Thebes (no. 51), showing the owner, his wife and mother drinking the water of paradise, *c.* 1280 BC.

desecrated since the days of Akhenaten were rebuilt and reconsecrated in the name of Ramesses II. For this purpose, his cartouches were superimposed over those of former kings. As a result he has come to be regarded, perhaps unjustly, as the arch-appropriator of other men's works. It is clear, for instance, that like his son Merenptah, he found many of the statues of Amenophis III lying unfinished in the temple of Luxor, and had them completed and raised in his own name.

During his long reign a number of different chief craftsmen must have succeeded each other; and his enormous building enterprises must have brought into requisition temple workshops at Memphis, Thebes and other main centres of art, where somewhat different traditions prevailed. The colossal statues carved *in situ* out of the soft Nubian sandstone, as adjuncts to the temples he raised at Abu Simbel, Wadi es-Sebua, Derr and Gerf Hussein, demanded a broad treatment and squat proportions if they were to be structurally stable, and may have introduced the practice of coarse and hasty work among some at least of the royal artisans. The suspicion is that the king's ambitions outran his resources, particularly towards the end of his reign.

155

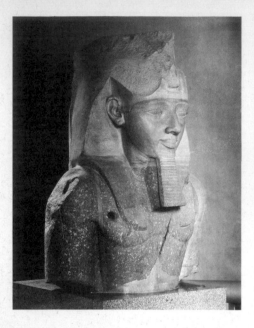

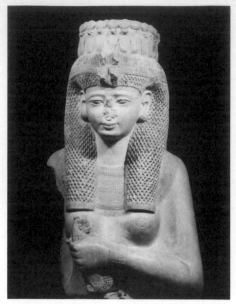

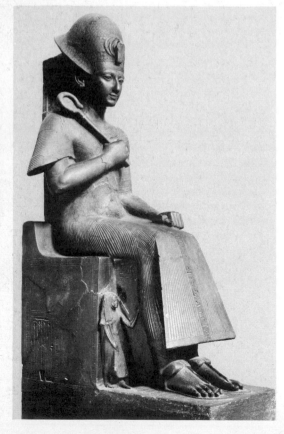

157 Upper part of a brown quartzite colossus of King Ramesses II, from the Ramesseum, *c.* 1250 BC.

158 Upper part of an indurated limestone statue of Queen Nofretari(?), from the Ramesseum, *c.* 1260 BC.

159 Black granite statue of King Ramesses II with diminutive figures of Queen Nofretari (not visible here) and their son Prince Amenhirkopshef on either side of the throne, from Karnak, *c.* 1278 BC.

For these reasons, the statuary of Ramesses II shows a wealth of examples, baffling in their varied quality and styles. The difficulty of dating them within his reign makes it virtually impossible in the present state of our knowledge to trace any development: nevertheless a number of observations may be made. It is clear that statuary produced for the series that was made for him at his coronation continues the tradition of fine work prevailing in the reign of his father. Of these the most impressive, for its size and technical excellence, is the large, black granite, seated statue in Turin, which shows Ramesses II in contemporary costume holding a crook-sceptre, his chief wife, Nofretari, and his eldest son by her, being carved on a *159* smaller scale beside his legs. The portrait is in the official style of Sethos I; so much so that it has induced one scholar to claim that it has been usurped from the earlier king, though this seems unlikely.

In the same group of early pieces characterized by fine workmanship are a number of statues of Nofretari, the chief queen of his youth, who appears on a smaller scale on some of the colossi usurped from Amenophis III at Luxor, where she probably replaces an original figure of Queen Tiye. She is also prominent at Abu Simbel, where on the façade of the smaller temple dedicated to her, she appears, three-quarters in the round, on the same huge scale as her husband. A number of statuettes, mostly fragmentary, may be accredited to her on stylistic grounds. Many of them are *ex votos* inscribed for the earlier queen Ahmose-Nofretari, whose worship underwent a popular resurgence in the reign of Ramesses II, and are made with the features and costume of the later queen. A life-sized bust in indurated limestone, found near the Ramesseum, the *158* mortuary temple of Ramesses II at Thebes, also without doubt represents the youthful Nofretari in all her finery, wearing the circlet of uraei of a queen, and holding the emblem of a high priestess of the goddess Hathor. This fragment is one of the masterpieces of Ramesside art, expressing the ideal of queenly grace in the New Kingdom, yet having a certain formal style that belongs as much to the period as the precise, somewhat stiff drawing, and the careful colouring of the paintings in her disintegrating tomb in the Valley of the Queens.

Another tradition is represented by the colossi that were hewn in great quantity during the long reign of Ramesses II. The largest was the seated example in the Ramesseum, which weighed over a thousand tons and was still celebrated in the time of Diodorus Siculus. Like other colossi of Ramesses at Luxor it was given a special name (Shelley's 'King of Kings') and was worshipped as an intermediary between man and the gods, having its attendant priesthood and being sited in the more public part of the temple. A hard limestone colossus, the sole survivor of a pair that stood with companions in red granite before the main pylon of the temple at Memphis, has the unmistakable features of Ramesses on a giant scale, with his large curving nose, the plastically rendered eyes and the lips fixed in the typical official smile of the reign. Sculpture of such a size, set up in the open, demanded a bold summary treatment to catch the light and make a proper effect at a distance. Stylization and a disregard for detail were inevitable in such work. The masterpiece in this style is the *157* great quartzite bust in the British Museum that Belzoni removed from the Ramesseum. The sculptor has cunningly selected the stone so that a golden stratum runs through the region of the head, as though the face were illuminated by a shaft of sunlight. With this statue the sculptors of Ramesses II reached an apogee in the representation of the benevolent god and heroic champion of Egypt. Such quality is not attained again in the large statuary of the New Kingdom.

The majority of sculptures of the reign of Ramesses II, both the colossal and the elegant, have been found on Upper Egyptian sites; even the examples from the temple of Ptah at Memphis were probably prepared at Aswan and Thebes. Such work is in the idealistic cast of traditional pharaonic statuary; but there is also evident a different and more realistic style which appears to originate in some Lower Egyptian studio, though such a circumstance may be entirely fortuitous, and the character of such pieces may have been determined by the appointment of a new chief sculptor of some originality later in the reign. Of such statues mostly from Delta sites, a standing example, a little more than life-size and found at Memphis, is the most complete. It shows the king wearing a long gown and holding a pair of temple staves, the bold cubic design of the body throwing into greater prominence the face which is round, even plump, and far removed in its severe expression from the benevolent cast of the colossi with their fixed smiles. The head of a similar quartzite statue of the king is on loan to the Brooklyn Museum.

Relief sculpture and wall paintings show the same general decline of resources and standards throughout the first century of the Ramessides. The early granite sunk reliefs of Ramesses II from Saft el-Hina, Heliopolis and other Delta sites, are competently executed in the style of Tuthmosis III; and the painted limestone reliefs from his *160* temple at Abydos are little inferior to those of his father, Sethos I, perhaps through the persistence of a trained team of craftsmen at this site. The tomb reliefs of Merenptah at Abydos and the Valley of the Kings, however, are more banal, mere mechanical interpretations of

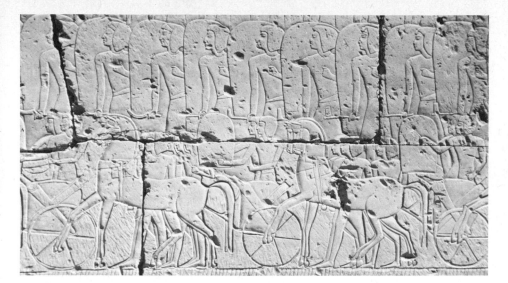

160 Egyptian chariotry and infantry waiting to go into battle, a limestone relief on the outer wall of the temple of King Ramesses II at Abydos, *c.* 1270 B C.

the standard formulae, though even here and there are surprises such as the correct delineation of the left and right foot of the king. Another departure from the norm is evident in a red granite statue in the Cairo Museum (no. C.1240) of two figures in conjunction. It shows Merenptah as the conquering king about to decapitate with his scimitar a Libyan prisoner whose head is turned to an angle of about 70°, thus disregarding Egyptian rules of frontality. The damage that this piece has sustained makes it difficult to assess its quality, but there is no doubt of its originality which may have inspired the sculptor of the better-known composition of Ramesses VI mentioned below.   *164*
Towards the end of the Nineteenth Dynasty, there was a revival of standards under Sethos II when chapels were built to the Theban triad and other constructions raised beyond the Second Pylon at Karnak. A number of damaged kneeling and standing statues in quartzite have been recovered from this site, the most complete of which is a seated example in the British Museum (no. 26), showing the youthful king holding a phylactery on his lap surmounted by the ram's head aegis of Amun. A head in New York (M M A no. 34.2.2) is also of excellent workmanship, and has been claimed for Ramesses II, as have a pair of colossi of this same king.

The private stone statuary of the Nineteenth Dynasty, most of which has been recovered from the Theban area, shows a steady decline in quality and range. Tomb-statues of a man and his wife, in the tradition of those of the late Eighteenth Dynasty, continue to be produced during the reign of Sethos I and in the earlier years of Ramesses II, though there is a falling off in size and excellence. There are, however, exceptions, and a high degree of skill is shown in the carving of statues, both in limestone and wood, which have been recovered from the necropolis of Deir Durunka, near Asyut, and which date to the earlier part of the dynasty. In particular, the statues of the king's scribe and steward Yuni, now in New York, are up to the standard of the best work of the Eighteenth Dynasty. The pair-statue of Yuni and his wife in their heavily pleated gala robes and festal wigs is the last good example of a genre which gives a charm and humanity to Egyptian statuary even in its most austere mood. Thereafter, with rare exceptions, figures of men and women in ancient Egypt exist apart.

161

The taste of the age, however, was for more stylized statues, especially *ex votos* for installation in temple precincts. The block statue recovers the esteem it had won in Tuthmoside times; but it is often adapted by the Ramesside sculptors to show the cloak goffered rather than plain, and incorporating a shrine held before the owner containing an image of a god, similar to that presented by kneeling donors. Such statues reduce the human body to a stark cuboid mass, and tend to divert interest to the individuality of the features of the

cf. 191

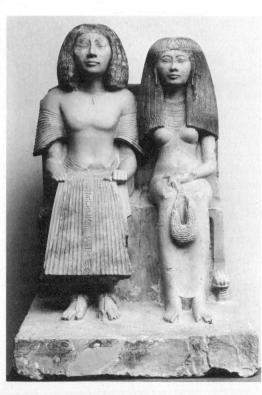

161   Limestone pair-statue of Yuni and his wife Renutet, from Deir Durunka, *c.* 1280 BC.

owner. Unfortunately, except in the case of one or two high officers of state, such portraits are often stylized and perfunctory, and the craftsmanship is frequently indifferent.

During the first three reigns of the Ramessides, the wooden figurines of men and women in the fashionable garb of the day continued to be produced as charming by-products of the sculptor's art. The statuettes of women are elegantly elongated and slim (e.g. Turin no. 3106; Louvre no. E.11523). They no longer appear naked in the erotic fashion of the dancers, musicians and handmaidens of the Eighteenth Dynasty, but are discreetly clad in pleated robes. The figures of men show them either with the shaven head of their priestly office or holding religious emblems, such as the staff surmounted by the ram's-head aegis of Amun (e.g. Louvre nos. N.854, 1575). A more sober spirit pervades these modest works, reflecting something of the same feeling that infuses Ramesside tomb paintings with their emphasis upon icons that illustrate the burial rites and the World of the Dead.

The renewal of artistic standards that is apparent in the royal statuary at the end of the Nineteenth Dynasty continues in the work of Ramesses III during the ensuing dynasty. The colossi of the reign were influenced, like much else at this period, by the examples of the king's vainglorious namesake, Ramesses II. They differ, however, in dispensing with the smile that purses up the lips into a near grimace with deep hollows drilled at the corners of the mouth. The expression is much less bland and may even be severe. The 'caryatid' figures in the first court of the mortuary temple at Medinet Habu, for instance, lack the benevolent appearance of similar colossi at Abu Simbel; and with elaborate crowns and trappings they are clumsily proportioned.

A more disciplined style is apparent in the smaller, free-standing statues at Medinet Habu. These examples, which often represent the king seated beside a god, or in one example standing between two deities whose hands he holds, are carved with great precision and skill in a rich, purplish-red granite and are finely polished. The most notable in this group is a restored triad in the Cairo Museum showing Ramesses III having his crown affixed by Horus and Seth, representing the gods of Upper and Lower Egypt. This piece is remarkable for its size and composition, and although analogous statues on a smaller scale are known they have not been so completely released from their fillings. The statues still *in situ* at the temple of Medinet Habu have suffered damage, particularly in the area of the king's face, but a head of Ramesses III, found on the site and now in Cairo, is exceptional for its realistic and individual portraiture. There are, nevertheless, other statues of this king in which a radically

162

different portrait appears with a round visage, flat cheeks and summarily modelled chin, eyes, nose and mouth. Whether this represents the king in the obesity of old age is doubtful, since the torso is not unduly corpulent, and the presumption is that as in the statuary of Ramesses II, the style owes its character either to the appointment of a different chief sculptor, or to the persistence of a particular school of sculpture with its own strong and distinct traditions. The Osiride effigy of Ramesses III on his sarcophagus lid in the Fitzwilliam Museum at Cambridge (no. E.1.1823) has a visage which is lean rather than rotund, and so has the statue of the king in the Cairo group.

The unusual qualities of the group in Cairo of Horus and Seth affixing the crown of Ramesses III, are well maintained in a number of statues of the Twentieth Dynasty, both royal and private, which, while they are not impressive in size, pay tribute to the invention and skill of the Egyptian sculptor at a time when the news from Thebes tells of decay, corruption and civil disorder. It may well be, however, that if the material remains from the northern residence cities had survived in an equal abundance, a different interpretation would be possible. Certainly the fragments of statues of Ramesses IX that have been recovered from Delta sites reveal admirable workmanship, and
163
the prostrating statue of this king in a green schistose stone is one of the best of this type to be preserved.

A distinct change of direction in fact may be detected in the reign of Ramesses IV, a king who was devoted to antiquarian research. The expedition that he sent to the Wadi Hammamat quarried large quantities of high-quality stone that may have been utilized for statuary during the rest of the dynasty, since in his short reign he was unable to complete his ambitious building projects. The great technical competence of the craftsmen of the preceding reign was harnessed to the production of statuary that looked back to what was now a classic style, that of Tuthmosis III. The characteristic Ramesside
Royal Protective cobra cf. 116, 162
uraeus, for instance, with a body coiled in a loop on either side of the hood, reverts in some examples to the familiar pattern of Tuthmoside statuary. It is probable that a number of statues, such as a large uninscribed group from Abydos in the Cairo Museum (no. J.49537), were left unfinished at the end of his reign and mostly usurped by his successors.

The distinctive full round face of Ramesses IV, for instance, is also present in statues of Ramesses VI, notably in an unusual, granite
164
triumphal statue of the latter pharaoh, accompanied by his pet lion, haling a pinioned Libyan by the hair. This is one of the masterpieces of Ramesside sculpture, bold in conception with its strong diagonal rhythms, and technically adventurous, making a striking contrast

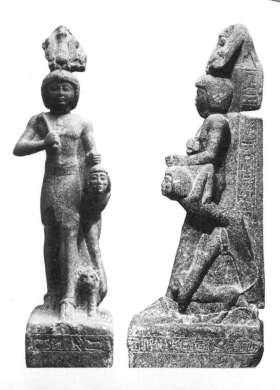

162   Red granite head from a statue of King
Ramesses III, from Medinet Habu, *c.* 1160 BC.

163   Green schist statue of King
Ramesses IX presenting a shrine
surmounted by a scarab beetle,
c. 1126 BC.

164   Red granite statue of King
Ramesses VI leading captive a
Libyan foe, from Karnak,
c. 1140 BC (front and side
views).

between the proud mien of the conquering king and the abject helplessness of his captive. The sculptor has handled the hard stone with complete assurance, incorporating into the design such diverse elements as the *Atef*-crown and the hovering falcon behind it. The concept of 'negative space' has assisted the realization of the bodies of the Libyan and the lion. A fragment of a similar statue in limestone may have been the model for this piece in the more intractable granite.

The temple reliefs of the Twentieth Dynasty show a somewhat mechanical approach to the problems of drawing. The battle scenes of Ramesses III at Medinet Habu, though they deal with more stirring and critical events than ever faced his predecessors, lack the originality and immediacy of the set-pieces of Sethos I at Karnak, and those of Ramesses II at Beit el-Wali and Abu Simbel. The relief showing the siege of Dapur by Ramesses II on a wall of the hypostyle hall in the

165 Mortuary temple of King Ramesses III at Medinet Habu, relief on the rear of the south tower of the first pylon, the king hunting the animals of the wild, *c.* 1160 BC.

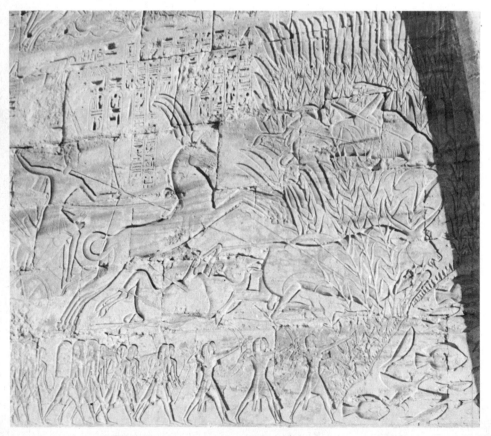

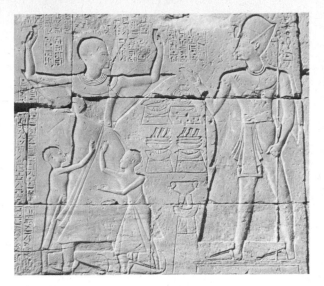

166 Sandstone relief of the high priest Amenhotep being decorated with gold collars in the presence of a statue of King Ramesses IX, at Karnak, c. 1110 BC.

Ramesseum, where the might of the king is shared with his sons who lead the assault groups, sets the pattern for similar scenes of triumph at Medinet Habu, such as the king as the slayer of the animals of the wild on the rear of the south tower of the First Pylon. The deep carving of these scenes in sunk relief gives a sharp edge to the contours, and attenuates the proportions of the figures. The design of the bull hunt in the marshes, and the pursuit of ass and gazelle in the desert, is not without merit in the tradition of the sporting subjects of the Eighteenth Dynasty; but nowhere do we find the masterly drawing and the poignancy of the lion-hunt scene on the painted box of Tutankhamun. The lion hunt at Medinet Habu is the uninspired assemblage and carving of a subject that probably now had only symbolical relevance. Even the scene of the great naval engagement which dispersed the Sea Peoples from the Nile mouths, and which has some claim to being the only original composition of the temple, lacks the dynamism of the earlier Ramesside battle scenes. Like the scenes of battle against the Libyans, and still more against the Sudanis, it takes its place in the decoration of the outer temple walls, not as an incident freshly recollected and recorded, so much as a prophylactic icon, in which the giant figure of the pharaoh opposes a disordered mass of human and animal foes, and so protects the holy precincts from evil.

Another icon of the late Ramesside Age, the investiture of an honoured official before a statue of the king acting as a substitute in his physical absence, receives its last variation in the scenes at Karnak carved on the rear wall of the apartments of the High Priest of Amun.

165

166

Icons of the Ramesside

Here Amenhotep, on a scale almost equal to that of the statue of Ramesses IX on its podium, is awarded gifts of gold and silver by three of the king's officials. The design is clear, with the chamberlains on a smaller scale as befits their insignificance, affixing collars and adjusting the priest's robes; and the carving is careful and competent. It should be observed that now the left and right feet of both the royal statue and the high priest have been differentiated. But the whole scene is little more than an elaborated hieroglyph, with the interior detail reduced to a minimum, though it may have been supplied in paint. Rather than an incident carefully observed and imaginatively reconstructed, we have two confronted symbols, reading 'high priest rejoicing' and 'king summoning'. The art of the period reflects the increasing contraction in the horizons and power of the Egyptian state, now beset with troubles abroad and at home.

cf. 134

The private sculpture of the Twentieth Dynasty is generally small in size and meagre in quality, though one or two examples reveal that even in the twilight years of the Ramessides, the Egyptian sculptor could still produce work of the highest quality when his patron was sufficiently concerned to command it. Among such pieces is the statue of Ramesses-nakht, one of the powerful High Priests of Amun, who from his seat in Thebes virtually ruled Upper Egypt at this period. This piece, showing Ramesses-nakht writing on his papyrus roll under the inspiration of the baboon of Thoth perched on his shoulders, brings to a fitting end the series of New Kingdom statues of scribes devoted to their craft.

167

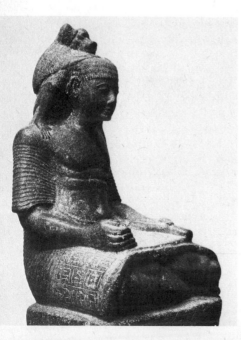

167 Grey granite statue of the high priest Ramesses-nakht as a scribe, from Karnak, *c.* 1130 BC.

Upper Egypt:
Thebes

Pylon - a gateway of an Egyptian Temple.

CHAPTER THIRTEEN

The Character of Late Egyptian Art
and the Tanite Period

Dynasty XXI

The dynasty of the Ramessides ended in civil strife. Egypt lost its Asiatic and African dependencies and fell apart into its two natural halves. Lower Egypt was governed by a new family of kings, ruling from Tanis in the Delta, who were loosely allied by marriage or other ties to the priestly administrators of the Thebaid, who controlled Upper Egypt. This pattern of rule was to persist, with interruptions, until the Persian conquest in the sixth century BC virtually extinguished the old Egyptian state.

Once more the kingship had suffered a fall in prestige and power from which it never recovered. The spiritual influence of the god incarnate in the pharaoh was transferred to the many city gods, among whom Amun of Thebes was the most wealthy and important, his oracles replacing royal judgment and decree in the government of Upper Egypt, at least. The kings no longer made their tombs in the Valley of the Kings, nor built mortuary temples in the plain beyond. They were content with modest monuments constructed in the protected precincts of temple complexes at their residence cities such as Tanis and Sais. Their high officials, with one or two exceptions, no longer sought burial near them, but replaced elaborate hypogea by family graves in the local necropolis, or at hallowed sites such as the vicinity of the Step Pyramid at Saqqara. Nevertheless, the immortality conferred upon the owner, and the confirmation of a family cult by the possession of a tomb-statue, were now secured by the erection of a votive statue in the precincts of the local temple.

The disappearance of the great royal and private tombs, except for some examples at Thebes in Kushite times (see below), led to a decrease in the employment of painters and sculptors. The destruction of monuments during three troubled centuries of dynastic wars and foreign invasions has resulted in the loss of nearly all works of art except sculpture. Moreover, as the kings of this period operated almost exclusively in Lower Egypt, little of their statuary has survived from that greatly ravaged region, and what has escaped complete destruction is usually only fragmentary, of modest size and almost exclusively in hard stone. The damp environment of the Delta has not been favourable to the preservation of objects in wood and limestone.

On the other hand, at Thebes less adverse conditions have permitted the survival of a number of its monuments, particularly those of its brief period of glory under the Kushite kings.

With the decline in the status of the pharaoh, there is a corresponding increase in the importance of the provincial governors, some of whose statues are of colossal size, such as those of Amenhotep in the Cairo Museum (no. C.1199). But the nature of these private statues, official rather than funerary, necessarily limits their design to a few hieratic poses. The seated statue, particularly of the owner and his wife, almost disappears and is replaced by the block statue of the 'hadji' squatting in his cloak, or kneeling to present an offering or sitting cross-legged in the manner of a scribe, reading or writing the sacred literature. The single standing statue of the magnate in all the pride and loneliness of his office, with a serene and benevolent gaze, replaces the pair or group statue designed for family worship and petition. The expression sometimes tends to become introspective, even ecstatic, before the god of the temple.

This is seen particularly in a new aspect of private sculpture: an individualistic portraiture. The facial appearance of the sitter in earlier times had tended to follow the family features of the ruling house, though in the case of an outstanding individual there was often a departure from the norm. In the late periods, however, more emphasis upon the idiosyncratic features of the sitter is apparent. The sculptor seems striving to portray an inner spiritual character by means of a realistic rather than an idealistic treatment of the head, which is now often stripped of its heavy wig, and delineated in all its shaven severity.

Moreover, as Bernard Bothmer has pointed out, this style of portraiture is evidently intended 'to denote the maturity of age, as distinguished from the immaturity of eternal youth'. We can perhaps see in such sculpture a progression from the funerary origin of much Egyptian statuary, where an attempt to create an immortal, forever vigorous and forever young, has become modified by a less materialistic view of man's fate. If the Egyptian exhibits a more sombre expression in the presence of his god, that may well be because external and internal affairs in Egypt must have given rise to much doubt and questioning.

Nevertheless, there were times, in the early Libyan Period and in the Saite Dynasty, when political stability and increased prosperity promoted a recrudescence of something of the old self-confidence and optimism. Then another feature of the age emerges: its dominant antiquarianism. A tendency to return to the proud traditions and style of a past epoch, that in retrospect seemed a Golden Age, was always

204

present in Egyptian consciousness, but only as a source of inspiration, a *reculement pour mieux sauter*. But in the later periods, particularly after the fall of the Libyan dynasties, a return to the styles of the great past became not a point of departure, but an end in itself, an academic ideal, and could embrace not one particular source of inspiration but several. We find, for instance, that the great connoisseur and patron of art, Mentuemhet, could revive with equal impartiality the styles of the Old, Middle and New Kingdoms almost in juxtaposition, particularly in his relief sculpture.

185, 186

This archaism may be but a reflection of that turning back upon itself which Egypt experienced in the political and spiritual field as a result of the constant failure of its foreign policy, its xenophobia, and the exclusion of other peoples with new ideas from the mass of its population. In the Saite Period, seminal influences from the emerging Hellenic world made little impact, and were carefully segregated. In Persian times to hate *Persicos apparatus* was a patriotic duty.

The impoverishment of the Egyptian state at the beginning of the Twenty-first Dynasty is seen in the paucity of building enterprises in the two capitals, Tanis and Thebes. The most that was attempted appears to be the renovation of some ruinous buildings and the usurpation of monuments of earlier days; even as late as the close of the dynasty, a statue of Tuthmosis III now in the Cairo Museum (no. C. 42192) was reinscribed for Psusennes II. At Thebes, the High Priests of Amun were equally unprincipled in carving their names on earlier work of the New Kingdom. The little original building that they had the resources to undertake was a continuation of the predominant style of the Ramessides at Thebes, and they contributed nothing of their own.

CHAPTER FOURTEEN

The Libyan Period
Dynasties XXII–XXIV

Sesonchis I – *great revival in arts*

The decline in pharaonic standards during the first millennium BC was arrested and even reversed with the accession of the energetic Great Chief of the Ma, Shoshenq, who as Sesonchis I became the inaugurator of a new Libyan dynasty. During the first century of this Twenty-second Dynasty, a great revival took place in the arts. Ambitious building schemes were promoted at Thebes, Tanis, Bubastis and Memphis, demanding their proper complement of reliefs, statues and equipment. Although a certain number of earlier works were still usurped during their dynasty, original statues were also created, particularly in metal.

Hollow cast statues, with an ash or clay core retained within, are known from the Eighteenth Dynasty, and may have been introduced in the late Twelfth Dynasty. In the tomb of Rekhmirē is a representation of the casting of the great bronze doors of the temple of Amun, in the reign of Tuthmosis III, proof that large-scale metal sculpture was well within the competence of the Egyptian craftsman. It was, however, especially vulnerable to the plunderer's melting-pot, and little has been recovered from earlier ages. The comparative wealth of examples that has survived from the Libyan Period must be regarded as largely owing to chance, but there can be little doubt that a great stimulus was now given to the work of the modeller and the bronze founder.

The most opulent of these sculptures, though on a small scale, are the gold Amun in New York (MMA no. 26.7.1412), and the gold and lapis lazuli Osirian triad of Osorkon II in the Louvre. Both pieces exhibit the characteristics of much of the art of the time, combining a return to the style of the great days of the New Kingdom, in this case the reign of Tuthmosis III, with certain contemporary features such as the perforated ear-lobe. There is, however, an original contribution of the Libyan Age in the emphasis upon elegance, achieved by the rather elongated proportions, the slim waists, the slender limbs and the meticulous finish. The tendency to produce a tripartite treatment of the torso, with the chest, rib cage and abdomen as separate elements, is an innovation of the time and becomes progressively more evident in the modelling of metal sculpture as the age advances. It also influences stone statuary, and an oscillation between a bipartite and a tripartite configuration of the torso is a characteristic of Late Period styles.

The earlier statuette of Osorkon I in Brooklyn (no. 57.92B) reveals a notable feature of these Libyan bronzes in the enrichment of the surface with gold, copper and silver inlays. The black bronze of the body of this particular statue acts as a foil for the gold damascening and recalls the earlier niello-work of the Aegean area. But the designs of these Libyan pieces are essentially Egyptian. The craftsmanship maintains a consistently high level throughout the period, as may be seen in the torso of Pedubast I in the Gulbenkian Museum at Lisbon (no. 52), with its gold and copper inlays, and in the elaborate designs on the gown worn by Takush.

cf. 131

169

This latter statue is on a larger scale, and the bold and sensuous modelling of the somewhat heavy forms and fleshy face makes it an early example of the impressive style of the Kushites, just then bursting upon the world in which Takush lived. The garment she wears is inlaid with silver, representing embroidered designs of gods and sacred emblems. Apart from the loss of the inlaid eyes and eyebrows, and her priestly emblems, the statue is unusually complete. It probably came from the Delta, and represents the best work of the

cf. 183

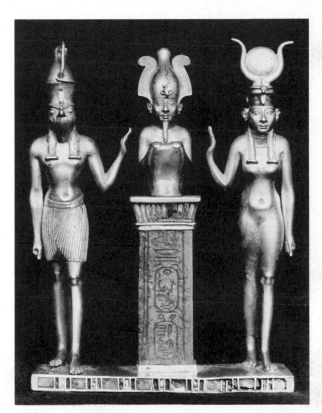

168 Gold and lapis lazuli pendant of the Abydene triad, Horus, Osiris and Isis, inscribed with the names of King Osorkon II, *c.* 890 BC.

Tripartite treatment

Lower Egyptian school of metal sculptors, almost certainly still working there under royal patronage at Memphis.

An example in the different traditions of Upper Egypt, is the nearly contemporary statue of the Divine Consort of Amun Karomama, from her chapel at Karnak, the *chef d'œuvre* among this group of bronzes, and indeed one of the supreme masterpieces of Egyptian art. It shows the granddaughter of Osorkon I, about a third life-size, in her sacerdotal capacity, holding what were doubtless two sistra, now missing. Her gown is also embroidered with a design, less elaborate than that of Takush, and represented by a damascening of gold, silver and electrum. She wears a robe patterned with a feather design, and a floral collar; but most of the inlays are missing from the lower part of the figure, and only traces remain of goldleaf on the face and arms. The delicate features, at once youthful and introspective, and the slender limbs are in the idealistic style of the period, made under the inspiration of early Tuthmoside models, and expressing the

169   Bronze statue of Takush, inlaid with designs in silver, from near Sebennytos, *c.* 730 BC.

170   Bronze statue of the Divine Consort Karomama, inlaid with gold, electrum and silver, from Karnak, *c.* 870 BC.

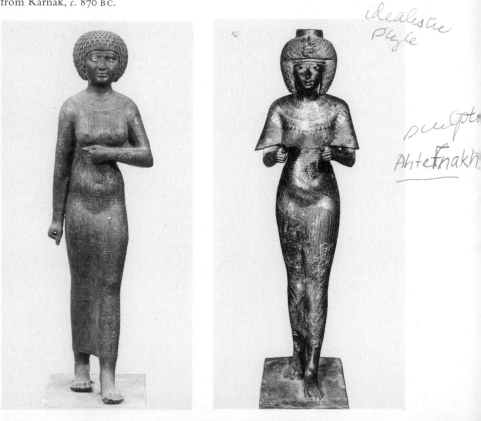

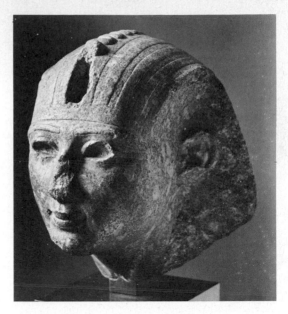

171　Grey granite head of a statue of
King Osorkon II, from Tanis, *c.* 890 BC.

perfection of feminine grace in the Egyptian fashion. By a happy
chance, the name of the sculptor who made this piece has survived.
He was an official of Karomama, called Ahtefnakht, and his name
should be honoured among the great craftsmen of antiquity.

Sesonchis I, and some of his successors, erected buildings at Thebes,
notably a great portal leading to the colonnaded court which was
planned in front of the Second Pylon at Karnak but never completed. *Reliefs*
The adjacent west wall of the southern tower of this pylon is
embellished with an unfinished scene of the campaign that Sesonchis
waged in Palestine, when the temple of Solomon was plundered. The
reliefs are carefully drawn and carved, with figures of Amun
presenting the sword of victory, and leading captured Palestinian
towns in chains, while Sesonchis, whose figure has not been
completed, would have been holding a batch of kneeling Semites by
the hair and raising his club to dispatch them. The design is purely
symbolic in the manner of Old Kingdom representations, such as that
of Phiops II, of the pharaoh prevailing over foes in the presence of the
god. Any attempt to present a graphic account of the campaign, as
depicted in the adjacent reliefs of Ramesses II, is avoided. Nevertheless
the Ramesside scenes have been the main source of inspiration for the
style, if not the iconography, of the reliefs of Sesonchis.

Although reference is made in the text on the Bubastite Portal to
the statues that were to stand in the colonnades of the court, nothing

Oso

of them now exists. Most of the kings of the dynasty, in fact, seem to have been content to usurp the monuments of earlier kings. With the advent of Osorkon II, *c.* 870 BC, however, a new vigour is apparent in all the sculptural arts. This king raised buildings at Tanis, Bubastis, Memphis, Karnak and elsewhere in Egypt. For these edifices statues must have been commissioned, but only from the temple at Tanis has any testimony survived of the style and craftsmanship of the new works of the reign. The earliest, and in many respects the most impressive of the statues of Libyan kings is the life-sized granite statue of Osorkon II, kneeling to present a stela inscribed with a petition to the gods of Tanis.

171

The statue is in a regrettably damaged state, the head being in Philadelphia while the rest is in Cairo; but the quality of the craftsmanship, the large size and the eager athletic posture, are at once apparent. It is clear that this piece revives the best traditions of the sculptors of the Tuthmoside Period, who had also provided a point of departure for early Ramesside sculptors. It is perhaps significant that before it was correctly identified by Bernard Bothmer, the isolated head was dated to the reign of Hatshepsut. The intractable stone, full of large quartz inclusions, has been handled with complete mastery. Bothmer, who from inscriptional evidence dates the statue to the first years of the reign, postulates that 'shortly after the coronation of Osorkon II, a great effort was made to create for him a monument of truly regal splendour.' Once more it is apparent that under vigorous and generous patronage, the Egyptian sculptor could return to the style of an earlier age with complete sympathy, and yet infuse it with something of his own sensibility.

172

This recall of the great traditions of the past is also seen in the broken limestone statue of Osorkon III launching a sacred boat, excavated at Karnak. The softer stone has allowed full scope to the sculptor to produce a piece of such elegance that were it not for the inscription, it would probably have been placed among the prostrating statues of the Tuthmoside Period. Even in such details as the design of the belt, the uraeus and ear-lobes, it follows a mid-Eighteenth Dynasty prototype, and gives rise to the unworthy suspicion that it may have been usurped.

The reliefs that were carved on the gateway to the great festival hall that was added to the temple at Bubastis for the jubilee of Osorkon II, reflect the energy and enterprise of the king. His artists, however, were trammelled by the subject-matter, which was strictly determined by an age-old and esoteric iconography. But even more of a restraint was the crystalline nature of the red granite in which these sunk reliefs are carved, and which made it difficult for the

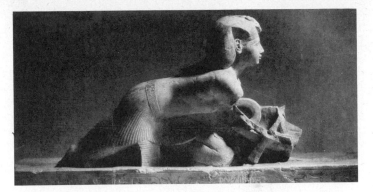

172   Limestone statue-fragment of King Osorkon III launching a model boat of the god Sokar, from Karnak, *c.* 790 BC.

sculptors to achieve any subtlety in the modelling, or sensitivity in the cutting of the contours. Perhaps this accounts for the uncertain drawing of the large-scale figures of the king and his chief wife, and the somewhat mediocre quality of the work.

While sculptures of the Libyan kings are rare and fragmentary, an unrivalled series of hard-stone statues of their children and near relatives, and their Upper Egyptian officials, has been recovered from Thebes. These private statues, in their superb craftsmanship and restrained treatment, are technically and artistically finer than anything produced during the New Kingdom after the Eighteenth Dynasty. They show a transition from the Tuthmoside style, which is their starting-point, to the more austere tradition to which the Kushites fell heir. In fact, the immediate and complete emergence of the fine monuments of the Twenty-fifth Dynasty must be attributed to the existence in Thebes of a flourishing school of sculptors well versed in the art of carving and inscribing statues in granite and other hard stones.

Most of these statues, which were votives in the Great Temple of Amun at Karnak, are of the squatting block-type which gave little opportunity for introducing bold innovations. They did, however, allow the sculptor scope for some modest variations upon the basic classical form, and they encouraged him to concentrate his powers on the precise cutting of the details and the inscriptions, and on the careful polishing of the surfaces. A representative example is the statue of the king's letter-writer, Hor, dated to the reign of Pedubast I *173* (fl. *c.* 800 BC). To the greatly stylized body of the owner, squatting with arms folded and elbows on drawn-up knees beneath his cloak,

211

has been added a head, carefully worked as an idealized portrait and probably bearing little resemblance to his true appearance. The inscriptions, with the opposed figures of Mentu and Osiris, are elegantly arranged and brilliantly cut.

175   The granite statue of the Lady Shebensopdu, the daughter of the High Priest, Namlot, and the granddaughter of Osorkon II, is a rare example of a seated statue of the time, and must be regarded as an equivalent of the stone statuary of the contemporary royal ladies in the absence of any representations of the Libyan queens. The engraving of figures of deities on the surfaces of the garment recalls the inlays in the metal sculptures of Takush and Karomama; but the formal pose, with one hand flat on the thigh and the other holding a lotus bud, and the long traditional tripartite wig, a little at variance with the flaring sleeves of the gown, give a much more monumental repose to this large votive piece.

In Lower Egypt a similar return to the artistic ideals of the part is also apparent in a number of contemporary pieces, but in the Memphite region there was a greater range of examples to inspire the artists. The great bronze statue of Pashasu in the Louvre (no. E. 7693), for instance, probably came from the casting shops at Memphis, and seems to have been produced under the influence of wooden archetypes with inlaid eyes dating to the Old Kingdom. When complete this statue would doubtless have shown the owner carrying a baton in his left hand and a long staff in his right. The close-fitting wig and the *shendyt* kilt and bare feet, comprise a dress long out of fashion in Libyan times; what is significant is the conscious attempt to revive a very ancient style, a notable example of that antiquarianism which is such a marked feature of the ensuing periods.

174   A transitional piece, showing an eclectic treatment of a traditional subject, is a faience panel carved in shallow low relief from a shrine dedicated at Thebes by the Delta kinglet Yewepet II, who held office as a vassal of the Kushite king, Pi[ankh]y, between 728 and 716 BC. The features of Yewepet are cast in the Nubian mould of his overlord, and he also wears the close-fitting cap, sewn with roundels, that was particularly favoured by the Kushite kings. But the style of dress, with the single knotted shoulder strap and the apron hanging from the belt, recalls the archaic garb of the kings of the Third Dynasty. Only the tripartite arrangement of the torso, with the kilt shortened and the belt set low to expose the navel, distinguishes the form of the figure from that of the early Old Kingdom. While, therefore, the designer of this panel has paid due deference to the fashion of portraiture and headgear preferred by the Kushite overlords, he has not abandoned his Memphite heritage in the process.

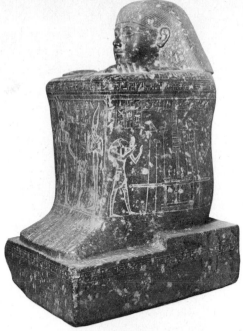

173 Grey granite block-statue of Hor, the front incised with figures of the gods Mentu and Osiris before an altar, from Karnak, *c.* 810 B C.

174 Faience plaque of King Yewepet II, from Thebes, *c.* 735 B C.

175 Granite statue of Shebensopdu, holding a lotus bud, her gown incised with figures of Osiris, Isis and Nephthys, from Karnak, *c.* 810 B C.

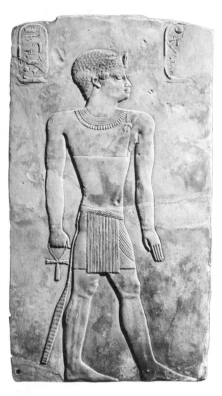

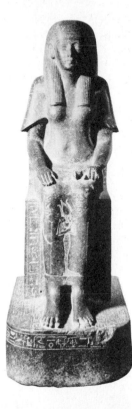

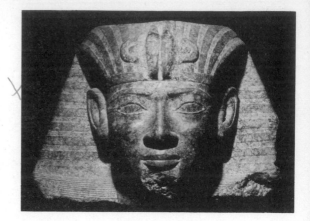

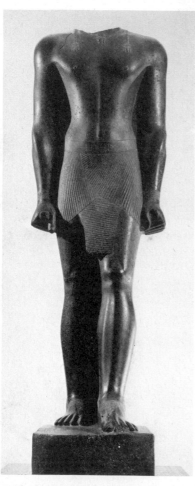

176   Granite head from a colossus of
King Shabaka, wearing the Double
Crown and two uraei (later re-cut), from
Karnak, *c.* 710 BC.

177   Black basalt headless statue of King
Tanutamun, from Gebel Barkal,
c. 660 BC.

178   Black granite head from a statue of
King Taharqa, from Karnak(?), *c.* 690 BC.

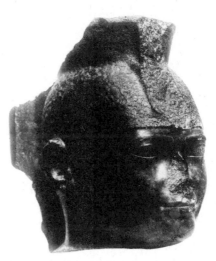

CHAPTER FIFTEEN

The Kushite Period

Dynasty XXV

Whether the Kushite kings of Nubia and the Lower Sudan, who form the Twenty-fifth Dynasty in Egypt, intervened of their own accord in the affairs of their great northern neighbour, or were invited to do so by the ruling faction at Thebes, tired of dynastic squabbles that particularly injured their interests, is now obscure. What is clear is that they were welcomed in Upper Egypt, and secured, by force of arms where necessary, the loyalty of Lower Egyptian princes as their vassals. They brought order and stability to a divided realm. A deep veneration for tradition was inherent in their religious outlook, and research was undertaken into ancient and sacred literature.

It is not surprising, therefore, that under their patronage the arts should have made a conscious return to the great examples of the past, particularly to those of the Theban Middle Kingdom. They thus accelerated the impact of ideas that were already abroad in the Libyan Period, but with their ambitious building schemes, and a programme of rehabilitation, they greatly increased the extent of such influences.

Thebes, as the great centre of Amun worship in Egypt, received the lion's share of donations from the Amun-worshipping Kushites. A new form of government, already in embryo in Libyan times, if not earlier, was introduced there. The secular and political power of the High Priest of Amun, the virtual ruler of Upper Egypt, was curbed by the divine marriage to the god of a princess endowed with great estates. This Divine Consort, a kind of Vestal Virgin, established a theocratic form of government in which her successor was adopted in turn from the daughters of the royal house. The Divine Consorts were assisted in their secular duties by major-domos appointed by the oracle of Amun. The political power thus remained in the hands of the pharaoh, his children filling high offices in the priesthood of Amun.

Under these new patrons, the pharaohs themselves, the Divine Consorts of Amun, and their officials, a great surge of activity is apparent in the arts, particularly in statuary, which is their only memorial to survive, now that their buildings have been largely destroyed. In general, two styles are dominant. There is firstly the continuation of the austere official mode which we have identified in the block statues and other monuments of the Theban area during the

Libyan dynasties. Besides works in this style, however, there exists more sombre and vigorous statuary which delineates with a searching realism the characteristic ethnic features and physiques of the more negroid Kushites.

To the first group belongs the upper part of a pink granite colossus 176 of Shabaka from Karnak. This work has been produced very much under the inspiration of the Middle Kingdom style of the colossal hard-stone statues of Sesostris I from the same site. There are, however, individual traits that could belong only to the Twenty-fifth Dynasty, such as the flat strap-like appliqués of the eyebrows, the broad cheeks, and the barely perceptible 'Kushite fold', which is the furrow of flesh that runs from the wings of the nose towards the corners of the mouth, and which always tends to be emphasized in Egyptian representations of Nubians. There is also the double uraeus, for which the Kushite kings showed a distinct preference, but in this case it has been altered to make it suitable for plastering into a single uraeus by the later pharaoh (probably Psammetichus II) who usurped the statue.

Another outstanding work in this genre is the headless statue of 177 Tanutamun from Gebel Barkal, which displays an emphatic bipartite treatment of the torso. The restrained but tensed musculature is in a classic tradition. There are, however, other headless, seated and standing statues, of Shabataka from Memphis and Taharqa from Karnak, which reveal in their fine craftsmanship and finish all the features of the early Twelfth Dynasty style, including, in one example, the slight slope in the upper surface of the block throne.

The more realistic portraiture of the second group is well 178 represented in the head of Taharqa from Karnak. This masterpiece infuses the classic style of the first group with an impressive representation of the Kushite physiognomy, emphasizing the broad round face, thick lips, horizontal eyebrows and folds of flesh at the corners of eyes and nose. If such works were produced under the inspiration of admired archetypes, it is perhaps in the distinctive portraits of the late rather than the earlier Twelfth Dynasty that their models must be sought. But they lack the withdrawn and brooding air of the hard-stone sculptures of Sesostris III and Ammenemes III. The expression is, by contrast, extroverted, even genial.

Statues of queens are unknown during this dynasty and their equivalents are to be found in the statues of the royal daughters who were adopted by their predecessors as human consorts of the god Amun of Thebes. A number of representations have happily survived, the most celebrated of which is the alabaster standing statue 179 of Amenirdis I from Karnak. This is a work in the idealizing style, the

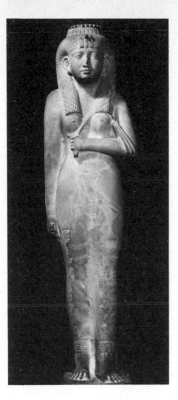

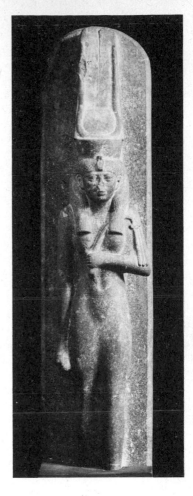

179　Alabaster statue of the Divine Consort
Amenirdis I, sister of King Shabaka, from the chapel
of Osiris Nebankh at north Karnak, *c.* 710 BC.

180　Granite statue of Amenirdas I dedicated by the
Divine Consort Shepenwepet II, from Luxor
(probably originally from Karnak), *c.* 665 BC.

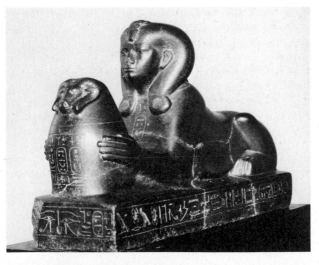

181　Black granite sphinx
of the Divine Consort
Shepenwepet II offering a
ram-headed vase, found in
the Sacred Lake at Karnak,
c. 665 BC.

cf. 169 broad features and plumpness of the Nubian female form being rendered with the utmost discretion in a semi-translucent stone that is apt to soften details and flatten the modelling. Nevertheless, the Kushite fold is apparent at the wings of the nose, and the details of dress, jewellery and coiffure have been meticulously rendered.

180 The posthumous granite statue consecrated to Amenirdis by her successor Shepenwepet is more realistic in its portraiture, and with the better proportions given to it by its tall crown, and the superior modelling of the body, is a much more appealing work of art. The 181 Berlin sphinx of Shepenwepet II, presenting a ram-headed vase of Amun, has been inspired by Middle Kingdom sphinxes of queens wearing the bouffant wig of Hathor; and the portraiture is in the same realistic mode, though lacking the Middle Kingdom serenity.

Statuettes of the Divine Consorts exist in bronze, stone and ivory. The most remarkable is a faience statuette in Cairo (no. C. 42199), unfortunately greatly damaged, showing Amenirdis I seated in the lap of the enthroned Amun, fervently clasped in a mutual embrace, a three-dimensional version of a design which also exists in relief.

The private statuary of the Kushite Dynasty comes almost exclusively from the great cache excavated in the court north of the Seventh Pylon at Karnak during the early years of this century. In its careful workmanship and fine finish it shows a development of the Theban official style of the Libyan dynasties but it is more adventurous in its choice of forms. It tends, for instance, to give its preference to the standing or kneeling statue as a votive piece. Where it adopts the form of the block statue for this purpose, it usually selects a pattern inspired by Eighteenth Dynasty examples, with exposed feet, hands grasping emblems, a curled wig of the kind fashionable in the reigns of Amenophis II to Amenophis III and the contours of the body revealed beneath the tightly wrapped cloak. For such models there must have been still many examples in the precincts of the temples of Thebes at this time. One of the most impressive of such statues, however, now in the Brooklyn Museum, comes from a Delta 182 site. It represents the official, Pedimahes, squatting with arms akimbo, his body closely swathed in his cloak but leaving his hands and feet free. The forms are more broadly modelled than those of the contemporary Theban block statues, and lack their fine, hard detail; but there is a rare sculptural cohesion between the various masses of the clothed body and the head with its large wig, summarily indicated. Attention is focused upon the features which are alert beneath their contemplative calm.

The contemporary standing statues of the Theban grandees, some of whom were near relatives of the Kushite kings, revert to the style of

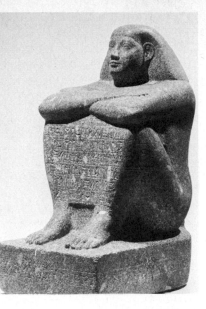

182　Granite squatting statue of the temple scribe Pedimahes from Tel el-Moqdam, *c.* 670 BC.

the royal statues of the early Twelfth Dynasty, themselves made under the inspiration of the Fourth Dynasty. With their broad-shouldered torsos, narrow waists, and legs braced in a muscular tension, they represent the ideal of male physical beauty from the days of the Old Kingdom; but the immediate comparison they invite is with statues of Sesostris I at Karnak. The influence of royal models is seen in the choice of the pleated *shendyt* kilt with its pendent codpiece, a distinctive kingly garment, and the carving of the name of the owner on the belt. The pose of the hands, too, grasping the rolled-up cylinder of cloth, is very seldom found in private statuary after the Old Kingdom.

cf. 35

cf. 36

The heads of such statues are shown shaven, or with a close-fitting tonsure, perhaps recalling late Middle Kingdom models, which also arrogated the *shendyt* kilt; but the features are cast in the contemporary idealizing mode, giving a modified portrait of the negroid physiognomy, with its broad cheeks, thick everted lips and flaring nostrils. These statues are carved in hard, intractable stones, quartzites, granites and basalts; some of them are finished with a fine polish.

By contrast, the grey granite statue of Iriketakana, who claimed to be a relation of a king, is in the more realistic and even brutal style of the dynasty. The grossly corpulent body, half concealed beneath a long gown, is far removed from the heroic ideal, though the pose is similar. The rendering of bulging masses of the body is repeated in the

183

219

broad treatment of the fleshy face. Fat men have not often stimulated the talents of the artist, but Iriketakana was fortunate in finding a sculptor of genius, and in inspiring him with the aim of producing a complete realization of his physical presence in a rare formal unity.

The great patron of artists during this period, however, was Mentuemhet, the most influential of the High Stewards of the Divine Consorts who have left extensive evidence of their activities at Thebes. An antiquarian and a sensitive connoisseur of the art of the past, Mentuemhet was able to commission artists to produce work in the style of all ages; but in statuary, he particularly favoured examples of Eighteenth Dynasty date. About a dozen statues of him in various poses, materials and fashions of dress testify to his eclectic tastes. One

184 of the most complete is the standing grey granite statue from Karnak, showing him almost life-size in the heroic, 'royal' pose of the time, with its powerful physique, *shendyt* kilt and inscribed belt; only the wig departs from the norm in copying a pattern popular in the mid-

183   Grey granite statue of Iriketakana, from Karnak, *c.* 670 BC.

184   Grey granite statue of Mentuemhet, from Karnak, *c.* 660 BC.

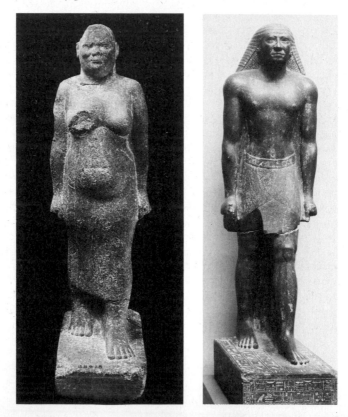

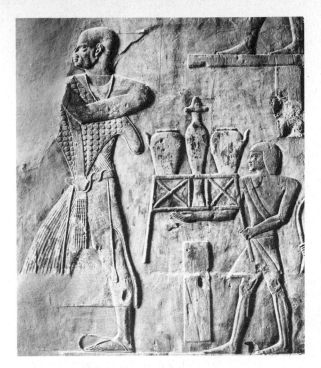

185   Limestone relief fragment
of Mentuemhet as a fourth
prophet of Amun with an
offering-bearer, from his tomb
at Western Thebes (no. 34),
c. 650 BC.

Eighteenth Dynasty. The face, with its distinctive traits, is rendered
with a masterly realism, its lines and furrows giving a resolute
expression to the owner who had the daunting tasks of clearing up
Thebes after its sack by the Assyrians, and coping with the pretensions
of the new Saite pharaoh in the North. The individual character of
this careful rendering must surely be the most authentic portrait of the
great man that has come down to us.

The statue of Mentuemhet in East Berlin (no. 17271), showing him
seated, wrapped in a long cloak, revives the official style of the early
Tuthmoside Period, though again with the later fashion of wig; but   *cf. 120*
the portrait is in an idealistic vein, giving a total impression of being a
conscious essay to recall the work of a particularly cherished past.

A similar antiquarianism with idealistic features, in an apparent
attempt not only to recall the past but to improve upon it, is seen in
the reliefs with which Mentuemhet and his contemporaries decorated
their vast tombs at Thebes. From the end of the Eighteenth Dynasty
private tombs had declined in size and quality and had virtually
disappeared in Ramesside times, being replaced by family burial
places. During the Twenty-fifth Dynasty, however, the great officials
at Thebes resurrected the idea of large hypogea, the walls carved with

221

raised reliefs in the best traditions of the past, just as their kings revived the pyramid for the design of their tombs at Kurru, near Gebel Barkal in the Sudan. Taharqa in 680 BC at Kawa in Nubia even made replicas of the reliefs of Sahurē and Phiops II referred to above (see Chapter Six). Fine raised relief in sandstone had been used for the decoration of the chapels of the Divine Consorts at Medinet Habu, where the near-by temple of Tuthmosis III and Hatshepsut, which was extended by Shabaka and Taharqa, doubtless provided the inspiration for figures of classic proportions and purity of line.

Most of these great Kushite and Saite tombs are in a very ruinous condition, however, and the decoration is largely concerned with funerary and religious texts. Offering scenes were evidently inspired cf. 111 by Hatshepsut's reliefs at Deir el-Bahri. Mentuemhet was influenced cf. 133, 134 principally by reliefs in the tombs of the reign of Amenophis III, though essays in the style of the Old Kingdom and the early Middle Kingdom were also attempted. It is clear that the monuments of the past were carefully studied for extracts that appealed to these students of antiquity. Their artists, however, did not copy them slavishly, but reinterpreted them, often in the idiom of their own time. Thus Ibi, an official of one of the Divine Consorts of the next dynasty, copied the Old Kingdom reliefs and inscriptions in the tomb of his namesake at Deir el-Gabrawi, over 200 miles to the north; but while he made use of the iconography of the earlier tomb in the grouping of figures and the choice of subject-matter, he introduced the different canon of proportions that prevailed in his own day, and certain contemporary fashions.

Mentuemhet's designer must have copied some of the minor details from the Eighteenth Dynasty tomb of Menna, doubtless at his patron's behest, which have also appealed to modern connoisseurs of 186 Egyptian art and life. Thus the fragment in Brooklyn copies two vignettes, in which a gleaner removes a thorn from her companion's foot, and a peasant woman nurses her child beneath a carob tree. That these were copied from the actual tomb of Menna admits of little doubt, for an infelicity in the drawing of the woman's lower legs has been reinterpreted here to show them as though crossed over each other at the ankles. The trees, too, have been rearranged and the pods removed from the branches of the carob. In contrast to the sketchy, fluid line of the original painting, Mentuemhet's relief is hard and precise in its contours, with fine crisp detail, in the manner of early Eleventh Dynasty reliefs. What is also original is the fantasticated furniture of wholly imaginary design, with elegantly turned legs incorporating floral motifs. These capriccios become more prominent in subsidiary parts of the design with such motifs as the

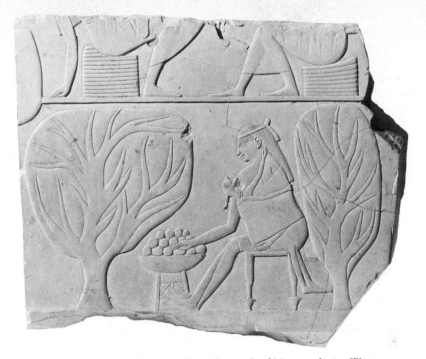

186 Limestone relief fragment from the tomb of Mentuemhet at Western
Thebes (no. 34), *c.* 650 BC.

slender, timidly stepping gazelle with a lotus flower dangling from its
mouth, or the crane or other shapely bird, with a similar flower on a
stalk hanging from its beak, and the great bouquets of 'artistically'
arranged flower and leaf.

Other reliefs from the tomb show a slightly different emphasis,
with the features of Mentuemhet realistically portrayed. Yet the
eclectic nature of the designs is equally apparent, such as the Old
Kingdom fashion of dress of the attendant, with his bandoleer and the
wide stripe to the pannier of his kilt. The disproportionate tray that
he carries, however, with its over-size vessels, is of New Kingdom
pattern. Similarly, for all the brutal realism of Mentuemhet's
physiognomy, his figure is elegantly elongated, and while his priestly
robe and apron have been stylized to formal patterns, his sandals have
a florid character with their long upcurving points, and a tasselled
cord is foppishly twined in his belt. Here the antiquarian recall of the
past is meant to appeal to other cognoscenti, and to make it part of a
new fashion.

185

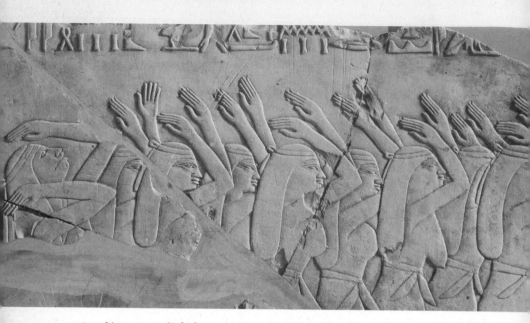

187   Limestone relief of mourning women from the tomb of the vizier Nespekashuti at Western Thebes (no. 312), *c.* 610 BC.

cf. 43

187
cf. 134

The greatly ravaged tomb of the almost contemporary vizier Nespekashuti was usurped from an Eleventh Dynasty official at Deir el-Bahri. For its new purpose, it was relined with fine limestone, though the decoration was never completed. The designer was greatly influenced by the reliefs in the nearby temple of Hatshepsut, even plagiarizing the queen's offering-lists for the benefit of the vizier. Some Old Kingdom scenes, such as the procession of estates, were also incorporated. The Voyage to Abydos, however, is in the style of the early New Kingdom, and scenes of mourning take their inspiration from later reliefs of the Eighteenth Dynasty. In all such scenes, the intention is to recall the glorious achievements of the past without any deep commitment to their meaning. The mourning women are reduced to a pattern of heads, coiffures, breasts and girdle-ties, beneath an arabesque flutter of hands pouring invisible dust over the hair. Any expression of grief is lacking, though the recollection of the *pompes funèbres* of a golden past is there for the connoisseur to appreciate. The spectator is now in a region where mannerism is beginning to dominate the representation of forms and to vitiate their meaning.

224

CHAPTER SIXTEEN

The Saite Period
Dynasty XXVI

The princes of Sais, who as vassals of Assyria had rallied Lower Egypt against their Kushite rivals, went on to become the pharaohs of an independent and prosperous Egypt, which they ruled as powerful merchant princes, having command of a large *corps d'élite* of Carian, Ionian and Lydian mercenaries, and control of a strong fleet. They neutralized the influence of Thebes, as the capital of Upper Egypt, by having their daughters adopted as Consorts of Amun, and they gradually replaced the old officials in the government of the South with their own nominees. In the reign of Psammetichus II, hostility against the Kushite power became more active with the dispatch of a punitive expedition into Nubia and the Lower Sudan. Thereafter names of the Kushite pharaohs were excised from the monuments.

Even before this, however, the Saites had shown their execration of all things Kushite by carefully stressing their own Lower Egyptian character. They wore for preference the Blue Crown, a form of headgear never assumed by the Kushite kings. They gradually relaxed the realistic representation of personal traits in their portraits. The portrait reliefs and statue-fragments accredited to Psammetichus I show a firm mouth, set in a grim line, but the later Saite kings adopt an idealized countenance, the features generally bland, the eyes set close together, the corners of the mouth lifted into a smile, presenting the portrait of the benevolent despot, who in the case of Amasis at least, did not disdain popular acclaim. Nevertheless, the populace turned their worship more to the local god, or to its tangible incarnation in animal form.

188
cf. 174, 178

188

The statues of Saite kings have survived only in fragments, and scarcely any of them have an undamaged inscription. The identification of various rulers has, therefore, been the concern of a few scholars working largely with the aid of a close stylistic analysis. A key piece in this research is a little schist head of Psammetichus II in the Jacquemart-André Museum, Paris (no. 438), which has an uncharacteristic melancholic expression, but which exhibits the traits of Saite portraiture in its formal stylization, technical mastery and high finish. It also reveals the peculiar details of the late version of the Blue Crown, with its flat tabs, curved parietal seams and a rolled border to the lower edge.

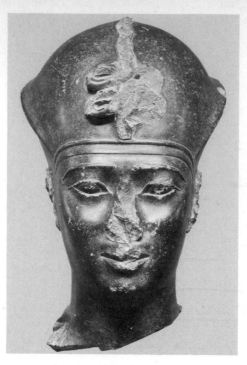

188 Black basalt head from a statue of King Apries wearing the later fashion of the Blue Crown, *c.* 580 B.C.

189 Green schist head from a statue of King Amasis, *c.* 560 B.C.

188

189

cf. 171

The successors of Psammetichus II introduced a uraeus with double S-coils behind the hood, as in the larger heads of Apries in the Louvre (no. E.3433) and Bologna. The latter example has part of the titulary visible on the back pillar and is the means of identifying portraits of this king. Other heads in Philadelphia (no. 14303), Cairo (no. J.53496), Berlin (*ill. 189*) and elsewhere, show a more pointed chin, and eyes set closer together, but with the same formally benign smile. These evidently represent Amasis, who dethroned Apries, and in whose long reign much rebuilding was undertaken. The head in Berlin has the same pattern of uraeus, but worn with the *nemes* wig-cover. Some other features of these heads of kings are the almost total disappearance of the cosmetic line at the outer corners of the eyes, and the absence of the royal beard even on statues of sphinxes.

The quality of these pieces is as faultless as the best of the Kushite royal sculptures, showing that the renaissance of standards achieved in the Twenty-fifth Dynasty was well maintained. The upper part of a quartzite prostrating statue of Amasis in Florence (no. 5625) is magnificently carved in the hard stone and recalls in its pose the Osorkon II of Cairo and Philadelphia, though it is of larger size and rather superior workmanship. The two large headless quartzite

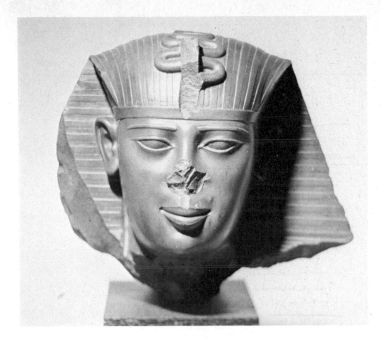

sphinxes of Apries in the museum at Alexandria (nos. 11218–9) are superb examples of Egyptian animal sculpture, lacking perhaps the tensed muscularity of the best earlier examples, but emphasizing the plastic qualities of the recumbent leonine bodies in repose.

It is reasonably certain that the casting of statues in metal was pursued with vigour during this century of prosperous activity; but all that has survived are votive statuettes of Necho II and Amasis and a small human-armed sphinx of Apries. The tradition of such sculpture is maintained until the end of dynastic Egypt, with statuettes of kneeling kings in London, Kansas City and elsewhere. By then, the mass production of votive statuettes of the gods was in full swing, and the art of casting metal sculptures on a small scale had been reduced to a mechanical exercise. Nevertheless, these are the antiquities that are now comprised in the term 'bronzes', and eagerly auctioned in the sale room.

Private statuary during the Twenty-sixth Dynasty continues the trends that were already prominent in Kushite times, but with an idealistic tradition steadily replacing work in a more realistic mode. The increasing importance and independence of the district officials is seen in the size of their statues. Some of these magnates even made

cf. 191

endowments to local cult centres, and accepted responsibility for building projects in temple precincts and for commissioning statues of deities. At the same time, foreign intervention and increasing contacts with peoples from the Eastern Mediterranean aroused in them a chauvinistic pride in their own past. The antiquarian study of the art of former periods, particularly that of the Old Kingdom, was pursued with even greater intensity as their cultural values were threatened by the new ideas of the Classical Age, now about to dawn in the Hellenic world.

This reverence for the past, and particularly the Lower Egyptian past, is seen in their restoration of ancient sites. The Step Pyramid complex at Saqqara received special attention, not so much as the tomb of a now legendary king, but as the monument of its architect Imhotep, the great hero of Egyptian culture who was shortly to be deified. Burial near the Step Pyramid was eagerly sought by the grandees of the time who demolished monuments of the Old Kingdom in order to sink their great pit tombs in the vicinity. The interior of the Step Pyramid was explored and consolidated, and selected reliefs were squared up for careful copying.

The Saite statues attempt to achieve in pose and expression that same withdrawn air of calm assurance that is seen in the statuary of the Old Kingdom and which was so lacking in the Egypt of their day, with the menace from Asia increasing year by year and the rule of the pharaoh precarious enough to be challenged by a rival. Whether the Saites showed the same preference for the painted limestone of their admired Old Kingdom models is unknown, as it is mostly sculpture in hard stones that has survived.

The statue of the vizier Nespekashuti as a squatting scribe, holding his papyrus roll open with two hands in order to read it, is a good example of the transitional style from Kushite realism to the softer, more impressionistic and more formalized manner of the Saite artists. The precisely cut contours and the bipartite treatment of the torso, defined by a channel running from the navel to the sternal notch, is in the Theban tradition of the Twenty-fifth Dynasty, but the incipient smile on the amiable features is a reflection of the 'Archaic smile' apparent in the portraits of contemporary pharaohs, and may have influenced sculptors from Archaic Greece, who doubtless were now exploring the monuments of Egypt from their base at Naukratis.

The temple statue showing the owner alone, participating in the cult by holding religious emblems, or a figure of the god, becomes more popular and elaborate. The large kneeling statue in black basalt of Wahibre, a great dignitary in the army and administration at this period, is a representative example of Saite art at its most official, with

228

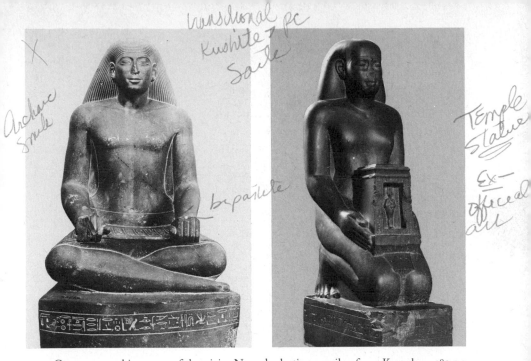

(handwritten annotations surrounding the images: "transitional pc Kushite → Saite" (top), "Archaic smile" (left), "bipartite" (centre), "Temple statue" and "Ex-officeal al" (right))

190 Grey-green schist statue of the vizier Nespekashuti as a scribe, from Karnak, *c.* 580 BC.

191 Black basalt kneeling statue of the district governor Wahibre presenting a statue of Osiris within an open shrine, from near Lake Marcotis, *c.* 550 BC.

the soft, impressionistic modelling of the masses of the body thrown into contrast with the sharp cubic forms of the shrine and the high podium. The kneeling pose with the owner sitting on his heels goes back to the earliest dynasties, but instead of having his hands clasped in supplication before him, or resting flat on his thighs in the manner of a contemporary official of Psammetichus II, whose large kneeling statue is in the Louvre (no. A.94), Wahibre presents the figure of Osiris in an open tabernacle. Such a composition was used from time to time for essentially dedicatory statues in the New Kingdom, as for example in the case of Senenmut of the Eighteenth and Yuni in the Nineteenth Dynasty; but in this statue of Wahibre, the recall of the remote past is seen in the choice of the royal *shendyt* kilt and in the absence of any jewels or insignia on the person. Only the bag-wig of the Saite Age is in the contemporary fashion.

The Egyptian sculptor periodically turned his attention to carving large statues of the animals which figured in his religious mythology. Impressive examples of guardian lions and sphinxes, rams,

cf. also 65

(handwritten note at bottom: "Archaic Smile = Inner satisfaction with life - beginning of Roman art")

hippopotami, vultures and falcons were produced at various periods. Late in the reign of Amasis, the high official Psamtek commissioned a statue of the goddess Hathor in her manifestation as a wild cow, protecting his own dedicatory figure. The composition was traditional, but the most famous example to have survived, the Hathor cow from Deir el-Bahri emerging from the primeval thicket, guards the figure of a king. Indeed, the Great Sphinx of Giza, and the crio-sphinxes at Karnak, Kawa and Sulb, had also taken the standing figure of a king under their protection. It is an eloquent comment on the Saite Period that the donor should now be a private courtier and Hathor should no longer protect her child, the pharaoh.

This monumental piece is in an almost perfect state of preservation and reflects the work of the idealistic school of the dynasty. An innovation is the re-emergence of the tripartite modelling of the torso, the muscles of the rib-cage below the breasts now being accentuated with the reduction of the vertical medial channel to a pear-shaped bulge surrounding the navel. A novel feature of the plastically modelled animal, which differentiates it from its prototype at Deir el-Bahri, is the sculptor's repudiation of the Egyptian concept of negative space. Four legs in a walking pose are shown on each side of the massive infill, two are three-quarters in the round, and two in raised relief. The udder, however, is seen only on the right side, the principal aspect, being obscured by the advanced rear leg on the opposite side.

Where this departure from tradition arose, it is not yet possible to say; but it may well be that it was brought from Assyria by Egyptian craftsmen commissioned to work on the palace reliefs of Assyrian kings. The Egyptian stonemasons were the most experienced and skilful in the Near East and were later employed by the Persian Achaemenides on their constructions at Persepolis. It is well within the bounds of possibility that they had earlier worked for other great kings elsewhere; the practice is at least as old as the Amarna Period, when the King of Babylon asked the pharaoh to commission craftsmen to produce objects for him in chryselephantine work.

The solution that Psamtek's sculptor offered to the problem of negative space, by his arrangement of the legs of the Hathor cow, appears to have been an aberration rather than part of a continuing tradition. A fragment of a similar group in the Cairo Museum (no. C.676) is of contemporary date and probably from the same studio: nevertheless a large limestone statue of an Apis bull in the Louvre, from the Serapeum, was carved about two centuries later in the Thirtieth Dynasty, and reverts to the form of the Deir el-Bahri cow, with two legs seen on each side of the massive infill.

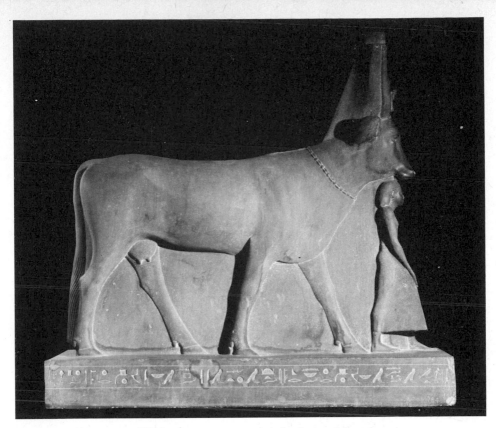

192   Grey schist statue of Hathor as a cow protecting the figure of the palace
official Psamtek, from Saqqara, *c.* 530 BC.

Seated statues of Isis and Osiris in the Cairo Museum (nos. C.38358,
38884), also dedicated by Psamtek and found with the Hathor cow,
are other classic pieces, preterhumanly perfect in their proportions
and finish, as befits images of the gods, and probably giving a
contemporary version of famous statues of the pair in one of their
great temples. But today the very perfection of the work, and the
sweetness of expression, cloy and discourage a sustained con-
templation, which, however, to the true believer must have had its
rewards. The subtlety of the modelling is only appreciated by long
inspection in the right lighting. It is then seen that the Saite ideal was
to achieve an art which in its excellence, secured by the highest
technical standards, would express that perfection and permanence
which men in the past had striven to attain, but which was singularly
lacking in the world of the sixth century BC.

231

193 Grey-green schist fragment of the statue of an official, from Memphis(?), c. 450 BC.

In Louvre

5th cent
B.C.

① Faithful rendering of the
   seamed & careworn face

② Its folds of flesh contrasting w/ the
   smoother, more idealistic rendering
   of the body.

CHAPTER SEVENTEEN

The Late Period
Dynasties XXVII–XXX

The conquest of Egypt by Persia in the reign of Psammetichus III brought entirely new factors into play. The Achaemenide kings came to stay as pharaohs: they organized their rich province under their satraps and collaborators with an efficiency that in due course their Greek and Roman successors could only copy. They opened the land to other peoples of their empire, to Persians, Greeks, Jews and Phoenicians. In the face of this foreign dominance, the Egyptians more than ever turned to the virtues they had learnt in recent centuries, of cultivating their past, resisting their conquerors with a xenophobic zeal and rising against them under native princes whenever an opportunity presented itself.

In the sphere of art, the antiquarian return to the great styles of the past was pursued with renewed fervour; and now added to the repertoire of acceptable forms was the art of the Saite Period itself, seen in retrospect as a Golden Age when Egyptian culture flourished under native kings before the Persian deluge.

The mental anguish of these times, particularly among the educated classes, had its effect upon the art of the period in several ways. Persian dress, particularly the long-sleeved gown, was sometimes worn by the collaborating high state officials. The melancholic introspection, already apparent in Saite times, became more pronounced in the resigned expressions with which the faces of the statues of this time gaze out into their troubled world. It was a period when the idea was steadily gaining ground that material success was wholly dependent upon virtuous conduct; and the portrait of the owner could, therefore, express that inner spiritual grace which had secured him high office and material rewards, such as the privilege of erecting a statue of himself in sacred precincts. Statues showing the owner in communion with his god by means of an image of the deity, or its symbol, increase in number. In a few rare cases, the sympathy can be expressed by an ecstatic pose, the face raised in the holy presence.

The upper part of a green schist statue of an unknown man in the *193* Louvre is one of the great portrait studies of the fifth century BC, remarkable for its faithful rendering of the seamed and careworn face, its folds of flesh contrasting with the smoother, more idealistic

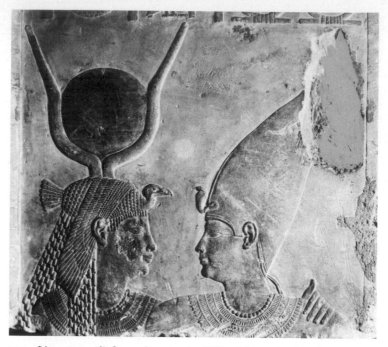

194 Limestone relief on a door-jamb of King Nectanebo II embraced by Isis, from the Serapeum at Saqqara, *c.* 350 BC.

cf. Berlin no.
12500

rendering of the body. Whether the famous Berlin head is also of this same period or of Ptolemaic date, must in the present state of our knowledge remain a matter of opinion. The idiosyncratic features of the Louvre head suggest that it is another example of what Bernard Bothmer has defined as true portraiture in the art of antiquity as distinct from 'schematic realism'. Such portraiture, with its searching delineation of the bony structure of the head beneath the flesh, now emerges in isolated examples from reign to reign during the Late Period, and is the chief glory it has bequeathed to posterity.

The resistance to their Persian overlords eventually won a brief century of independence for the Egyptians under the leadership of princes of Mendes and Sebennytos. These men ruled as pharaohs during the Twenty-ninth and Thirtieth Dynasties, and although they showed great energy in raising monuments of high quality in traditional style, scarcely any of their work survives intact. The monolithic shrine of Nectanebo II, which is the oldest part of the

234

present temple of Edfu, is of magnificent workmanship, superbly carved and polished in the hard grey granite, with elegant inscriptions crisply cut in glyphs of classical form. The town of Behbet el-Hagar is still not fully explored, but its extensive ruins bear witness to the ambitions and resources of Nectanebo II who built the great temple of Isis there in granite brought from Aswan at the other end of the kingdom. The decoration was finished by Ptolemy II, but until proper investigation is made, it is impossible to say what exactly his contribution was to the reliefs and inscriptions. The style of the last native dynasty was continued in the ensuing Ptolemaic Period by rulers who were anxious to represent themselves as the inheritors of a continuous tradition. The reliefs of Nectanebo II revive the tripartite management of the torso, whereas the bipartite treatment prevailed *cf. 192* during the earlier years of the Thirtieth Dynasty, and is particularly to be seen in the headless statues of Nectanebo I in London (BM no. 1013) and Paris (Louvre no. E.25491). With the elongated proportions of these reliefs goes an internal sculptural modelling which is as eloquent as the drawn outlines themselves.

The main features of this distinctive style are seen in the painted limestone relief from the Serapeum in the Louvre, where the bulbous *194* modelling of chin, lips and nose-tip gives a peculiar character to the facial appearance, which with slight exaggerations and distortions

195 Limestone relief of offering-bearers on a lintel from the tomb of Thanufer, from Heliopolis, *c.* 360 BC.

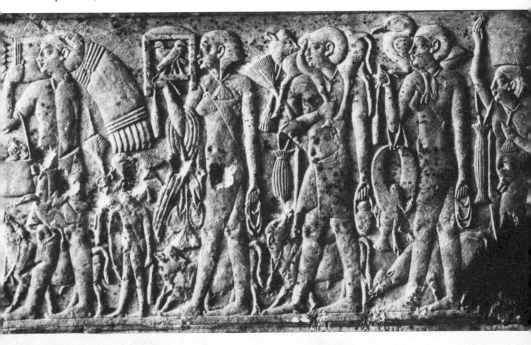

caused by constant copying, was to become the mannerism of the Ptolemaic and Roman reliefs.

Another feature of this Late Period art, is the revival of an erotic element, best seen in a number of carved architraves to which the epithet of 'neo-Memphite' has been applied, though not all the pieces come from Memphis, nor do they exactly copy the work of the Old Kingdom. It is rather the art of the late Eighteenth Dynasty which is their chief source of inspiration, as may be seen in such details as the version of the short Nubian wig often worn by the women in the scenes, and the two lines in the neck under the chin. The style varies slightly from piece to piece, but all seem to be the work of a particular studio and are characterized by exquisite, perhaps slightly precious drawing, and by great technical skill in the carving. The best of the work has a haunting quality, the last plaintive song of the Egyptian relief sculptor, with his recall of Old Kingdom subjects in the manner of the late Eighteenth Dynasty, and yet with a descant of his own in the varied poses of the animals in the procession. The sensuous modelling of the fleshy limbs is also new; and despite the vestiges of garments on their upper torsos, the women bearers are shown as virtually naked, like the serving maidens of the mid-Eighteenth Dynasty.

Whether the revived cult of the nude was influenced by contemporary imports from Greece is very doubtful. Egyptian art existed on its own traditions and lived in an entirely different world of space from that of Greece. Only Petosiris, the High Priest at Hermopolis, a much-travelled and highly cultured man, incorporated foreign elements in his fourth-century tomb-chapel at Tuna el-Gebel, and he apparently employed a Greek designer for the scenes of everyday life on the exterior portions of his funerary monument. But his example inspired no imitators. The features of the neo-Memphite reliefs, with their suave internal modelling of the forms and their accent on the female erogenous zones, become stylized in the icons of goddesses and queens in the Late Period, and crystallize into the empty formulae of Ptolemaic and Roman representations.

Very few complete statues of the kings of the Late Period have survived. Disparate fragments reveal that the sculptors of the age reverted to the work of the Saite Dynasty for their inspiration, with a bipartite treatment of the torso, and idealized features of the pharaoh, emphasizing his benevolence and god-like detachment. So closely was the style of the Saites followed by the Sebennytes, that isolated heads are attributed indiscriminately to Apries, Amasis or the Nectanebos. A notable case in point is the large green schist head of a

236

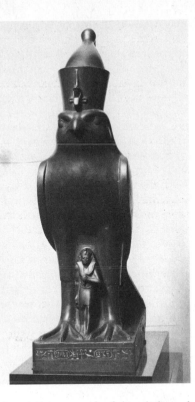

196   Green schist statue of King
Nectanebo II protected by the falcon
of Horus, from Heliopolis, c. 380 BC.

king in the British Museum (no. 97), with its wonderful polish and
superb carving, about which opinion is divided as to whether it
should be attributed to the Twenty-sixth or Thirtieth Dynasty. A
dating criterion may be the single group of figure-of-eight coils
behind the hood of the uraeus, which seems to differentiate the later
examples from the earlier with their double set of loops.   cf. 189

   Statues of the ruler under the protection of a god incarnate in an
animal continue to be produced up to the very end of Egypt's history   cf. 32
before the onset of the Christian era. Several statues of Nectanebo II
standing between the legs of a falcon have survived and are now in
Paris, Lyons and New York. The last example, with the king holding   196
a scimitar in one hand and a portfolio in the form of a jubilee-festival
glyph in the other, compose a rebus on his name. But the largest and
most impressive pieces of animal sculpture to have survived from this
period are the pink granite lions of Nectanebo I in the Vatican   197
Museum. These are the latest versions of the recumbent animal lying
on its side, his head turned inwards at right angles, the one forepaw

placed upon the other. Such guardian figures are designed in pairs to flank thresholds, the earliest examples to have survived being the couple originally commissioned by Amenophis III for his temple at Sulb. The Nectanebo specimens lack the majesty and breadth of handling of the earlier pair, but they give impressive renderings of relaxed animal muscular power. They have been an inspiration to artists since the Renaissance in Europe, when they were rediscovered in the ruins of the Iseum near Rome, whither they had been brought in the days of the Emperors.

The private statues of this period show similar features to the royal sculpture – consummate craftsmanship, a somewhat hieratic formalism and an archaistic recall of the glorious past. Their expressions are generally benign and bland, with the fixed smile of their royal exemplars emphasized by the drill holes at the corners of the mouth. Such pieces as the 'Dattari' statue in Brooklyn (no. 52.89), the 'Tyskiewicz' statue in the Louvre (no. E.10777) and the Djed-hor in Cairo (no. J.37861), represent a Lower Egyptian school.

A rather different emphasis is found in the statue of Osir-wer, of which the head is in Brooklyn and the body in Cairo. It is in grey-green schist and comes from the Karnak cache. Osir-wer wears the sleeved Persian jacket beneath the long wrap-over kilt, and holds a

150

198

197 Pink granite statue of a recumbent lion of King Nectanebo I, *c.* 370 BC.

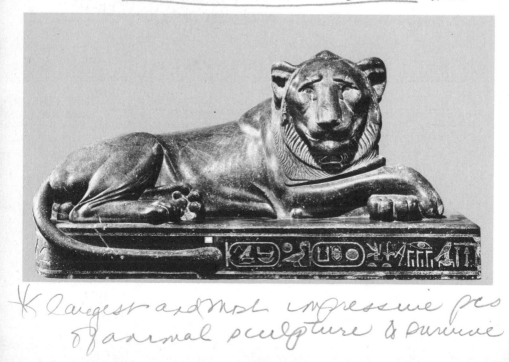

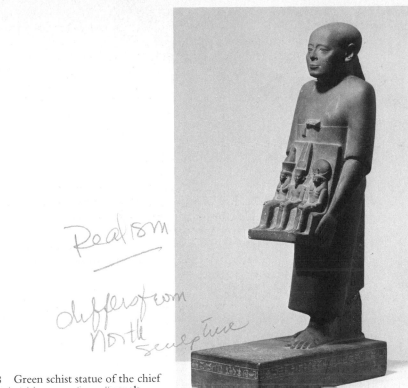

198 Green schist statue of the chief prophet Osir-wer, from Karnak, *c.* 350 BC.

votive statuette of the Theban trinity. While it has the same unity of form and style in its somewhat restrained modelling of both head and body, it differs from contemporary sculpture in the North in its more conservative approach. The sculptor is still working in the traditions of the earlier Persian Period with its more realistic portraiture. The head lacks all idealism: the mouth is pursed and unsmiling, there is no play of light over the features, which though finely worked are not highly polished. The structure of the skull beneath the skin, particularly the cranium and cheek-bones and the jutting chin, has been carefully realized. The total effect gives a compelling portrait of a particular individual. The ear with all its convolutions has been most expertly carved and this is a feature which is not always carefully rendered, even on important statues. It is in such details that this head proves to be in the tradition of the realistic portraits that now take their place beside the idealistic productions of the next three centuries.

239

Epilogue

The intervention of the victorious Alexander of Macedon in the affairs of Egypt in 332 BC was regarded by the official classes as the liberation of the land from the Persian yoke. The recognition of Alexander by the oracle of Amun at Siwa as his true son and the heir of all the pharaohs engendered a goodwill that was not dissipated for a century. Egypt thereafter became a part of the Hellenistic world. Alexandria, its new capital, had an international reputation for promoting learning and the arts, but made scarcely any impact upon the Egyptian populace. For all the lip-service that was paid to the ancient cults, and the attempt to introduce an ecumenical state religion with the worship of Serapis, the Greek kings never achieved the understanding between rulers and subjects which had been the accomplishment of pharaonic government at its best.

In these circumstances, Egyptian religion, except for the cult of Isis, retired more and more into itself, supported indeed by the state, but divorced from its needs and those of its citizens, and becoming an esoteric mystery to all but a few adepts. The support of the state made it possible to erect the great temples that were built on ancient foundations during Ptolemaic and Roman times, particularly at Dendera, Esna, Edfu, Kom Ombo and Philae. These edifices, in their fine craftsmanship, their noble proportions, their lavish use of sandstone and granite, their complex floriated capitals and their meticulous attention to detail, have a solemn grandeur. They were made according to a standardized building system, codified in a manual that was said to have fallen from heaven at Saqqara in the days of Imhotep. The reliefs and inscriptions, however, are deplorable, a lifeless formula followed without inner conviction.

The art which had given expression to Egyptian religious beliefs suffered a parallel alienation. Only in one respect did the dying artistic consciousness burst into a last bright flame. Throughout its long history, Egyptian sculpture had occasionally produced a portrait that transcended the conventions of its age, and attempted not only a more individual rendering of the facial appearance of the sitter at a certain period of his life, but also something of his mood and character. In the Ptolemaic Period, statues appear with realistic portrait heads grafted on to bodies that are no more than a banal stylization, producing a dichotomy to match the schism in Egyptian beliefs, which were now being subverted by ideas from the Hellenistic and Judaic worlds. But so searching are these portraits of grave men in the resignation of maturity, that they compel comparison with the portrait busts of Republican Rome, which indeed they appear to have influenced.

33, 84, 147, 184, 193, 198

Select Bibliography

General

Badawy, A. *A History of Egyptian Architecture*, vols, I–III, Giza 1954 and Los Angeles 1966–8.

Brooklyn Museum. *Five Years of Collecting Egyptian Art, 1951–56*, Catalogue of the Exhibition. Brooklyn 1956.

Edwards, I.E.S., Gadd, C.J., Hammond, N.G.L. and Sollberger, E. *The Cambridge Ancient History*, vol. I (chapters XI, XIV, XX), vol. II (chapters II, III, VIII, IX, XIX, XXIII, XXXV), 3rd edn, Cambridge 1975.

Hayes, W.C. *The Scepter of Egypt, I–II*, New York 1952–9.

Hornung, E. *Der Eine und die vielen*, Darmstadt 1971.

Lange, K. and Hirmer, M. *Egypt, Architecture, Sculpture, Painting*, 4th edn, London 1968.

Leclant, J. (ed.). *Le monde égyptien, Les Pharaons*, vols I–VI (L'Univers des Formes), Paris 1978–80.

Smith, W.S. *The Art and Architecture of Ancient Egypt*, Harmondsworth 1965.

Vandersleyn, C. *Das alte Ägypten* (Propyläen Kunstgeschichte, 15), Berlin 1975.

Vandier, J. *Manuel d'archéologie égyptienne*, vols I–VI, Paris 1952–78.

Chapter One

Fischer, H.G. *Egyptian Studies, II: The Orientation of Hieroglyphs*, pt I, *Reversals*, New York 1978.

Peck, W.H. and Ross, J.G. *Drawings from Ancient Egypt*, London 1978 (published in U.S. as *Egyptian Drawings*, New York 1978).

Schäfer, H. *Principles of Egyptian Art*, edited by E. Brunner-Traut, translated and edited by J. Baines, Oxford 1974.

Chapter Two

Clarke, S. and Engelbach, R. *Ancient Egyptian Masonry*, London 1930.

Lucas, A. *Ancient Egyptian Materials and Industries*, 4th edn, revised by J.R. Harris, London 1962.

Chapter Three

Emery, W.R. *Archaic Egypt*, Harmondsworth 1961.

Lauer, J.-P. *Histoire monumentale des pyramides d'Égypte*, vol. I, Cairo 1962.

Quibell, J. and Green, F.W. *Hierakonpolis*, vols I and II, London 1900–02.

Chapter Four

Lauer, J.-P. *La Pyramide à degrés*, vols I–IV, Cairo 1936–59.

Quibell, J. *The Tomb of Hesy*, Cairo 1913.

Ricke, H. *Bemerkungen zu ägyptischen Baukunst des Alten Reiches*, vols I–II, Zürich 1944 and Cairo 1950.

Wildung, D. 'Two Representations of Gods from the Early Old Kingdom', in *Miscellanea Wilbouriana*, vol. I, Brooklyn Museum 1972.

Chapter Five

Edwards, I.E.S. *The Pyramids of Egypt*, London and New York 1972.

Fakhry, A. *The Monuments of Sneferu at Dahshur*, vol. II, *The Valley Temple*, Cairo 1963.

Holscher, U. *Das Grabdenkmal des Königs Chephren*, Leipzig 1912.

Junker, H. 'Zu dem Idealbild des menschlichen Körpers in der Kunst des Alten Reiches', in *Anzeiger, Österreichische Akademie der Wissenschaften, Wien*, 84 (1948).

Reisner, G.A. *Mycerinus*, Cambridge, Mass., 1931.

Simpson, W.K. *The Mastaba of Queen Merysankh III*, Boston 1973.

Smith, W.S. *A History of Egyptian Sculpture and Painting in the Old Kingdom*, Oxford 1946, Boston 1949.

Chapter Six

Bissing, F.W. von, *et al. Das Re-Heiligtum des Königs Ne-Woser-Re*, vols I–III, Leipzig 1905–28.

Borchardt, L. *Denkmäler des Alten Reiches*, Cairo 1937–64.

Borchardt, L., *et al. Das Grabdenkmal des Königs Sahu-Re*, vols I–III, Leipzig 1910–13.

Davies, N. de G. *The Mastaba of Ptahhetep and Akhethetep*, vols I–II, London 1900–01.

Duell, P. *The Mastaba of Mereruka*, vols I–II, Chicago 1938.

Edel, E. and Wenig, S. *Die Jahreszeitenreliefs aus dem Sonnenheiligtum des Königs Ne-user-re*, Berlin 1974.

Epron, L., Daumas, F. and Wild, H. *Le Tombeau de Ti*, vols I–III, Cairo 1939–66.

Jéquier, G. *Le Monument funéraire de Pépi II*, vols I–III, Cairo 1936–40.

Lauer, J.-P. *Saqqara*, London and New York, 1976.

Macramallah, R. *Le Mastaba d'Idout*, Cairo 1935.

Moussa, A.M. and Altenmüller, H. *The Tomb of Nefer and Ka-hay*, Mainz 1971.

Chapter Seven

Borchardt, L. *Statuen und Statuetten*, vols I–V, Berlin 1911–36.

Junker, H. 'Das lebensware Bildnis in der Rundplastik des Alten Reiches', in *Anzeiger, Österreichische Akademie der Wissenschaften, Wien*, 87 (1951).

Shoukry, M.A. *Die Privatgrabstatue im Alten Reich*, Cairo 1951.

Chapter Eight

Chassinat, E. and Palanque, C. *Une campagne de fouilles dans la nécropole d'Assiout*, Cairo 1911.

Dunham, D. *Naga-ed-Der Stelae of the First Intermediate Period*, London 1937.

Fischer, H.G. *Dendera*, Locust Valley, N.Y. 1968.

Chapter Nine

Arnold, D. *Der Tempel des Königs Mentuhotep von Deir el-Bahari*, vols I–II, Mainz 1973–74.

Bisson de la Roque, F. *Tod (1934 à 1936)*, Cairo 1937.

241

Blackman, A.M. and Apted, M.R. *The Rock Tombs of Meir*, vols I–VI, London 1914–53.

Bothmer, B.V. 'Block Statues of the Middle Kingdom', in *Bulletin of the Brooklyn Museum*, 21 (1959–60) and 22 (1960–61).

Cottevieille-Giraudet, R. *Medamoud (1931), Les monuments du Moyen Empire*, Cairo 1933.

Evers, H.G. *Staat aus dem Stein*, vols I–II, Munich 1929.

Newberry, P.E. and Griffith, F.L. *Beni Hasan*, vols I–IV, London 1893–1900.

Smith, W.S. 'Paintings of the Egyptian Middle Kingdom at Bersheh', in *American Journal of Archaeology*, 55 (1951).

Winlock, H.F. *Excavations at Deir el Bahari (1911–1931)*, New York 1942.

Chapter Ten

Arnold, D. *Wandrelief und Raumfunktion in ägyptischen Tempeln das Neuen Reiches*, Berlin 1962.

Otto, E. *Egyptian Art and the Cults of Osiris and Amon*, London 1968.

Winlock, H.E. *Rise and Fall of the Middle Kingdom in Thebes*, New York 1947.

Chapter Eleven

Aldred, C. *Akhenaten and Nefertiti*, London 1973.

Davies, Nina. *Ancient Egyptian Paintings*, vols I–III, Chicago 1936.

Legrain, G. *Statues et Statuettes*, vols I–III, Cairo 1906–25.

Naville, E. *The Temple of Deir el Bahari*, vols I–VI, London 1894–1908.

Schäfer, H. *Amarna in Religion und Kunst*, Leipzig 1931.

Chapter Twelve

Calverley, A.M. and Broome, M.F. *The Temple of King Sethos I at Abydos*, vols I–IV, London and Chicago 1933–58.

Chicago University, Oriental Institute. *Medinet Habu*, vols I–VIII, Chicago 1930–70.

Piankoff, A. *The Tomb of Ramesses VI*, New York 1954.

Chapters Thirteen and Fourteen

Aldred, C. 'The Carnarvon Statuette of Amun, in *Journal of Egyptian Archaeology*, 42 (1956).

Bothmer, B.V. 'The Philadelphia-Cairo Statue of Osorkon II', in *Journal of Egyptian Archaeology*, 46 (1960).

Chicago University, Oriental Institute. *Reliefs and Inscriptions at Karnak*, vol. III, *The Bubastite Portal*, Chicago 1954.

Montet, P. *La nécropole de Tanis*, vol. II, *Les constructions et le tombeau de Psousennès*, Paris 1951.

Chapter Fifteen

Leclant, J. *Montouemhat, Quatrième Prophète d'Amon*, Cairo 1961.

Leclant, J. *Recherches sur les Monuments Thébains de la XXVe Dynastie*, vols I–II, Cairo 1965.

Russmann, E.R. *The Representation of the King in the XXVth Dynasty*, Brussels and Brooklyn 1974.

Chapters Sixteen and Seventeen

Bösse, K. *Die menschliche Figur in der Rundplastik der ägyptischen Spätzeit*, Glückstadt and Hamburg 1936.

Bothmer, B.V. *Egyptian Sculpture of the Late Period, 700 B.C. to A.D. 100*, Brooklyn 1960.

Müller, H.W. 'Der Torso eine Königsstatue', in *Studi in Memoria di Ippolito Rosellini*, vol. II, Pisa 1955.

Müller, H.W. 'Ein Königs Bildnis der 26 Dynastie', in *Zeitschrift für Ägyptische Sprache*, 80 (1955).

Müller, H.W. 'Löwenskulpturen in der ägyptischen Sammlung des Bayerischen Staates', in *Müncher Jahrbuch der bildenden Kunst*, XVI (1965).

List of Illustrations

Measurements are given in inches and centimetres; figures after museums are registration numbers.

Frontispiece: Wooden statue of King Tutankhamun from his tomb in the Valley of the Kings. Ht 32 (81.3). Griffith Institute, Ashmolean Museum, Oxford, no. 275c.

1 Map of ancient Egypt. Drawn by Hanni Bailey.

2 Gesso-coated wooden board with line drawing of King Tuthmosis III, from a tomb at Thebes. Ht 14½ (36.4). British Museum, London, no. 5601.

3 Wooden stela of Hesy from Saqqara. Ht 45 (114). Egyptian Museum, Cairo, no. C. 1427.

4 Two fragments of the slate 'Battlefield Palette'. W. 11¼ (28.7).

Top, Ashmolean Museum, Oxford, no. 1171.1892. Bottom, British Museum, London, no. 0791. Photo British Museum.

5 Reverse of slate palette from Hierakonpolis. Ht 17 (43). Ashmolean Museum, Oxford, no. E. 3924.

6, 7 Reverse and obverse of slate palette of King Narmer, from

Hierakonpolis. Ht 25 (63.5). Egyptian Museum, Cairo, no. J. 14716.

8 Ivory label of King Den, from Abydos. W. 2⅛ (5.4). British Museum, London, no. 55586.

9 Steatite and alabaster disc of King Den, from Saqqara. Diam. 3½ (9). Egyptian Museum, Cairo, no. J. 70104. Photo Hirmer Fotoarchiv.

10 Reconstruction of the mastaba tomb of Queen Merneith at Saqqara. Drawing by Martin Weaver after Lauer.

11. Limestone funerary stela of King Djet, from Abydos. W. 25½ (65). Louvre, Paris, no. E. 11007.

12 Schist statue of King Khasekhem, from Hierakonpolis. Ht 22 (56). Egyptian Museum, Cairo, no. J. 32161.

13 The Step Pyramid at Saqqara, entrance porch. Photo Cyril Aldred.

14 The Step Pyramid at Saqqara, relief panel of King Djoser in the south tomb. W. 23 (59). Photo Hirmer Fotoarchiv.

15 The Step Pyramid at Saqqara, shrines in the Jubilee Court. Photo Cyril Aldred.

16 The Step Pyramid at Saqqara, the 'House of the South'. Photo Cyril Aldred.

17 Statue of King Djoser, from the mortuary temple to the Step Pyramid at Saqqara. Ht 55¼ (140). Egyptian Museum, Cairo, no. J. 49158. Photo Hirmer Fotoarchiv.

18 Granite corbel with heads, from the Step Pyramid at Saqqara. W. 18 (46). Egyptian Museum, Cairo, no. J. 49613.

19 Diorite statue of a god holding a knife. Ht 8⅜ (21.3). Brooklyn Museum, New York, Charles Edwin Wilbour Fund, no. 58.192.

20 Granite statue of Bedjmes. Ht 26 (66). British Museum, London, no. 171.

21 Painted limestone statues of Rēhotep and Nofret, from Meydum. Av. ht 48 (122). Egyptian

Museum, Cairo, nos. C. 3 and C. 4. Photo Peter Clayton.

22 Plan of the Valley Temple of the Bent Pyramid of King Snoferu at Dahshur. Garth Denning after Fakhry 1969.

23 Hall in the Valley Temple of King Khephren at Giza. Photo Cyril Aldred.

24 Detail of limestone funerary stela of King Snoferu, from Dahshur. Total ht c. 197 (500).

25 Limestone relief of Prince Khufukaf and his wife at Giza. W. 30 (76.2). Museum of Fine Arts, Boston.

26 Frieze of geese from the mastaba of Itet at Meydum. Ht 11¼ (28.4). Egyptian Museum, Cairo, no. C. 1742. Photo Hirmer Fotoarchiv.

27 Painted limestone stela of the Princess Nofretyabet, from Giza. Ht 14¾ (37.5). Louvre, Paris, no. E. 15591. Photo Musées Nationaux.

28 Limestone reserve head of the wife of the prince in ill. 29, from Giza. Ht 12 (30.5). Museum of Fine Arts, Boston, no. 14.719.

29 Limestone reserve head of a prince, from Giza. Ht 10½ (26.7). Museum of Fine Arts, Boston, no. 14.718.

30 Limestone statue of Prince Hemon, from Giza. Ht 62 (157). Pelizaeus-Museum, Hildesheim, no. 1962. Photo Peter Clayton.

31 Quartzite head of King Djedefrē, from Abu Roash. Ht 11 (28). Louvre, Paris, no. E. 12626. Photo Musées Nationaux.

32 Diorite statue of King Khephren, from Giza. Ht 63 (160). Egyptian Museum, Cairo, no. C. 14.

33 Limestone bust of Ankh-haf, from Giza. Ht 20 (51). Museum of Fine Arts, Boston, no. 27.442.

34 The pyramid of King Kheops with the Great Sphinx at Giza. Photo Cyril Aldred.

35 Schist pair-statue of King Mykerinus and Queen Khamerernebty

II, from Giza. Ht 56 (142). Museum of Fine Arts, Boston, no. 11.738.

36 Schist triad of King Mykerinus, Hathor and the personified Hare nome, from Giza. Ht 33 (84). Museum of Fine Arts, Boston, no. 09.200.

37 Painted limestone group of Seneb and his family, from Giza. Ht 13 (33). Egyptian Museum, Cairo, no. J. 51281.

38 Reconstruction of the sun temple of King Niuserre near Abusir. From Mendelssohn 1974.

39 Plan of the mortuary temple of King Sahurē at Abusir. Garth Denning after Edwards 1972.

40 Fragmentary painted relief of offering-bearers from pyramid temple of King Phiops II at Saqqara. Ht of each register 50 (127). From Smith 1946.

41 Limestone relief of King Sahurē hunting, from Abusir. Ht 59 (150). Ägyptisches Museum, Berlin DDR, no. 21783.

42 Limestone relief of the goddess of Upper Egypt suckling King Sahurē, from Abusir. Egyptian Museum. Cairo, no. J. 39533.

43 Limestone relief of the estates of King Sahurē. Ht 24 (61). Egyptian Museum, Cairo, no. J. 39534.

44 Painted limestone relief of the presentation of cranes, geese and cattle, tomb of Ptah-hotep at Saqqara. Ht of each register 16½ (42). Photo Hirmer Fotoarchiv.

45 Painted relief of butchers, tomb of the Princess Idut at Saqqara. Ht 9¾ (25). Photo Hirmer Fotoarchiv.

46 Painted limestone relief, tomb of Ti at Saqqara. Ht of each register 15 (38). Photo Hirmer Fotoarchiv.

47 Relief from tomb of Ptah-hotep at Saqqara. Ht 16½ (42). From J. Quibell, *The Ramesseum*, London 1896, pl. XXXII.

48 Drawing of a relief of the hunt in the desert, tomb of Ptah-hotep at

Saqqara. Ht 16½ (42). From N. de G. Davies 1900.

49 Main offering chamber of the mastaba tomb of Mereruka at Saqqara. Photo Albert Shoucair.

50 Diabase head of a king wearing the White Crown. Ht 23 (58). Freer Gallery of Art, Smithsonian Institution, Washington, D.C., no. 38.11.

51 Colossal granite head of King Userkaf, from Saqqara. Ht 26 (66). Egyptian Museum, Cairo, no. J. 52501. Photo Hirmer Fotoarchiv.

52 Copper standing statues of King Phiops I, from Hierakonpolis. Hts 70 and 23¾ (178 and 60). Egyptian Museum, Cairo, nos. J. 33034–5.

53 Alabaster statue of King Phiops II seated in the lap of his mother. Ht 12 (30.2). Brooklyn Museum, New York, Charles Edwin Wilbour Fund, no. 39.119.

54 Alabaster statuette of King Phiops I seated in jubilee attire. Ht 10 (25.5). Brooklyn Museum, New York, Charles Edwin Wilbour Fund, no. 39.120.

55 Schist statuette of King Phiops I kneeling to offer libation vessels. Ht 6 (15.3). Brooklyn Museum, New York, Charles Edwin Wilbour Fund, no. 39.121.

56 Painted limestone statue of Rē-nofer, from Saqqara. Ht 72¾ (185). Egyptian Museum, Cairo, no. C. 18.

57 Painted limestone statue of Rē-nofer, from Saqqara. Ht 70¾ (180). Egyptian Museum, Cairo, no. C. 19.

58 Painted limestone statue of a scribe, from Saqqara. Ht 19½ (49.5). Egyptian Museum, Cairo, no. C. 36. Photo Hirmer Fotoarchiv.

59 Painted wooden statue of Methethy, from Saqqara. Ht 31½ (80.3). William Rockhill Nelson Gallery of Art, Atkins Museum of Fine Arts, Kansas City, no. 51.1.

60 Painted wooden statue of Methethy, from Saqqara. Ht 24¼ (61.5). Brooklyn Museum, New York, Charles Edwin Wilbour Fund, no. 51.1.

61 Painted limestone group of Penmeru and family, from Giza. Ht 61 (155). Museum of Fine Arts, Boston, no. 12.1484.

62 Limestone statue of Niankhrē, from Giza. Ht 27½ (70). Egyptian Museum, Cairo, no. J. 6138.

63 Limestone statue of Iruka-ptah and family, from Saqqara. Ht 29 (73.5). Brooklyn Museum, New York, Charles Edwin Wilbour Fund, no. 37.17E.

64 Limestone pair-statue of Memisabu and his wife, from Giza. Ht 24 (61). Metropolitan Museum of Art, New York, Rogers Fund, no. 48.111.

65 Painted limestone statue of the funerary priest Ka'emked, from Saqqara. Ht 17 (43). Egyptian Museum, Cairo, no. C. 119.

66 Painted statuette of a brewer straining mash, from Saqqara. Ht 10½ (26.7). Egyptian Museum, Cairo, no. J. 66624.

67 Wooden statue of the chancellor Nakhti, from Asyut. Ht 69 (175). Louvre, Paris, no. E. 11937. Photo Musées Nationaux.

68 Painted statue of King Mentuhotep II, from Deir el-Bahri. Ht 72 (183). Egyptian Museum, Cairo, no. J. 36915. Photo Hirmer Fotoarchiv.

69 Relief on the sarcophagus of the Princess Kawit, from Deir el-Bahri. Ht 18¾ (47.6). Egyptian Museum, Cairo, no. J. 47397.

70 Relief on the shrine of King Mentuhotep II, from Dendera. Ht 32¼ (82). Egyptian Museum, Cairo, no. J. 46068. Photo B. V. Bothmer, Brooklyn Museum.

71 Painted limestone relief of a papyrus-bearer, from Deir el-Bahri. Ht 18½ (47). Musée d'Art et d'Histoire, Geneva, no. 4583.

72 Relief of King Mentuhotep II and deities, from Tod. Ht c. 20 (51). Egyptian Museum, Cairo, no. J. 66330. Photo B. V. Bothmer, Brooklyn Museum.

73 Relief of King Mentuhotep III being crowned, from Tod. Egyptian

Museum, Cairo, no. J. 66333. Photo B. V. Bothmer, Brooklyn Museum.

74 Painted wooden models of offering-bearers, from the tomb of Meket-rē at Deir el-Bahri. Average ht 44 (112). Egyptian Museum, Cairo, no. J. 46725 (left) and Metropolitan Museum of Art, New York, no. 20.3.7 (right).

75 Limestone relief of offering-bearers from the pyramid temple of Sesostris I at Lisht. Ht 55 (139). Metropolitan Museum of Art, New York, Rogers Fund, no. 09.180.13A.

76 Painted wooden model of offering-bearers, from Bershah. Ht 17 (43). Museum of Fine Arts, Boston, no. 21.326. Photo Peter Clayton.

77 Relief on the limestone jubilee kiosk of Sesostris I at Karnak. W. 20½ (52). Photo Cyril Aldred.

78 Rebuilt limestone jubilee kiosk of Sesostris I at Karnak. Ht 189 (480). Photo Cyril Aldred.

79 Copy of a wall-painting in the tomb of Khnum-hotep at Beni Hasan, with men gathering figs. Ht 12½ (31.5). From Nina Davies 1936.

80 Copy of a wall-painting in the tomb of Khnum-hotep at Beni Hasan, with men feeding oryxes. Ht 13½ (34.5). From Nina Davies 1936.

81 Relief on a limestone pillar of King Sesostris I embraced by Ptah, from Karnak. W. 34¾ (88). Egyptian Museum, Cairo, no. J. 36809.

82 Drawing of a relief of Senbi hunting in the desert, from his tomb at Meir. Ht 27 (69). From Blackman and Apted 1914–53.

83 Grey granite head of King Sesostris III, from Medamud. Ht 11½ (29). Egyptian Museum, Cairo, no. C. 486.

84 Brown quartzite head from a statue of King Sesostris III. Ht 6½ (16.5). Metropolitan Museum of Art, New York, Carnarvon Collection, Gift of Edward S. Harkness, 1926, no. 26.7.1394.

85 Sphinx of King Ammenemes II, from Tanis. Ht 81 (206). Louvre, Paris, no. A. 23. Photo Musées Nationaux.

86 Sphinx of King Ammenemes III, from Tanis. Ht 39 (99). Egyptian Museum, Cairo, no. C. 394.

87 Fragment of dyad of Hathor and King Sesostris I. Ht 23½ (60). Egyptian Museum, Cairo, no. C. 42008.

88 Limestone statue of King Sesostris I, from his pyramid temple at Lisht. Ht (whole) 78¼ (199). Egyptian Museum, Cairo, no. C. 418.

89 Statue of King Sesostris I. Ht 30 (76). British Museum, London, no. 44. Photo Bildarchiv Foto Marburg.

90 Green schist head of King Ammenemes III(?). Ht 14½ (37). Kunsthistorisches Museum, Vienna, no. 37. Photo B. V. Bothmer, Brooklyn Museum.

91 Black granite statue of Sennu, from Kerma. Ht 66 (168). Museum of Fine Arts, Boston, no. 14.720.

92 Statue of King Ammenemes III, from Hawara. Ht 63 (160). Egyptian Museum, Cairo, no. C. 385.

93 Head of a female sphinx. Ht 15¼ (39). Brooklyn Museum, New York, Charles Edwin Wilbour Fund, no. 56.85.

94 Group of Ukh-hotep with his wives and daughter, from Meir. Ht 12½ (31.5). Egyptian Museum, Cairo, no. C. 459.

95 Statue of Queen Nofret, from Tanis. Ht 44 (112). Egyptian Museum, Cairo, no. C. 381.

96 Statue of Amenemhēt. Ht 20 (50.8). British Museum, London, no. 462.

97 Block-statue of Si-Hathor, from Abydos. Ht 17 (43). British Museum, London, no. 570.

98 Statue of Gebu, from Karnak. Ht 36½ (93). Ny Carlsberg Glyptotek, Copenhagen, no. AEIN 27.

99 Statue of Kherti-hotep, from the Asyut region. Ht 30 (76.2). Staatliche Museen, Berlin DDR, no. 15700.

100 *Ka*-statue of King Hor Awibrē, from Dahshur. Ht 70 (177.8). Egyptian Museum, Cairo, no. C. 259.

101 Wooden cult statues of an unknown king, from Lisht. Average ht 22 (56). Metropolitan Museum of Art, New York, no. 14.3.17 and Egyptian Museum of Art, Cairo, no. J. 44951. Photo Egyptian Expedition, Metropolitan Museum of Art.

102 Upper part of seated statue of Sennufer and his wife. Ht 26 (66). Egyptian Museum, Cairo, no. C. 42126.

103 Towers flanking the eastern gateway to the mortuary temple of King Ramesses III at Medinet Habu, Western Thebes. Photo Cyril Aldred.

104 The mortuary temple of King Ramesses II at Western Thebes, showing the Second Court with Osiride pillars and the hypostyle hall. Photo Cyril Aldred.

105 Upper part of stela of King Amosis, from Abydos. W. 39 (99). Egyptian Museum, Cairo, no. C. 31002.

106 Alabaster human-handed sphinx of King Amenophis I. L. 8 (20.4). Egyptian Museum, Cairo, no. J. 42033. Photo B. V. Bothmer, Brooklyn Museum.

107 Upper part of a statue of a queen, from Deir el-Bahri. Ht 11 (28). Metropolitan Museum of Art, New York, Rogers Fund, 1916, no. 16.10.224.

108 Painted limestone relief of King Amenophis I. W. 21⅝ (55). Royal Scottish Museum, Edinburgh, no. 1968.626.

109 'Proto-Doric' colonnade of the Anubis Chapel, in the mortuary temple of Queen Hatshepsut at Deir el-Bahri. Photo Cyril Aldred.

110 General view of the mortuary temple of Queen Hatshepsut at Deir el-Bahri. Photo Cyril Aldred.

111 Painted limestone relief of offering-bearers, from the cult

chapel of Queen Hatshepsut in her mortuary temple at Deir el-Bahri. Ht 20 (51). Photo Royal Scottish Museum, Edinburgh.

112 Painted limestone relief of soldiers rejoicing, from the Hathor chapel in the mortuary temple of Queen Hatshepsut at Deir el-Bahri. Ht 20 (51). Photo Cyril Aldred.

113 Kneeling granite colossus of Queen Hatshepsut wearing the White Crown, from Deir el-Bahri. Ht 110⅝ (281). Metropolitan Museum of Art, New York, Rogers Fund, 1930, no. 30.3.1.

114 Indurated limestone statue of Queen Hatshepsut in the costume of a pharaoh, from Deir el-Bahri. Ht 77 (196). Metropolitan Museum of Art, Rogers Fund and contribution from Edward S. Harkness, 1929, no. 29.3.2.

115 Painted limestone sphinx of Queen Hatshepsut, from Deir el-Bahri. Ht 24 (61). Metropolitan Museum of Art, New York, no. 31.3.94.

116 Statue of King Tuthmosis III, from Karnak. Ht 35⅜ (90). Egyptian Museum, Cairo, no. C. 42054.

117 Statue of King Amenophis II, from Karnak (front view). Ht 22⅜ (57). Egyptian Museum, Cairo, no. C. 42077.

118 Statue of King Amenophis II, from Karnak (side view). Ht 22⅜ (57). Egyptian Museum, Cairo, no. C. 42077.

119 Statue of Senenmut holding the Princess Nefrurē, from Karnak(?). Ht 20⅜ (52.7). Field Museum of Natural History, Chicago, no. 173.988.

120 Statue of Senenmut nursing the Princess Nefrurē, from Karnak(?). Ht 28 (71). British Museum, London, no. 174.

121 Statue of Pehsukher kneeling and raising his hands in a hymn to the sun-god. Ht 16 (41). Royal Scottish Museum, Edinburgh, no. 1910.75.

122 Granite relief of King Tuthmosis III kneeling to be crowned by the god Amun, at Karnak. W. 65½ (166.5). Photo Cyril Aldred.

123 Copy of a wall-painting in the tomb of Menkheperresonb at Western Thebes, showing Aegeans bringing gifts to the pharaoh. Ht 17 (45). From Nina Davies 1936.

124 Copy of a wall-painting in the tomb of Menna at Western Thebes, showing the owner and his family fishing and fowling in the marshes. Ht 31 (78.7). From Nina Davies 1936.

125 Wall-painting in the tomb of Userhet at Western Thebes, showing the owner hunting desert game from his chariot. Ht 33 (84). Photo Hirmer Fotoarchiv.

126 Drawing from a wall-painting in the tomb of Rekhmirē at Western Thebes, showing sculptors at work. Ht 21¼ (54). From N. de G. Davies, *Rekhmirē*, 1943.

127 Drawing from a wall-painting in the tomb of Rekhmirē at Western Thebes, showing masons using boning rods on a block of stone. Ht 22⅜ (57). From N. de G. Davies, *Rekhmirē*, 1943.

128 Wooden statuette of the high priestess Tuyu. Ht 15⅜ (39). Louvre, Paris, no. E. 10655. Photo Giraudon.

129 Wall-painting in the tomb of Rekhmirē at Western Thebes, showing maidservants waiting upon women guests. Ht of each register 19¼ (49). Photo Hirmer Fotoarchiv.

130 Head of a statue of King Amenophis III wearing the Blue Crown. Ht 24 (61). Brooklyn Museum, New York, Charles Edwin Wilbour Fund, no. 59.19.

131 Kneeling bronze statuette of King Tuthmosis IV offering libation vessels. Ht 5½ (14). British Museum, London, no. 64564.

132 The temple of Amun at Luxor, the hypostyle hall of King Amenophis III. Photo Cyril Aldred.

133 Relief in the tomb of Kheruef at Western Thebes, showing foreign princesses pouring libations. Ht 45 (115). Photo Hirmer Fotoarchiv.

134 Relief in the tomb of Khaʿemhet at Western Thebes, showing the investiture of officials. Ht 13¾ (35). Photo Metropolitan Museum of Art, New York.

135 Head of a statuette of Queen Tiye, from Serabit el-Khadim. Ht 3½ (9). Egyptian Museum, Cairo, no. J. 38257.

136 Statue of Amenhotep-son-of-Hapu as a scribe, from Karnak. Ht 50⅜ (128). Egyptian Museum, Cairo, no. J. 44861.

137 Statue of Amenhotep-son-of-Hapu carved to represent an aged man, from Karnak. Ht 56 (142.2). Egyptian Museum, Cairo, no. C. 42127.

138 Relief of King Akhenaten and Queen Nofreteti. Ht 50⅜ (105). Egyptian Museum, Cairo, no. 30.10.26.12. Photo Hirmer Fotoarchiv.

139 Sculptor's model relief with portraits of King Akhenaten and Queen Nofreteti from Amarna. Ht 8¾ (22.1). Brooklyn Museum, New York, Charles Edwin Wilbour Collection, no. 16.48.

140 Stela of King Akhenaten, his wife and three of their daughters, from Amarna. W. 15¼ (38.7). Ägyptisches Museum, Berlin, no. 14145. Photo courtesy Corpus of Late Egyptian Sculpture, the Brooklyn Museum.

141 Wall-painting from the tomb of Nebamun at Western Thebes, showing musicians entertaining guests at a meal. Ht 24 (61). British Museum, London, no. 37984.

142 Limestone relief fragment of a hand offering an olive branch to Aten, originally from Amarna, found at Hermopolis. Ht 9 (23). Collection Mr and Mrs Norbert Schimmel, no. 244. Photo B.V. Bothmer, Brooklyn Museum.

143 Relief fragment of a stand of wheat, originally from Amarna, found at Hermopolis. Ht 9 (23). Collection Mr and Mrs Norbert Schimmel, no. 265. Photo B.V. Bothmer, Brooklyn Museum.

144 Sarcophagus of King Tutankhamun, *in situ* in his tomb in the Valley of the Kings. Ht 58 (147.3). Photo Egyptian Expedition, Metropolitan Museum of Art, New York, no. 240.

145 Quartzite torso from a statue of Queen Nofreteti, from Amarna(?). Ht 11⅝ (29.4). Louvre, Paris, no. E. 25409. Photo B. V. Bothmer, Brooklyn Museum.

146 Painted portrait bust of Queen Nofreteti. Ht 23 (58.5). Ägyptisches Museum, Berlin, no. 21.300. Photo Hirmer Fotoarchiv.

147 Original plaster cast of a modelled portrait mask of a man, from Amarna. Ht 7 (17.8). Ägyptisches Museum, Berlin, no. 21.356. Photo B. V. Bothmer, Brooklyn Museum.

148 Limestone head of Queen Nofreteti in process of being carved. Ht 11¾ (29.8). Ägyptisches Museum, Berlin, no. 21.352. Photo B. V. Bothmer, Brooklyn Museum.

149 Painted sandstone colossus of Akhenaten, from Karnak. Ht 70 (178). Egyptian Museum, Cairo, no. J. 49528.

150 Guardian lion of King Tutankhamun, originally from the temple of King Amenophis III, at Sulb. Ht 48 (122). British Museum, London, no. 34.

151 Limestone relief of Asiatic rebels, from the tomb of Haremhab at Saqqara. Ht 31 (78.7). Rijksmuseum van Oudheden, Leiden, no. C. 1.

152 Limestone relief of King Sethos I crowning the image of Atum in his temple at Abydos. Photo K. Lange.

153 Relief of King Sethos I worshipping Amun and Mut in the hypostyle hall of the temple of Amun at Karnak. Photo Cyril Aldred.

154 Relief of King Ramesses II smiting a Libyan chieftain, in the main temple at Abu Simbel in Nubia. Photo Cyril Aldred.

155 Façade of the main rock-hewn temple of King Ramesses II at Abu Simbel in Nubia. Photo Cyril Aldred.

156 Copy of a wall-painting in the tomb of Userhet at Western Thebes, showing the owner, his wife and mother drinking the water of paradise. Ht 54¾ (139.2). From Nina Davies 1936.

157 Upper part of a quartzite colossus of King Ramesses II, from the Ramesseum. Ht 105 (267). British Museum, London, no. 19.

158 Upper part of a limestone statue of Queen Nofretari(?), from the Ramesseum. Ht 28¾ (73). Egyptian Museum, Cairo, no. C. 600.

159 Black granite statue of Ramesses II, from Karnak. Ht 76½ (194). Museo Egizio, Turin, no. 1380.

160 Egyptian chariotry and infantry waiting to go into battle, a limestone relief on the outer wall of the temple of King Ramesses II at Abydos. Photo Cyril Aldred.

161 Pair-statue of Yuni and his wife Renutet, from Deir Durunka. Ht 33¼ (84.6). Metropolitan Museum of Art, New York, Rogers Fund, 1915, no. 33.2.2.

162 Granite head from a statue of King Ramesses III, from Medinet Habu. Ht 36½ (92.7). Egyptian Museum, Cairo, no. J. 54477. Photo B. V. Bothmer, Brooklyn Museum.

163 Green schist statue of King Ramesses IX presenting a shrine surmounted by a scarab beetle. L. 18½ (47). Royal Scottish Museum, Edinburgh, no. 1965.1.

164 Red granite statue (front and side views) of King Ramesses VI leading captive a Libyan foe, from Karnak. Ht 29 (74). Egyptian Museum, Cairo, no. C. 42152. Photo Bildarchiv Foto Marburg (front view).

165 Mortuary temple of King Ramesses III at Medinet Habu, relief on the rear of the south tower of the first pylon. Photo Cyril Aldred.

166 Relief of the High Priest Amenhotep being decorated in the presence of a statue of King Ramesses IX, at Karnak. Photo Cyril Aldred.

167 Statue of the High Priest Ramesses-nakht as a scribe, from Karnak. Ht 31½ (80). Egyptian Museum, Cairo, no. C. 42162.

168 Gold and lapis lazuli pendant of the Abydene triad, Horus, Osiris and Isis. Ht 3½ (9). Louvre, Paris, no. E. 6204. Photo Musées Nationaux.

169 Bronze statue of Takush, inlaid with designs in silver, from near Sebennytos. Ht 27¼ (69). National Museum, Athens, no. 110. Photo courtesy Corpus of Late Egyptian Sculpture, the Brooklyn Museum.

170 Bronze statue of the Divine Consort Karomama, inlaid with gold, electrum and silver, from Karnak. Ht 23¼ (59). Louvre, Paris, no. N. 500. Photo Musées Nationaux.

171 Granite head of a statue of King Osorkon II, from Tanis. Ht 13¼ (33.5). University Museum, University of Pennsylvania, Philadelphia, no. E. 16199.

172 Statue-fragment of King Osorkon III launching a model boat of the god Sokar, from Karnak. Ht 7¼ (18). Egyptian Museum, Cairo, no. C. 42197. Photo André Vigneau, © Editions Tel-Vigneau.

173 Granite block-statue of Hor, from Karnak. Ht 43 (109). Egyptian Museum, Cairo, no. C. 42226.

174 Faience plaque of King Yewepet II, from Thebes. Ht 11½ (29.3). Brooklyn Museum, New York, Charles Edwin Wilbour Fund, no. 59.17.

175 Granite statue of Shebensopdu, holding a lotus bud. Ht 34¼ (87). Egyptian Museum, Cairo, no. C. 42228.

176 Granite head from a colossus of King Shabaka, from Karnak. Ht 38¼ (97). Egyptian Museum, Cairo, no. C. 42010. Photo courtesy Corpus of

Late Egyptian Sculpture, Brooklyn Museum.

177 Headless statue of King Tanutamun, from Gebel Barkal. Ht 86½ (220). Toledo Museum of Art, no. 49.105.

178 Head from a statue of King Taharqa, from Karnak(?). Ht 13¾ (35). Egyptian Museum, Cairo, no. C. 560.

179 Statue of the Divine Consort Amenirdis I, from the chapel of Osiris Nebankh at north Karnak. Ht 65⅝ (167). Egyptian Museum, Cairo, no. C. 565.

180 Statue of Amenirdis I, from Luxor (probably originally from Karnak). Ht 39⅜ (100). Egyptian Museum, Cairo, no. J. 67871. Photo courtesy Corpus of Late Egyptian Sculpture, Brooklyn Museum.

181 Granite sphinx of the Divine Consort Shepenwepet II, found in the Sacred Lake at Karnak. Ht 19¾ (50). Ägyptisches Museum, Berlin DDR, no. 7972.

182 Statue of the temple scribe Pedimahes from Tel el-Moqdam. Ht 18¼ (46.3). Brooklyn Museum, New York, Charles Edwin Wilbour Fund, no. 64.146.

183 Statue of Iriketakana, from Karnak. Ht 17¾ (45). Egyptian Museum, Cairo, no. J. 38018.

184 Statue of Mentuemhet, from Karnak. Ht 52¾ (134). Egyptian Museum, Cairo, no. C. 42236. Photo Bildarchiv Foto Marburg.

185 Relief fragment of Mentuemhet as a fourth prophet of Amun, from his tomb at Western Thebes. Ht 20¼ (51.3). William Rockhill Nelson Gallery of Art, Atkins Museum of Fine Arts, Kansas City, no. 48.28.

186 Relief fragment from the tomb of Mentuemhet at Western Thebes. Ht 9½ (24). Brooklyn Museum, New York, Charles Edwin Wilbour Fund, no. 48.74.

187 Relief of mourning women from the tomb of the vizier Nespek-

ashuti at Western Thebes. Ht 10¾ (27.5). Brooklyn Museum, New York, Charles Edwin Wilbour Fund, no. 52.131.3.

188 Black basalt head from a statue of King Apries. Ht 15¾ (40). Museo Civico, Bologna, no. 1801.

189 Green schist head from a statue of King Amasis. Ht 9¾ (25). Ägyptisches Museum, Berlin DDR, no. 11864. Photo courtesy Corpus of Late Egyptian Sculpture, the Brooklyn Museum.

190 Grey-green schist statue of the vizier Nespekashuti as a scribe, from Karnak. Ht 31½ (80). Egyptian Museum, Cairo, no. J. 36662.

191 Kneeling statue of the district governor Wahibre, from near Lake Mareotis. Ht 71 (180.3). British Museum, London, no. 111.

192 Grey schist statue of Hathor as a cow protecting the figure of the palace official Psamtek, from Saqqara. Ht 33⅛ (84). L. 41 (104). Egyptian Museum, Cairo, no. C. 784.

193 Fragment of the statue of an official, from Memphis(?). Ht 9¾ (25). Louvre, Paris, no. N. 2454. Photo Musées Nationaux.

194 Limestone relief of King Nectanebo II embraced by Isis, from the Serapeum at Saqqara. Louvre, Paris, no. N. 402. Photo courtesy Corpus of Late Egyptian Sculpture, Brooklyn Museum.

195 Limestone relief of offering-bearers on a lintel from the tomb of Thanufer, from Heliopolis. Ht 12 (30.5). Egyptian Museum, Cairo, no. J. 10976.

196 Statue of King Nectanebo II protected by the falcon of Horus, from Heliopolis. Ht 29 (73.5). Metropolitan Museum of Art, New York, no. 34.2.1.

197 Pink granite statue of a recumbent lion of King Nectanebo I. L. 77⅝ (197). Vatican Museum, Rome, no. 16. Photo Alinari-Anderson.

198 Statue of the chief prophet Osirwer, from Karnak. Ht 27¾ (70.3). Head, Brooklyn Museum, New York, no. 55.175. Body, Egyptian Museum, Cairo, no. J. 38664. Photo courtesy Corpus of Late Egyptian Sculpture, Brooklyn Museum.

Index and Glossary

Italic figures are illustration numbers

fl=floruit; k=king; q=queen; loc=location

All dates are BC unless otherwise indicated

Abu Gurab (loc, near Abusir) 79
Abu Simbel (loc, in Nubia) 144, 146, 189, 191, 193, 197, 200, *155*
Abusir (loc) 78, 79
Abydos (loc), tomb sites 37, 39, 40, 43, 44, 45, 50; temples 135, 146, 147, 187, 189, 194, 198; pilgrimage to 123, 133, 138, 224
Aegeans 30, 32, 141, 162, 163, *123*
Ahmose-Nofretari (q, fl 1550) 193
Ahtefnakht (steward, fl 870) 209
Akhenaten (k, 1356–1339) 172–83; works 27, 28, 142, 158; period 8, 159, 163, 170, 191, *138–40, 142, 149*
Akhet-hotep (vizier, fl 2430) 89
Amarna (loc, also Tell el-Amarna) 22, 27, 143, 144, 158, 172–83, 185, 186; period 8, 42, 164, 189, 230
Amasis (k, 570–526) 226, 227, 230, 236, *189*
Amenemhēt (nomarch, fl 1910) 123
Amenemhēt (official, fl 1890) 133, *96*
Amenhotep (High Priest of Amun, fl 1090) 202, *166*

Amenhotep-son-of-Hapu (Scribe of Recruits, fl 1360) 20, 21, 42, 170, *136, 137*
Amenirdis I (divine consort, fl 710) 216–17, *179, 180*
Amenophis I (k, 1527–1497) 147, 150, *106, 108*
Amenophis II (k, 1427–1394) 150, 156, 163, 170, *117, 118*
Amenophis III (k, 1384–1345) works 20, 21, 24, 42, 142, 150, 164, 167–72, 191, 193; period 19, 143, 186, 222, *130, 132*
Amenophis IV *see* Akhenaten
Ammenemes I (k, 1991–1962) 118, 124, 187
Ammenemes II (k, 1929–1895) 118, 126, *85*
Ammenemes III (k, 1878–1842) 126, 127, 128–9, 137–8, 142, 148, 153, 186, 216, *86, 90, 92*
Amosis (k, 1552–1524) 140, 141, 146, 147, *105*
Amun (god of Thebes) 12, 115, 118,

145, 187, *153*; barque 167, 169; priesthood 201, 202, 215, 216; as a ram 195, 197, 218, 230; as a sponsor 151, 152, 159, 203, 209, *122*; temple 20, 126, 144, 163, 206, 211
Andjib (k, 2940–2900) 46
Ankhesenamun (q, fl 1329) 142, 174, *140*
Ankhesenpaaten (princess, later Queen Ankhesenamun) *140*
Ankh-haf (vizier, fl 2560) 77, *33*
Ankhmahor (vizier, fl 2390) 89
Ankhnesmeryrē (q, fl 2350) 96, *53*
antiquarianism 105, 118, 128, 150, 170, 198, 204, 212, 215, 220, 223, 224, 233, *186*
Anubis (dog-headed god of embalming) 151
ape 123, 170, 202, *167*
Apries (k, 589–570) 226, 227, 236, *188*
Armant (loc, near Thebes) 113, 158
Ashru (sacred lake south of Karnak) 142, 167

248

Asia 20, 38, 141, 163, 166, 189, 203, 228
Asiatics 30, 32, 34, 80, 107, 139, 140, 162, *8*, *151*; *see also* Semites
Assyria 221, 225, 230
Aswan (loc) 45, 80, 124, 152, 194, 235, 238
Asyut (loc) 109, 110
Aten (god of the sun's disc) 158, 172, 174, 175, 177, 178, *138*, *140*
Atum (primordial god of the sun cult at Heliopolis) 59, 77, 152
Ay (k, 1329–1324) 179, 183, 185

Baal (Canaanite god of storm, war, etc.) 141
baboon *see* ape
back-pillar (of a statue) 56, 91, 133
Bak (chief sculptor, fl 1355) 21, 170, 182
barque 47, 59, *38*
Bedjmes (shipwright, fl 2700) 58, *20*
Behbet el-Hagar (loc, near Seben-nytos, with temple to Isis) 235
Beit el-Wali (temple site in Lower Nubia) 200
Bekenkhons (high priest of Amun, fl 1250) 20
Belzoni, G.B. (Italian explorer, AD 1778–1823) 194
ben-ben (sacred stone of Heliopolis) 59, 79
Beni Hasan (loc, with rock tombs) 122–4, 132, *79*, *80*
Bershah (loc, with rock tombs) 115, 122, 124, *76*
Biyahmu (loc, in Faiyum) 124
block-pattern border 13, 178, *124*
block statue 133, 135, 157, 196, 204, 211, 218, *97*, *173*, *182*
Book of the Dead 190
Bubastis (loc), Bubastite 8, 206, 210
Bubastite Portal (in the first court of the temple of Amun at Karnak) 209
Busiris (holy city of Osiris near Sebennytos) 123
bust 72, 174, 182, *33*, *146*
Buto (holy city and prehistoric capital of the Delta) 34, 87, 88, 123
Byblos (loc, in Lebanon near Beirut) 20, 113

canon of proportion 13
casting, in metal 24–5, 206, 227; in plaster 182, *147*
causeway (in pyramid complex) 59, 60, 79, 80, 88, 106, *38*
cavetto *see* cornice

cenotaph 37, 40, 47, 50, 187
child 17, 174, *37*, *119*, *120*, *140*
climate 106–7, 139, 187
cobra *see* uraeus
coffin 110; *see also* sarcophagus
colossus 12, 26, 42, 142, 186, 204: in Old Kingdom 92; in Middle Kingdom 124; in New Kingdom 152, 153, 166–8, 180, 182, 191, 193–5, 197, *51*, *113*, *149*, *155*, *157*
composite statues 182, 189
Consort, Divine, of Amun 21, 208, 215, 216, *222*, *225*, *170*, *179*, *180*, *181*
copper statue 24, 45, *62*
corbel 55, 81, *18*
cornice 50, 53, 62, *78*
coronation 82, 193, 197, *122*
cosmetic line (round the eyes) 91, 226
craftsman (in title) 12
crio-sphinx (ram-headed sphinx) 230
Crown, Blue 147, 158, 186, 225, *122*, *130*, *188*; Red 111, *68*; White 34, 44, *50*; others 96, 159, 174, 200, *164*

Dahshur (loc) 31, 59, 60, 61, 118, 137
Dapur (loc, in eastern Syria) 200
Deir Durunka (loc, near Asyut) 196
Deir el-Bahri (loc, in Western Thebes) 20, 111, 112, 114, 142, 151, 157, 222, 224, 230, *110*
Delta 31, 32, 34, 36, 124, 139, 140, 187, 194, 198, 203, 207, 212, 218; *see also* Lower Egypt
Den (k, 3000–2940) 36, 45, *8*, *9*
Dendera (loc) 109, 112, 240
Derr (loc, in Nubia) 191
Diodorus (Sicilian historian, fl 40) 193
Djedefrē (k, 2583–2575) 70, 72, 73, 75, 96, *31*
Djer (k, 3079–3033) 39
Djet (k, 3033–3000) 15, 40, *11*
Djoser (k, 2687–2667) 20, 45–56, 59, 61, 65, 70, 78, 150, 180, *14*, *17*
drawing 13, 15, 18, 26–8, 56; in painting 88, 122, 162, 163, 193, 201; in relief 40, 64, 112, 114, 159, 168, 185, 189, 200, 211, 236, *2*
dress 98, 123, 138, 156, 164, 182, 184, 186, 212, 223, 233, 238; *see also* wig
dyad (pair-statue) 73, 128, *35*, *64*, *87*

ebony *see* wood
Edfu (loc) 234, 240
engraving 27, *8*, *72*, *105*
eroticism 163, 182, 186, 197, 236, *145*, *195*

ex votos 17, 36, 44, 135, 138, 143, 193, 196, 203, 218

Faiyum (oasis in Libyan desert) 113, 118, 124
falcon (of Horus) 34, 35, 40, 46, 95, 200, 237, *6*, *11*, *32*, *54*, *196*
false door 19, 64, 65, 66, 85, 98, 162, *49*
famine 113, 139
First Time (of Creation) 11, 15, 32, 39, 52, 78, 84, 144, 146

gargoyle 146
Gebel Barkal (loc, in the Sudan) 216, 222
Gebel es-Silsileh (loc, with sandstone quarries) 31, 143
Gebu (chancellor, fl 1750) 98
Gerf Hussein (loc, in Nubia) 191
gesso 24, 28
Giza (loc) 42, 60, 61, 62, 63, 66, 68, 69, 76, 78, 84, 92, 142, *34*
God's Wife of Amun *see* Consort, Divine
Greeks 225, 228, 233, 236, 240
grid 26, 28, *2*

Haremhab (general, later k, 1324–1296) 179, 183, 185, *151*
Hathor (goddess of maternity, love, deserts, etc.) 73, 112, 115, 128, 133, 151, 152, 158, 193, 218, 230, *36*, *87*, *192*
Hatshepsut (q, 1478–1457) 20, 142, 148, 150–6, 157, 158, 159, 210, 222
Hawara (loc, in the Faiyum) 142
Heliopolis (city of the sun religion) 7, 20, 21, 43, 59, 79, 124, 145, 146, 172, 194
Helwan (loc, near Memphis) 40, 45
Hemon (vizier, fl 2580) 20, 67, 91, *30*
Heracleopolis (loc) 109, 110, 113
Hermopolis (loc) 118, 190, 236
Hesy (official, fl 2670) 30, 54, 65, 66, *3*
hesy (sanctified person) 133, 204, *97*; *see also* block statue
Hetepheres II (q, fl 2560) 77, 102
Hierakonpolis (loc) 33, 44, 95
hieroglyphs 13, 15–18, 28, 36, 40, 173, 174, 202, 235, *3*
Hittites 141, 142, 187
Hor (scribe, fl 810) 211, *173*
Hor Awibrē (k, fl 1760) 25, 137, *100*
Horus (god as king) 34, 36, 78, 95, 146, 150, 197, 198, 224, *frontispiece*
Huny (k, 2654–2630) 53, 58
Hyksos (usurping Semitic kings, 1668–1545) 139, 140, 141, 147, 150

hypogea see rock tomb
hypostyle hall (with ceiling supported by columns) 114, 118, 144, 145, 151, 152, 189, 200

Ibi (official, fl 595) 222
iconoclasm 152, 159, 173, 183, 216
Idut (princess, fl 2410) 88, 89, 45
Imhotep (chancellor, fl 2680) 20, 21, 45–52, 59, 105, 228, 240
Iriketakana (Kushite prince, fl 670) 219–20, 183
Iritisen (sculptor, fl 2000) 21
Iruka-ptah (official, fl 2500) 102, 63
Isis (goddess of the kingship, etc.) 231, 235, 240, 168, 194
Itet (princess, fl 2630) 66, 26
Iteti (chamberlain, fl 2390) 66
It-tawi (residence-city near Lisht) 124, 140
ivory 25, 26, 8

Jemdet-Nasr (site of fourth-millennium proto-literate culture in Iraq) 38
jubilee 43, 49, 50, 52, 53, 80, 82, 111, 118, 126, 168, 195, 54, 68, 78, 133

ka, ka-statue (spiritual personality) 137, 138, 143, 100
Ka'emked (priest, fl 2410) 104, 65
Kagemni (vizier, fl 2400) 89
Karnak (site of temples on east bank at Thebes) 27, 28, 91, 115, 118, 119, 121, 124, 147, 150, 159, 167, 180, 182, 183, 189, 195, 200, 201, 209, 210, 216, 219, 220, 230, 238
Karomama (consort of Amun, fl 870) 21, 208, 209, 212, 170
Kawa (loc, in Lower Sudan) 222, 230
Kawab (prince, fl 2585) 75, 96
Kawit (princess, fl 2030) 69
Kem-ten (scribe, fl 2530) 77
Kenamun (steward, fl 1425) 20, 28, 158, 159
Kha'emhet (official, fl 1355) 143, 163, 174, 176, 134
Khamerernebty II (q, fl 2540) 76, 35
Khasekhem (k, 2732–2720) 44, 55, 56, 12
Khasekhemwy (k, 2720–2705) 45
kheker (ornamental frieze) 52, 16
Kheops (k, 2606–2583) 66, 67, 68, 75, 78, 84, 34
Khephren (k, 2575–2550) 60, 61, 66, 70, 72, 73, 75, 78, 92, 95, 128, 150, 32
Kherti-hotep (official, fl 1780) 136, 99

Kheruef (steward, fl 1350) 168, 174, 176, 133
Khnumhotep II (nomarch, fl 1890) 122, 123, 79, 80
Khons (moon-god of Thebes) 144
Khufukaf (prince, fl 2560) 25
kiosk 118, 119, 121, 174, 78
Kom Ombo (loc) 105, 240
Koptos (loc) 93
Kush (region of Upper Nubia and Lower Sudan), Kushite 8, 203, 204, 207, 211, 212, 215–24, 225

Labyrinth (mortuary temple of Ammenemes III at Hawara) 142
lapis lazuli 38
Lebanon 20, 24, 113, 187
Libya 113
Libyan period 7, 25, 204, 216
Libyans 32, 35, 80, 82, 107, 189, 195, 198, 201
lion 18, 38, 62, 127, 146, 148, 153, 184, 198, 201, 237–8, 4, 7, 86, 115, 130, 197
Lisht (loc) 118, 124, 128, 137
literature 104, 107, 118, 138, 150, 163, 190, 215
Lower Egypt 20, 31, 39, 140, 147, 150, 194, 203, 212, 215; see also Delta
Luxor (temple site at Thebes) 20, 142, 167, 191, 193, 132

Ma (tribe of Libyans) 206
maet (the rightness of the world at its creation) 11, 32
Mahu (vizier, fl 2390) 89
Mahu (chief of police, fl 1345) 179
Manetho (historian, fl 300) 7, 9, 139, 140
mask 68, 127, 153, 147
mastaba (bench-like superstructure over a tomb) 37–9, 46–8, 50, 58–60, 63, 64, 66, 77, 84, 114, 121, 122, 10, 49
Medamud (loc, near Thebes) 126
Medinet Habu (site of temples and palaces on west bank at Thebes) 142, 197, 200, 201, 222, 103, 165
Medinet Madi (loc, in Faiyum) 118
Meir (loc) 121, 122, 124, 132
Meket-rē (chancellor, fl 2000) 115, 74
Memi-sabu (official, fl 2370) 64
Memnon (Colossus) 26, 167
Memphis (capital city of united Egypt) 11, 20, 31, 45, 95, 109, 113, 124, 140, 185, 189, 191, 206, 208, 210, 212, 216

Memphite 50, 90, 96, 107, 108, 128, 148
Men (chief sculptor, fl 1360) 21, 170
Mendes (loc, in the Delta) 234
Menes (k, 3168–3113) 7, 31, 32, 34, 50, 172
Menkauhor (k, 2466–2458) 95
Menkheperrēsonb (second prophet of Amun, fl 1430) 123
Menna (official, fl 1380) 174, 222, 124, 186
Mentu (falcon god of the Thebaid) 115, 141, 145, 212, 72
Mentuemhet (steward of the Divine Consorts, fl 660) 205, 220–3, 184–6
Mentuhotep II (k, 2061–2010) 27, 111, 112, 118, 124, 147, 68, 70, 72
Mentuhotep III (k, 2010–1998) 113, 118, 147, 73
Merenptah (k, 1212–1202) 168, 191, 194, 195
Mereruka (vizier, fl 2390) 66, 89, 49
Meresankh III (q, fl 2540) 67, 76, 77, 100
Merka (official, fl 2870) 40
Merneith (q, fl 3000) 10
Meryankhrē (k, fl 1660) 138
Meryrē I (High Priest of the Aten) 178
Mesopotamia 38
Methethy (official, fl 2370) 99, 110, 59, 60
Meydum (loc) 53, 58, 59, 60, 66
Min (fertility god of the desert at Koptos) 112
mines, gold 113, 142, 187
Minmose (architect, fl 1450) 20, 21
Minnakht (general, fl 1335) 184
Mo'alla (loc) 108, 109
Mouth, Opening of the, (rite) 18, 21, 42
Mut (mother-goddess of Thebes) 142, 158, 167, 153
Mykerinus (k, 2548–2530) 19, 66, 73, 76, 77, 78, 91, 93, 96, 128, 133, 35, 36

Nakhti (chancellor, fl 2050) 110, 67
Narmer (=Menes?, k, 3168–3113) 33–6, 6, 7
Necho II (k, 610–595) 227
Nectanebo I (k, 381–362) 235, 237–8, 197
Nectanebo II (k, 360–343)
Nefer-her-ptah (chief barber, fl 2415) 88
Neferhotep I (k, 1751–1740) 43, 138

nemes (striped headcloth) 70, 126, 184, 186, 226, *116*
neo-Memphite 236, *195*
Nespekashuti (vizier, fl 610) 224, *187*
Nespekashuti (vizier, fl 580) 228, *190*
Neterikhet (k) *see* Djoser
Niankhptah (artist, fl 2450) 47
Niankhrē (physician, fl 2370) 102, *62*
Nile 22, 80, 87, 114, 122, 143, 201
Nile, inundation 11, 13, 31–2, 106–7, 113, 136, 139, *187*
Niuserrē (k, 2477–2466) 79, 89, 91
Nofret (princess, fl 2630) 58, *21*
Nofret (q, fl 1910) 133, *95*
Nofretari (q, fl 1260) 186, *158*
Nofreteti (q, fl 1348) 173, 174, 182, 193, *138–40*
Nofretyabet (princess, fl 2580) 27
Nofru (q, fl 2050) 111
Nofrurē (princess, fl 1475) 157, *119, 120*
nome (district governed by a nom-arch) 50, 73, 80, 93, *36*
Nubia (district between First and Second Cataracts of the Nile) 55, 113, 126, 140, 163, 190, 191, 215, 222, 225
Nubian(s) 30, 32, 124, 216, 218

obelisk 20, 79, 151, 159, *38, 122*
offering-list 40, 42, 85, 224, *27*
Osiride 143, 198, 206, *168*
Osiris (god of the kingship, the Nile, etc.) 43, 78, 123, 128, 135, 138, 144, 152, 162, 187, 189, 212, 229, 231, *104, 191*
Osiwer (chief prophet, fl 350) 238, 239, *198*
Osorkon I (k, 916–913) 207, 208
Osorkon II (k, 890–860) 206, 210, 212, 226, *171*
Osorkon III (k, 797–767) 210, *172*

'palace-façade' (panelled wall de-coration) 37, 39, 46, 60, *10, 11*
Palermo Stone (in the museum at Palermo recording fragments of early annals) 9, 43, 45, 94
Palestine 38, 141, 187, 189, 209
palette 32–6, 82, *4–7*
Parennefer (chief craftsman, fl 1350) 176
Pashasu (prince, fl 770) 212
Pedimahes (official, fl 680) 218, *182*
Pedubast I (k, 828–803) 207, 211
Pehsukher (general, fl 1450) *121*
Penmeru (official, fl 2410) 100, 101, *61*

Persia 8, 203, 205, 230, 233–4, 238, 239
perspective 15, 177, 180
Petosiris (High Priest of Thoth, fl 360) 236
Phiops I (k, 2390–2361) 24, 90, 94, 95, 96, *52, 54, 55*
Phiops II (k, 2355–2261) 80, 82, 84, 90, 93, 96, 104, 106, 112, 118, 150, 152, 209, 222, *40, 53*
Pi(ankh)y (k, 753–713) 212
pigments 28–9
pilgrimage 87, 133, 138
plaster, casting in 182, *147*
plaster, modelling in 22
portrait 54, 58, 68–70, 157, 170, 182, 197, 204, 240
pose 99–100, 102
'proto-Doric' column 123, *109*
Psammetichus I (k, 664–610) 225
Psammetichus II (k, 595–589) 216, 225, 226, 229
Psammetichus III (k, 526–525) 233
Psamtek (official, fl 530) 230–31, *192*
pseudo-group 100
Psusennes II (k, 960–946) 205
Ptah (creator-god of Memphis) 11, 12, 19, 21, 44, 93, 98, 194, *81*
Ptah-hotep (vizier, fl 2450) 89, *44, 47, 48*
Ptolemy I (k, 323–285) 7
Ptolemy II (k, 285–246) 235
Punt (spice land near Horn of Africa) 152
pylon gateway to a temple 20, 119, 145–6, 150, 167, 189, 194, 195, 201, 209, 218
pyramid 59, 60, 61, 66, 67, 78, 84, 114, 118, 136–7, 139, 146, 222, *22, 23, 34, 39, 75*
Pyramid, Step 20, 46–58, 59, 65, 150, 203, 228, *13, 15, 16*
Pyramid Texts 60

Qa'a (k, 2890–2860) 40, 43, 44, 50
quarry 51, 113, 143; *see also* Tura

Ramesses II (k, 1279–1212) 19, 20, 41, 168, 189, 190–4, 195, 196, 197, 198, 200, 209, *154, 157, 159, 160*
Ramesses III (k, 1182–1151) 197–8, 200, *103, 162, 165*
Ramesses IV (k, 1151–1145) 20, 142, 198
Ramesses V (k, 1145–1141) 25
Ramesses VI (k, 1141–1134) 195, 198, *164*

Ramesses IX (k, 1126–1108) 198, 202, *163, 166*
Ramesses-nakht (High Priest of Amun, fl 1130) 20, 202, *167*
Ramesseum (mortuary temple of Ramesses II at Western Thebes) 193, 194, 200, 202, *104*
Ramessides (kings of dynasties XIX–XX) 8, 146, 186
Ramose (vizier, fl 1356) 176
Rē, Rē-Herakhty (the sun-god in his active form at Heliopolis) 20, 45, 78, 79, 145, 151, 172
Rēhemu-ankh (official, fl 1760) 136
Rēhotep (prince, fl 2630) 20, 58, 67, *21*
Rekhmirē (vizier, fl 1430) 23, 158, 159, 162–3, 206, *126, 127, 129*
relief, 'bastard' 27, 89
Rēneb (k, 2830–2815) 40
Rēnofer (High Priest of Ptah, fl 2520) 96, 98, *56, 57*
'reserve' heads 68, 91, *28, 29*
rock tombs, Old Kingdom 67, 76, 107; Middle Kingdom 110, 114, 121, 122; New Kingdom 21, 28, 143, 146, 158, 176, 178, 186, 190; Late 203, 221–2
Ruskin 184

Sabef (official, fl 2870) 40
Saft el-Hina (loc, near Bubastis) 194
Sahurē (k, 2517–2505) 19, 60, 80, 84, 93, 222, *41, 42*
Sais (loc) 34, 203, 225
Saite period 8, 22, 204, 205, 221, 222, 225, 231, 233, 236
Saqqara (necropolis of Memphis) 37, 39, 40, 43, 44, 45, 46, 53, 78, 84, 92, 118, 142, 185, 240
sarcophagus 111, 122, 175, 179, 198, *69, 144*
Scorpion (predynastic king before 3170) 105
Sea Peoples (migrating piratical peoples in Eastern Mediterranean during the twelfth century BC) 201
Seasons, Room of the 80, 88, 119
sceptre 96, 147, 158, 193, *149, 179*
Schimmel Collection 177, *142, 143*
Sebennytos (loc) 234, 236
Sed Festival *see* jubilee
Sekhemkhet (k, 2667–2660) 53
Sekhmet (goddess of fire at Mem-phis) 142
Semites 123, 139, 209
Semna (fortress area at Second Cataract) 124

Senbi (nomarch, fl 1900) 121, *82*

Seneb (scribe, fl 2530) 77, *37*

Senenmut (steward, fl 1470) 20, 157, *119, 120*

Sennu (wife of a nomarch, fl 1920) 132, *91*

Sennufer (mayor of Thebes, fl 1395) 21, *102*

Serapeum (burial-place of sacred bull of Memphis where later Serapis was worshipped) 235, 240

serdab (sealed chamber for statues in Old Kingdom tombs) 44, 53, 96, 102, 129

Serabit el-Khadim (temple loc in Sinai) *135*

Serpent (k) 15, 105, *11; see also* Djet

servant statue 42, 102, 104, 110, 115, 65, 66, 76

Sesonchis I (k, 946–913) 206, 209

Sesostris I (k, 1971–1928) 24, 118, 124, 128, 137, 147, 216, 219, *75, 77, 81, 87–9*

Sesostris II (k, 1897–1878) 128, 133

Sesostris III (k, 1878–1842) 124, 126, 129, 132, 139, 216, *83, 84*

Seth (god of storm, violence, deserts, etc.) 141, 197, 198

Sethos I (k, 1291–1279) 187–8, 193, 194, 196, 199, *152, 153*

Sethos II (k, 1199–1193) 195

Shabaka (k, 713–698) 216, 222, *176*

Shabataka (k, 698–690) 216

Shebensopdu (granddaughter of Osorkon II, fl 810) 212, *175*

shendyt kilt 212, 219, 220, *116*

Shepenwepet (II) (divine consort, fl 670) 218, *180, 181*

Shepherd Kings *see* Hyksos

Shepseskaf (k, 2530–2526) 19, 91

Shoshenq (Libyan chief) *see* Sesonchis I

shrine 37, 53, 56, 78, 112, 144, 146, 151, 153, 157, 158, 174, 229, *15, 70, 100, 191*

Si-Hathor (treasurer, fl 1900) 135, *97*

Si-kahika (steward, fl 1775) 136

Sinai (loc) 113, 141, 170

Smenkhkarē (k, 1342–1339) 184

Snoferu (k, 2630–2606) 58, 59, 63, 78, *24*

Sobek-rē (crocodile god) 145

Solomon (king of Israel) 209

space, concept of 13, 36, 173, 175–80

space, negative 18, 56, 230

sphinx 18, 62, 80, 92, 118, 126, 127, 146, 147, 226, 227, 230, *34, 85, 86, 106*; as queen 133, 148, 151, 152, 218, *93, 115; see also* lion

star 47, 59, 60, 84, 145

stave 186, 194

stela 21, 40, 56, 60, 65, 66, 85, 132, 135, 138, 158, 174, *11, 15, 24, 27, 105, 121*

stone 22–4, 26, 27

studio *see* workshop

Sudan 113, 201, 215, 222, 225

Sulb (loc, in Sudan) 144, 184, 230, 238

Surer (steward, fl 1350) 176

Syria 38, 141, 187, 189

Taharqa (k, 690–664) 216, 222, *178*

Takush (priestess, fl 730) 207, 208, 212, *178*

Tanis (loc) 8, 203, 205, 206, 210

Tanite period 7, 8

Tanutamun (k, 664–656) 216, *177*

Tell el-Amarna (loc) 8, 173; *see also* Amarna

Tell el-Moqdam (loc, modern site of Leontopolis) 219

temple, origin of 144–6

Tephenis (goddess in Heliopolis) 175

Teti (k, 2400–2390) 90, 94

Thanufer (priest, fl 360) 195

Thebes (capital of Upper Egypt) 12, 20, 21, 28, 109, 111, 115, 118, 121, 140, 143, 144, 147, 148, 151, 152, 158, 187, 190, 191, 194, 198, 202, 203, 205, 206, 209, 211, 215, 220, 221, 225; *see also* Deir el-Bahri, Karnak, Luxor, Medinet Habu

Thinis (ancient site near Abydos) 109

Thoth (god of learning in Hermopolis) 170, 202

Ti (curator of monuments, fl 2450) 30, 88, *46*

timber *see* wood

Tiye (q, fl 1360) 21, 166, 167, 170, 193, *135*

Tod (loc) 27, 113, 147

tomb *see* rock-tombs

tool 22–4

triad 73, 146, 195, 206, *168*

Tuna el-Gebel (necropolis of Hermopolis) 236

Tura (limestone quarries opposite Memphis) 19, 46, 63, 67, 84, 110, 121

Turin Canon (damaged king-list in the museum at Turin) 9

Tutankhamun (k, 1339–1329) 24, 137, 159, 175, 179, 183–5, 201, *frontispiece*

Tuthmose (sculptor, fl 1340) 21, 182, 183

Tuthmosides (kings of the mid-XVIIIth Dynasty, 1500–1380)

Tuthmosis I (k, 1507–1495) 146, 148, 150

Tuthmosis III (k, 1479–1425) 20, 26, 146, 148, 158, 159, 162, 163, 183, 194, 198, 205, 206, 222, *2, 116, 122*

Tuthmosis IV (k, 1397–1384) 25, 163, 167, *131*

Tuyu (high priestess, fl 1390) 166, *128*

Ukh-hotep (nomarch, fl 1870) 132, *94*

Unas (k, 2430–2400) 60, 80, 84, 88, 185

Upper Egypt 31, 32, 33, 39, 114, 122, 147, 194, 202, 203, 211, 215, 225

uraeus (royal protective cobra) 48, 70, 136, 186, 189, 193, 198, 210, 216, 226, 237

Uriren (official, fl 2450) 104

Uruk (site of fourth-millennium prehistoric culture in Iraq) 38

Userhet (scribe, fl 1395) 125

Userhet (priest, fl 1280) *156*

Userkaf (k, 2524–2517) 91, 92, 93, *51*

Valley of the Kings (loc, at Western Thebes) 146, 187, 194, 203

Valley of the Queens (loc, at Western Thebes) 193

votive(s) *see ex votos*

Wadi es-Sebua (loc, in Nubia) 191

Wadi Hammamat (loc) 20, 142, 198

Wahibrē (nomarch, fl 550) 228–9, *191*

White Walls (loc, later Memphis) 31, 50

wig 54, 138, 148, 164, 196, 212, 218, 220, 229, *128; see also* dress

wood 24, 25

workshop 107, 126, 182

Yewepet II (k, fl 735) 212, *174*

Yuni (scribe, fl 1280) 196, *161*

Yuti (sculptor, fl 1360) 21